# PATTERN CUTTING FOR WOMEN'S TAILORED JACKETS:

## CLASSIC AND CONTEMPORARY

WINIFRED ALDRICH

Blackwell
Science

Blackwell Science Ltd
Editorial Offices:
Osney Mead, Oxford OX2 0EL
25 John Street, London WC1N 2BS
23 Ainslie Place, Edinburgh EH3 6AJ
350 Main Street, Malden
MA 02148 5018, USA
54 University Street, Carlton
Victoria 3053, Australia
10, rue Casimir Delavigne
75006 Paris, France

Other Editorial Offices:

Blackwell Wissenschafts-Verlag GmbH
Kurfürstendamm 57
10707 Berlin, Germany

Blackwell Science KK
MG Kodenmacho Building
7–10 Kodenmacho Nihombashi
Chuo-ku, Tokyo 104, Japan

Iowa State University Press
A Blackwell Science Company
2121 S. State Avenue
Ames, Iowa 50014-8300, USA



First published 2002

Set in 9/10pt Times
by DP Photosetting, Aylesbury, Bucks

DISTRIBUTORS

Marston Book Services Ltd
PO Box 269
Abingdon
Oxon OX14 4YN
(*Orders:* Tel: 01235 465500
Fax: 01235 465555)

USA
Blackwell Science, Inc.
Commerce Place
350 Main Street
Malden, MA 02148 5018
(*Orders:* Tel: 800 759 6102
781 388 8250
Fax: 781 388 8255)

Canada
Login Brothers Book Company
324 Saulteaux Crescent
Winnipeg, Manitoba R3J 3T2
(*Orders:* Tel: 204 837-2987
Fax: 204 837-3116)

Australia
Blackwell Science Pty Ltd
54 University Street
Carlton, Victoria 3053
(*Orders:* Tel: 03 9347 0300
Fax: 03 9347 5001)

A catalogue record for this title is available from the British Library

ISBN 0–632–05467–0

Library of Congress
Cataloging-in-Publication Data

Aldrich, Winifred.
Pattern cutting for women's tailored jackets: classic and contemporary/Winifred Aldrich.
p. cm.
Includes bibliographical references.
ISBN 0-632-05467-0 (alk. paper)
1. Jackets. 2. Dressmaking—Pattern design.
3. Tailoring (Women's) I. Title.

TT535 .A43 2001
646.4′5704—dc21

2001037727

For further information on
Blackwell Science, visit our website:
www.blackwell-science.com

# CONTENTS

# ACKNOWLEDGEMENTS

Many people and organisations have contributed to the production of this book; it could not have been completed without their support. I would like to give the following people my sincere appreciation for their interest and help.

The Leverhulme Trust for providing the grant which enabled the project to be undertaken.

Professor Edward Newton for his continuing encouragement and advice.

Kathleen Farrell for administrative support and James Aldrich for the photography, layout and research assistance which were needed to bring the book to its fruition.

The following organisations, libraries, archives and museums for help in researching pattern journals and costume examples or who have given me permission to reproduce some of the images in Chapter 1.
The Archives Lavigne, ESMOD, Paris
Bibliothèque Nationale of France, Paris
Bibliothèque Forney, Paris
Bankfield Museum, Halifax
Bradford Art Galleries and Museums
Chethams Library, Manchester
EMAP Publishing (Nederland) BV
The British Library, London
The Butterick Co. Inc. Archives, New York
The Hagley Museum and Library, Delaware
The London Centre for Fashion Studies, London
The Library of Congress, Washington
The New York Public Library
The Nottingham Museum of Costume
The Nottingham Trent University Library
The Metropolitan Museum of Art * The Costume Institute, New York
Musee de la Mode et du Costume, Palais Galliera, Paris
The Platt Hall Gallery of Costume, Manchester
Public Record Offices in Leicester, Manchester and Leeds.
The Smithsonian Institution, Washington
The Victoria and Albert Museum, London
The Winterthur Library, Delaware

The following companies who have kindly taken time to find the most appropriate images for Chapter 5.
assyst bullmer, Barnsley
echzeit AG, Germany
Durkopp Adler AG, Germany
Gerber Technology, Manchester
Telmat Industrie, France
Veit GmbH & Co., Germany

Some copy on page 10 and Figures 8 and 9 were published in W. Aldrich, 'Tailors' Cutting Manuals and the Growing Provision of Popular Clothing 1750–1870, *Textile History*, November 2000. These are included by courtesy of the Pasold Research Fund.

# INTRODUCTION

The aim of this book is to explain the wide range of cutting methods used to produce garments which claim the term a 'tailored' jacket. Although the main focus of the book is modern methods of producing clothing, it acknowledges and uses a cutting heritage which is rich and complex. Libraries and museums of costume provide a rich resource for students and over the last decade American publishers such as R. L. Shep and Dover Books have made available facsimiles of old cutting books. However, to inspire the modern garment designer or to recover methods that retain their validity today, an understanding of the development of cutting methods and sizing is needed.

The term 'tailored' has changed as methods of manufacture and the retailing of clothes have evolved. Until the second half of the eighteenth century, tailors cut men's and women's garments which had little relationship to the tailored garments produced by the middle of the nineteenth century. High quality men's and women's jackets were crafted, moulded and shaped with layers of canvas and stitching. Today there are tailors who still believe that the word 'tailored' should only be ascribed to a garment crafted by these methods. From the middle of the nineteenth century, the growth of the ready-to-wear industry and retail outlets, and the tremendous increase in professional dressmakers, meant that the word 'tailored' or 'tailor-made' began to be used to describe a style or to infer quality.

It is possible to cut and 'fit-up' a woman's jacket with interlinings and linings using almost identical methods to those used in men's structured tailoring. This is very rarely required; today very few women's jackets are either bespoke tailored or engineered to create this effect. Although fashion sometimes dictates a structured high shoulder line, most high quality women's jackets are influenced by the softer tailoring methods of the style made famous by the Italian designer Armani. As men are opting for less structured jackets, the internal construction of men's and women's jackets has become more similar. Today, the increasing cost of labour has meant that not only are very few jackets hand-made, but that the machinery of mass production thrives on the repeatability of styles. This has resulted in a sameness about many of the jackets offered in the major retail stores.

This book sets out to explain in a simple way the evolution of the cutting and grading of women's jackets. It makes clear the different approaches to 'tailored' cutting by describing it under three headings: *bespoke cutting, engineered cutting* and *style cutting.* The rich heritage of the latter came from the tremendous creativity that was unleashed by women's emancipation at the turn of the twentieth century and the merging of tailored styles with fashionable clothing. The section on style cutting has derived some of the cutting techniques from that period, thus demonstrating their relevance to current methods of production.

**Note** Chapter 1, 'The Evolution of the Woman's Tailored Jacket', is a summary; the subject is covered in more detail by the author in 'Tailors' Cutting Manuals and the Growing Provision of Popular Clothing; 1750–1870', *Textile History*, November 2000. A further article covering the later period is in the process of preparation.

# 1 THE EVOLUTION OF THE WOMAN'S TAILORED JACKET

# The Evolution of the Woman's Tailored Jacket

The woman's tailored jacket has changed its shape, methods of construction, and its cutters and makers during the last two centuries. During the nineteenth century, the tailored jacket became an accepted and essential part of the wardrobe of most men and women creating a large market which could no longer be satisfied by the bespoke tailors and mantle makers. Methods of mass manufacture and workshops using sweated labour provided garments at prices which most of the population could afford.

The word 'tailored' creates a problem. Vincent, a tailor of men's and women's garments, stated in 1924 that the difference in the construction methods of tailors and dressmakers was that dressmakers worked from the 'inside', creating a lining that fitted the body, then covering it with the cloth, whilst tailors worked from the 'outside', moulding and fitting the outer cloth to the form of the body and then inserting a lining[1]. Although a significant proportion of the jackets made by dress and mantle makers during the nineteenth century were based on the 'inside' approach (Fig. 1), by 1924 the influences of fashion and mass manufacture had radically changed the cut of jackets and their construction. The new methods became the foundation of the garment industry today. This chapter explains the evolution of jacket manufacture, the methods we have inherited and their potential for further change.

## Before the Nineteenth Century

The background of the tailored jacket is well recorded. It emerged in earlier centuries as riding wear, but it was also used as a practical alternative to court dress for morning wear. In France, the jacket and skirt were catalogued mainly as the costume of the working classes, and it was not until the second half of the eighteenth century, during the Revolution of 1789, that the jacket and skirt became the new fashion, very certainly under the influence of the bourgeoisie who occupied an increasingly important place in the economic and social life of the Parisien. The costume was seen as representing the new spirit of the age[2]. In England it was common for the jacket and the greatcoat to be worn by women of all classes for many practical and social pursuits throughout the seventeenth and eighteenth centuries (Fig. 1). Pepys in 1664 said, 'Walking in the gallery at Whitehall, I find the ladies of honour dressed in their riding garbs, with coats and doublets with deep skirts, just for all the world like mine.'[3] Women's gig coats, spencers, pelisses, and riding habits were offered by both tailors and clothiers across a wide range of quality and prices catering for a much wider class of people than is apparent from many of the costume history books.

The well-established second-hand trade of clothes provided a variety of garments for the poorer classes, but as the textile mills produced cheaper cloth and the provincial towns expanded, there were opportunities for drapers and the new ready-to-wear warehouses to expand[4]. Tailors and dressmakers were at the heart of this expansion; large-scale hand-production was of major significance in industrial growth. Women were working in both the dress and tailoring trades in small workshops or outworking. The scale of their productive capacity is often ignored by many economic historians because of their invisibility in records, but it was the labour of these women in Britain, France and America which underpinned the expanding ready-made clothing industry[5].

Knowledge of the actual appearance and structure of tailored garments for men or women in the seventeenth and eighteenth centuries is limited to examples that survive in museums, written descriptions and images in paintings and illustrations. The main interest of costume historians seems to have been the garments of the aristocracy or occasionally peasant costume, and they therefore give little information about the garments of the middle classes. The fashion plates which appeared in the latter half of the eighteenth century were intended to influence fashion and stimulate purchasing, and were aimed, therefore, at the affluent groups in society. It was not until the books and magazines for tailoring, dressmaking and fashion trades spread, during the early part of the nineteenth century, that the literature began to expose clearly the costume of the middle and aspiring working classes. From the middle of the nineteenth century, increasing amounts of information began to become available, generated by the proliferation of women's magazines, department store trade catalogues and the growing popularity of the photographic image.

Few garment drafting books written before the nineteenth century for dressmakers or tailors have survived. But it is clear that cutting systems used by tailors and dressmakers were simple point to point instructions which enabled them to cut basic garments or a fashionable coat shape[6]. They used notched strips of card to record the body size (Fig. 2). Many women's garments were draped on the body or patterns copied from existing gowns (Fig. 2). Who invented the inch or metric tape measure is disputed amongst historians. Dressmakers were using marked pieces of ribbon in the eighteenth century but the adoption of the tape measure by tailors seems to have occurred at the beginning of the nineteenth century. The most important factor at this time was the standardisation and use of units of measurement, the inch and the centimetre. These were units which could be divided easily and they allowed more complex drafting and sizing systems to be developed[7].

Fig. 1 Detail from *Vaux-hall*, Thomas Rowlandson, 1785.
*By permission of The Victoria and Albert Museum*

Fig. 2 Dressmaking and tailoring as different crafts.
*The Book of English Trades and Library of Useful Arts*, 1824. *By permission of The British Library, 1420.d.2*

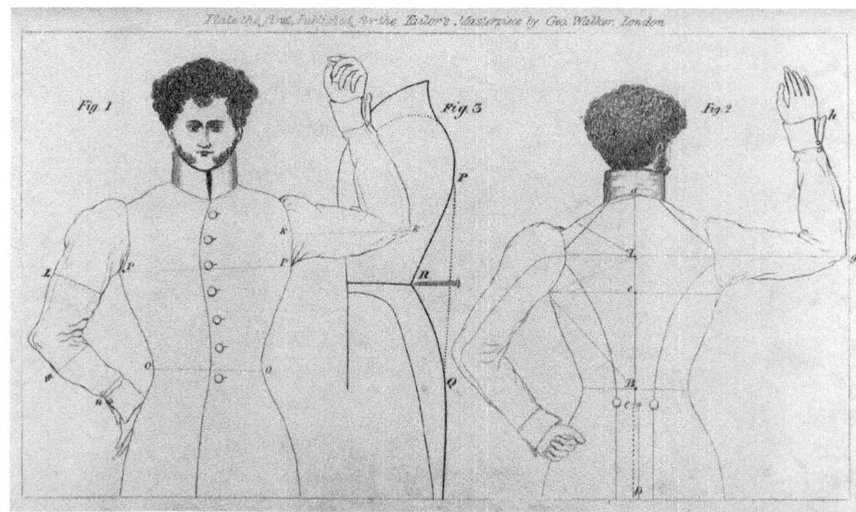

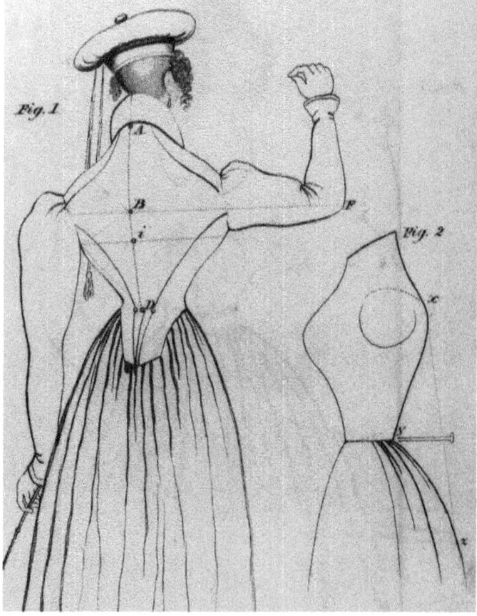

Fig. 3 A comparison of Walker's measurement positions for men and women. George Walker, *The Tailor's Masterpiece, The Art of Cutting all Kinds of Coats*, 1834; *The Tailor's Masterpiece, The Art of Cutting Ladies' Riding Habits, Pelisses, Gowns, Frocks &c*, 1836. *By permission of The British Library, RB23.a.17302*

## The Emergence of Drafting Systems 1800–1860

During the first half of the century, many tailors' drafting systems appeared; the tailors were competitive and vigorously criticised each other's systems. Whilst there were some women working in the tailoring trade (a tailor's drafting book by Amanda Jones published in 1822 has survived)[8], it was dominated by men who began to allude to it as the practice of science and art. The use of the tape measure stimulated interest in the human body and its proportions. Places and points on the body were identified with recognition of the male and female differences (Fig. 3). Complicated harnesses and measuring machines were patented[9]. The number of body measurements taken increased; these were later refined and became accepted as the basic landmarks on the body which could be used for drafting and graduation. The few dressmaking books that have survived from this period give minimal instructions for taking measurements and it is not until the middle of the century that they began to contain measurement diagrams[10].

The strong image that emerges from the early nineteenth century fashion plates is the similarity of the cut of women's and men's garments that were worn outside the home (Fig. 4); both were close-fitting with narrow backs and full sleeve heads. By the middle of the century, garments became more related to the form of the body (Fig. 5) as cutters strove to create 'anatomical' drafting systems.

It is clear that the production of ready-made and 'mass produced' made-to-measure clothing for men and women owes a debt to the cutting and sizing methods created by the early nineteenth century tailors, who shared their knowledge in full scale drafts, pamphlets and books.

An amazing number of different tailor's drafting systems emerged in the years from 1800–1850. The dominant ones which have survived are: *divisional*

Fig. 4 The similar cut of male and female jackets
*Costumes Parisiens*, 1812 and 1826. *Personal Collection*

Fig. 5 The cut of the jackets begins to reflect the figure shape
*Le Bon Ton, 1840 and 1842. Personal Collection*

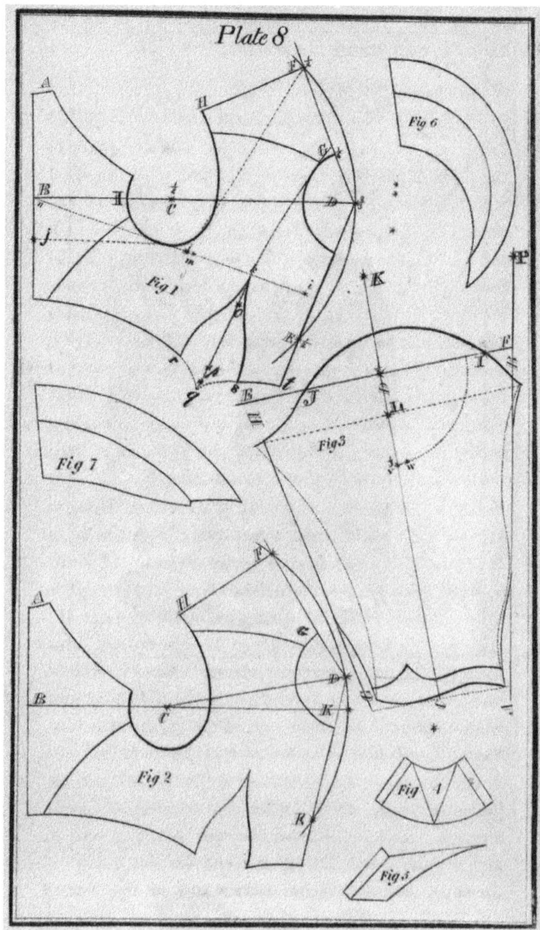


Fig. 6 A *combination system* used to construct a riding habit. Hamlet Hadfield, *The Tailor's Preceptor*, 1826.
*By permission of The British Library, 1043.b.37*

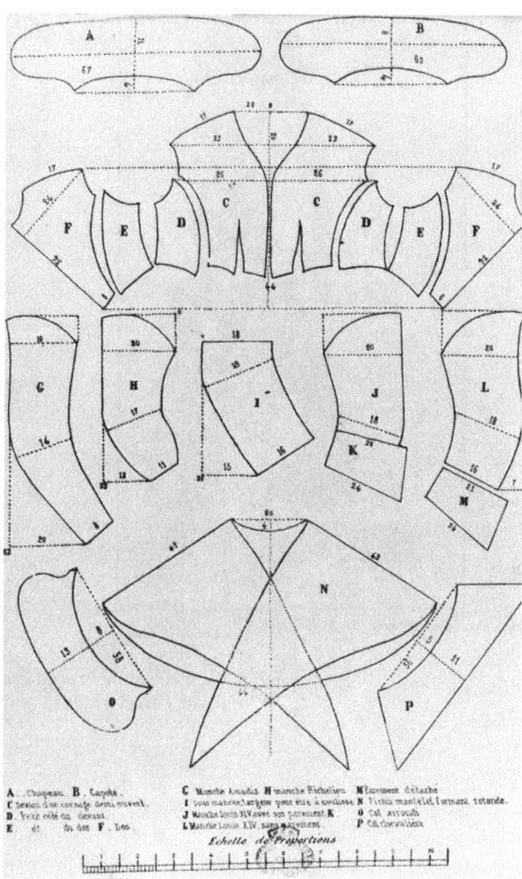

Fig. 7 A bodice pattern with a sizing scale printed on the back of a fashion plate. *Le Bon Ton*, 1841.
*By permission of The Victoria and Albert Museum*

*systems,* which divide major measurements proportionally; *direct measurement systems*, which identify most points by body measurements; *combination systems*, which are a mixture of the two. Most of the systems were developed by male bespoke tailors, and it is important to distinguish between systems that were simply a mathematical means of reproducing a garment shape and those based on anthropometry.

Systems based solely on proportions of the breast dominated the tailors' publications during the early part of the century, but many cutters saw this as illogical and recognised that height was also a factor. They also realised its limitations in the cutting of women's garments. Most women's garments constructed from the drafts were by direct measurement or combination systems (Fig. 6). However, anatomical theories of cutting and the use of the rectangle as a base for drafts and block patterns were developed[11]. These were important; they were ideally suited to the mass produced 'made-to-measure' trade which was beginning to emerge. The invention of graduated scale measures (Fig. 8) meant that ready-to-wear jackets could also be produced in proportionate sizes (Fig. 9); it also allowed dressmakers to scale patterns (Fig. 7). By focusing on a few basic measurements, the manufacturer could create and modify block patterns to offer 'custom made' garments. Many bespoke tailors who developed made-to-measure garments also used their knowledge to produce size charts which were a foundation to the idea that garments could be made for people using *average measurements.*

Before 1860 few drafting systems were developed specifically for dressmaker or mantle makers; many simply gave measurements (Fig. 10), and the earliest drafts were modified tailors' systems[12]. Whilst the ready-to-wear trade adopted proportionate systems many dressmakers used or developed direct measurement systems as body fitting styles dominated women's fashions for the next sixty years.

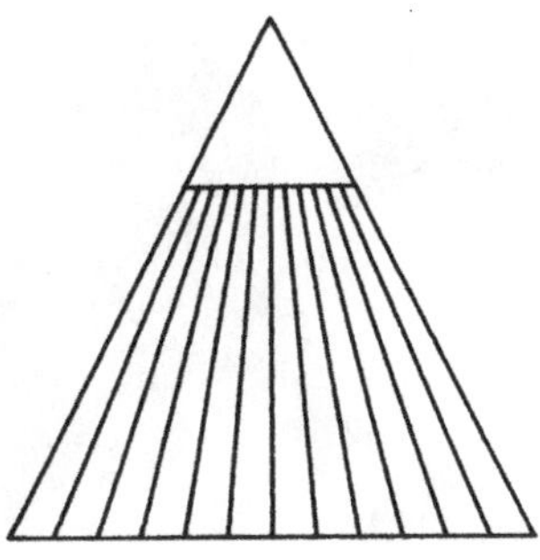

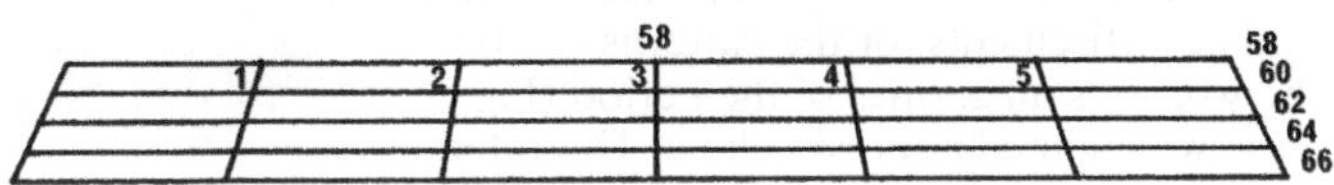


Fig. 8 Compaing's idea for scaling patterns and graduated tapes. Guillaume Compaing, *L'Art du Tailleur: Application de la Géométrie à La Coupe de L'Habillement*, 1828.

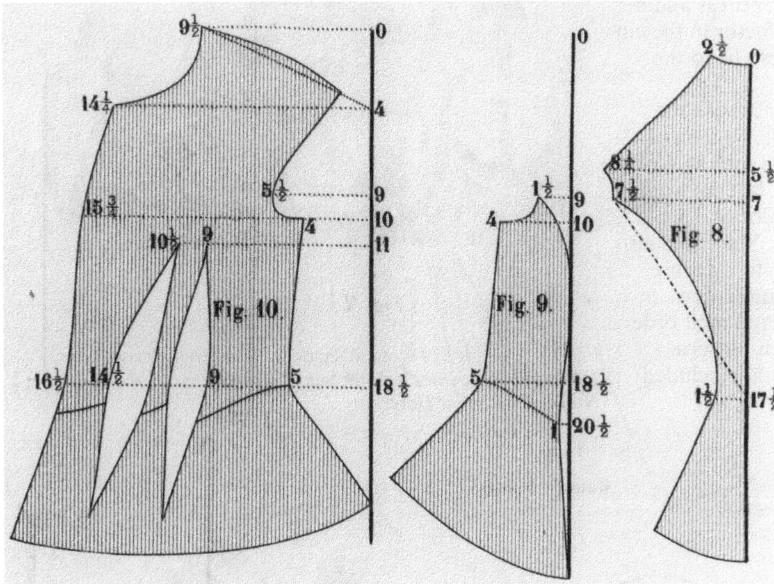


Fig. 9 The tailor's draft for a paletot based on the cut of a habit. Charles Compaing and Louis Devere, *The Tailors' Guide; a Complete System of Cutting Every Kind of Garment to Measure*, 1856. *By permission of The British Library, 1269.b.6*

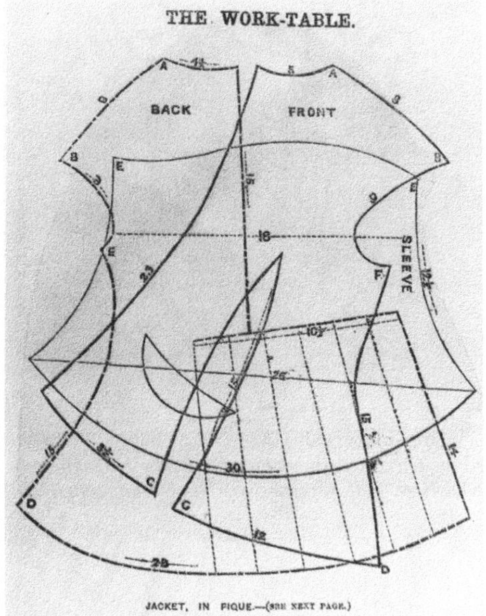

Fig. 10 The design and draft for a 'dressmaker' jacket. *The Englishwoman's Domestic Magazine* 1858. *Courtesy of Nottingham Museum of Costume*

## Close-Fitting Jackets 1860–1910

By 1860 a range of overgarments such as mantles and paletots were available from tailors, dressmakers or ready-to-wear establishments (Fig. 11). But it was the close-fitting jacket based on the riding jacket which became the dominant cut of the second half of the nineteenth century. Contrary to the popular myth that only tailors made riding habits (Fig. 12), illustrations of habits and advertisements for the patterns can be found in the women's magazines of the period (Fig. 13), and these were aimed at dressmakers. The fitted jacket was worn in a simple practical form for riding, sports and walking, or it was highly decorated and embellished for fashionable wear (Fig. 14). Although the silhouette of the woman both in her dress and her body changed during this period, one factor in the cut of jackets remained constant – the close fit to the upper body (Figs 14, 15, 16 and 17).

The draft of the jacket depended on where the woman bought or had her jacket made.Women of society patronised couture dressmakers such as Worth or top bespoke tailors such as Redfern, but the woman of lesser means could use her local tailor or dressmaker to copy the current modes. She could also purchase jackets ready-made or made-to-measure from the garment warehouses, or from the new department stores many of which offered mail order catalogues. There was an abundance of patterns offered in women's magazines which also included instructions for the home dressmaker.

Fig. 11 A range of women's jackets. *The Englishwoman's Domestic Magazine*, Vol. IX Sept. 1870. *Courtesy of The Nottingham Trent University*

Fig. 12 Riding, sporting and walking jackets cut by the tailor Lavigne during the 1860s. *L'Archives de Lavigne. Courtesy of ESMOD, Paris*

Fig. 13 Dressmakers also made riding habits, a pattern offered by *The Englishwoman's Domestic Magazine*, Vol. XIX Nov. 1875. *Courtesy of The Nottingham Trent University*

Fig. 14

Fig. 14 A fashionable jacket based on the riding habit, a pattern offered by *The Englishwoman's Domestic Magazine*, Vol. XIV April 1873. *Courtesy of The Nottingham Trent University*

Fig. 15 Copies of Paris suits offered as ready-mades in *Strawbridge & Clothier's Quarterly*, Spring 1882. *Courtesy of The Hagley Museum and Library, Delaware*

Fig. 16 Bespoke tailored jackets, illustrations for drafts offered to tailors. *The Ladies' Tailor*, Vol. 1 June 1884. *Courtesy of The Nottingham Trent University* ©EMAP Publishing (Nederland) BV

Fig. 17 Ready-to-wear jackets from the mail order *Autumn & Winter Catalogue*, 1908, of Strawbridge & Clothier. *Courtesy of The Hagley Museum and Library, Delaware*

Fig. 15

Fig. 16

Fig. 17

## The Tailors 1860–1910

During the latter half of the nineteenth century, ladies' tailoring expanded. The tailored jacket became a fashionable yet practical garment for society women, particularly the young, to wear as they emerged into public places to shop, make visits and engage in sports. The tailored jacket became more than a fashionable garment, it became an expression of the 'new woman' who was gaining independence through the expansion of education, professional and white-collar work.

By 1880 tailors' journals and drafting books no longer just included riding habits, but offered drafts for an increasing range of outer garments. The most famous tailoring journal, *The Tailor and Cutter,* which began publishing in 1875 (Fig. 18), found that the demand became such, that by 1884 they had to publish a journal specifically for women's tailoring, *The Ladies Tailor*. Although tailoring was principally a male trade, a room was specially set apart in the Tailor and Cutter Academy 'for teaching Ladies the Art and Science of Cutting'[13].

During this period, the techniques of the tailor were quite different from those of the dressmaker. The tailor created drafts which would produce a garment shape that accommodated the changing fashionable shape of the woman's body and also a shirt or 'waist' that was worn beneath. The cloth pieces of the jacket were moulded to the body but it was also padded where this would enhance the final shape. The jacket was then lined.

The drafts were mainly combination systems but they relied heavily on direct measurements. The tailors began to develop drafts that systematically produced a three-dimensional form for the bust. The method of swinging the front forward then darting the waist fullness to create the bust prominence remained popular well into the twentieth century (Figs 19 and 20)[14].

British tailor-made women's jackets were renowned for their quality but also for their rather severe and military styling (Fig. 21). Although the journals often claimed they were influenced by Paris fashion, the styles they offered were certainly not as complex, lavish or ornamented as those illustrated in the French or American journals (Fig. 22).

Whilst most tailors created different drafts for each style and made only minor modifications to block patterns, the American tailor Charles Hecklinger identified the possibilities of creating a large variety of styles from a basic pattern[15]. This was a technique that was to become adopted widely by the ready-to-wear trade.

Fig. 18 An illustration of the original offices of *The Tailor and Cutter*, Vol. 8 No. 324 1872. *Courtesy of The Nottingham Trent University*
©EMAP Publishing (Nederland) BV

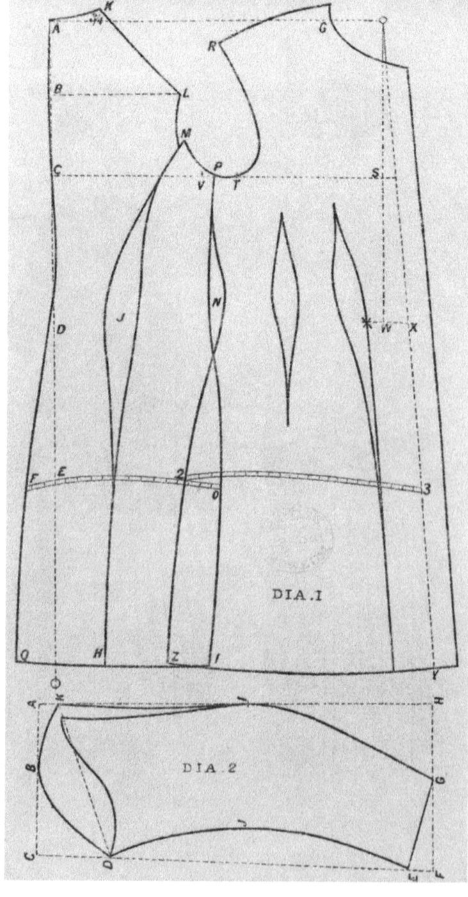


Fig. 19 An example of a jacket block, the bust darting achieved by swinging the front line. J. F. Davies, *The Pioneer System of Cutting Ladies' Fashionable Garments, 1881. By permission of The British Library, 7743.f.9*

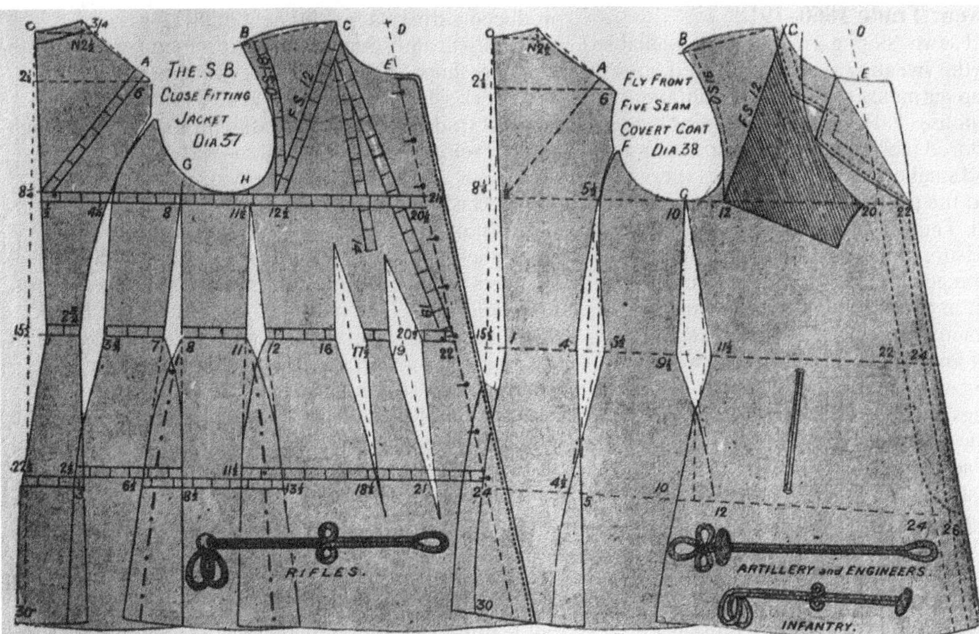


Fig. 20 A later example of the same technique of swinging the front in 1904. Vincent was still using it in his 10th edition in 1924. W. D. Vincent, *The Cutters' Practical Guide. Ladies' Garments, Seventh Edition*, 1904. *Personal collection*

Fig. 22 The more elaborate style offered by some American tailors, highly influenced by Paris. *The American Ladies' Tailor*, Vol. 1 No. 3, March 1903. *Courtesy of the Library of Congress*

Fig. 21 The simple styles of the British tailor. W. D. Vincent, *The Cutters' Practical Guide. Ladies' Garments, Seventh Edition*, 1904. *Personal collection*

## The Ready-to-wear Trade 1860–1910

Ready-made hand sewn 'slop' garments were available for the poor, and the sweating system produced large quantities of cheap garments both for the military and the clothing warehouses[16]. However, a different type of ready-to-wear tailored jacket and coat trade began to flourish. Large and smaller department stores sprang up in the capitals and the provincial towns of Europe and America (Fig. 23). The garment departments offered both made-to-measure and ready-made coats and jackets in a wide range of qualities. Some stores offered personal attention in comfortable fitting rooms (Fig. 24). Cheaper garments were housed in more spartan premises (Fig. 25) and the jackets and coats were usually easy-fitting, eliminating the need for complicated fittings and alterations (Fig. 26).

America became famous not only for the popularity of the woman's ready-made tailored suit and mail order catalogues, but also for its methods of mass production based on the cutting and sectional making-up systems of the men's garment trade. Between 1860 and 1910 the women's ready-to-wear trade multiplied by fifty times[17]. The use of average measurement tables enabled the further development of the craft of proportionate grading. By 1904 the wholesale trade was producing sophisticated grading systems[18]. Many American cutting systems were tailoring methods simplified and adapted for women's wear and were ideally suited for this type of production (Fig. 27). Large factories produced garments for the new retail stores and warehouses, and some stores set up their own factories and workshops (Fig. 28). But it was Seventh Avenue, New York which became the centre of the women's garment trade. Eastern European immigrants with high skills developed the 'task system' within their workshops and produced high quality ready-to-wear tailored fashions at low cost[19].

In Britain the large tailoring factories were established in Leeds but few produced women's garments and these were very simple styles based on male tailoring[20]. The major production was in London and Manchester, where like New York, immigrants with tailoring skills set up small workshops and produced ready-to-wear stylish garments. There was great exploitation of workers in these workshops which were difficult to regulate. The sweating system[21] was used not only by the warehouses but also by many of the so-called reputable retailers.

Paris led the world in fashion, and their designs were imported, copied and modified by both the American and British trade. Most of the tailored fitted jackets were produced by mass made-to-measure techniques, that is proportionate graded sizes, were altered to the few basic measurements given by the customer. This work was often farmed out to small immigrant workshops or home workers, high quality craftsmen and women working for low returns.

Fig. 24 The comfortable fitting room of the suit department of Strawbridge & Clothier 1890s. Stawbridge & Clothier documents, box 78. *Courtesy of the Hagley Museum and Library*

FITTING ROOMS IN SUIT DEPARTMENT.
Direct from Photograph.

Fig. 23 The Department Store of Strawbridge & Clothier, Philadelphia. Established in 1862, the illustration shows a part of the rebuilt and expanded store in 1898. *Courtesy of the Hagley Museum and Library*

Fig. 25 The more spartan surroundings of the saleroom at Kennard & Co., Philadelphia, 1906. *Courtesy of the Hagley Museum and Library*

Fig. 26 Two tailored garments from the Kennard & Co., *Catalogue of Women's and Misses' Ready To Wear Garments and Furs*, 1906. *Courtesy of the Hagley Museum and Library*

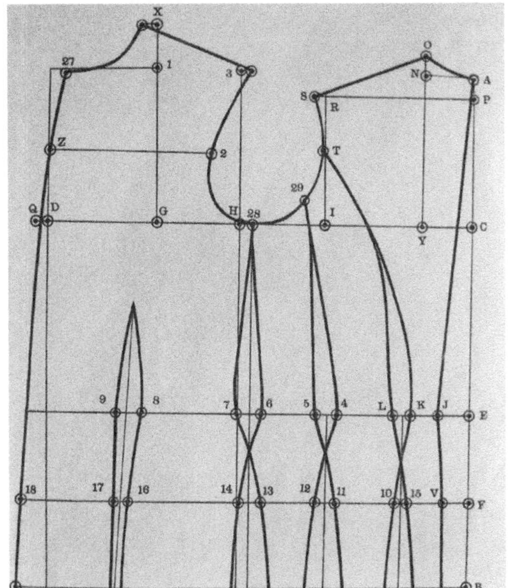


Fig. 27 An example of a simpler tailored jacket draft with less bust shaping. *The American Garment Cutter for Women*, 1904. *Courtesy of the Library of Congress*

Fig. 28 The main operating room of the women's garment factory, *Strawbridge & Clothier Store Chat*, Vol. VI No. 4 March 15 1912. *Courtesy of Hagley Museum and Library*

## The Dressmakers 1860–1910

The dressmakers began to adopt the 'drafting to measure' methods of tailors. These were simple at first (Fig. 29), but they also began to adopt many of the tailors' measuring and drafting techniques and tools to create more complex combination drafts (Figs 30 and 31). Most of the dress cutting systems were influenced by tailors' methods and advertised that they were, *'based on mathematical principles and similar to the cutting methods used by the best tailors'*[22]. Many of them were written by the growing number of 'man-dressmakers', particularly in America. However, from 1880 there began a deluge of publications of direct measure dressmaker systems[23].

The cuirass jacket (Fig. 32), so popular for day wear, was based mainly on cutting the garment in a similar way to that of tailors' direct measure drafting. But most of the drafts for dressmaker 'tailored' jackets were employed to construct the lining body that perfectly fitted the corseted body shape. The jacket was then mounted on the lining body. Easier fitting jackets were created by adding ease to a dress block. There was great pride in producing a perfectly fitting 'body'; Harriet Brown, an American dress cutter, visited Worth in Paris, who stated that he could not obtain a better fit in the cutting of a 'body'[24].

Many new direct measure drafting systems, drawing aids, sizing templates and cutting machines were developed by dressmakers (Figs 33, 34 and 35). These tools allowed them to cut and size patterns without the complicated mathematics of the drafts; they simply had to pencil in dots at appropriate places. Most of the early examples appear to have originated in America[25], but their production was swiftly adopted by British dressmakers.

Tailors had *inserted* bust darts in early drafts, but as tailoring methods were absorbed into dress cutting new methods of *drafting* bust darts emerged (Figs 36 and 37).

By learning to draft patterns or use a drafting tool a dressmaker could start her own business or double the pitiful salary she earned by sewing in sweatshops.

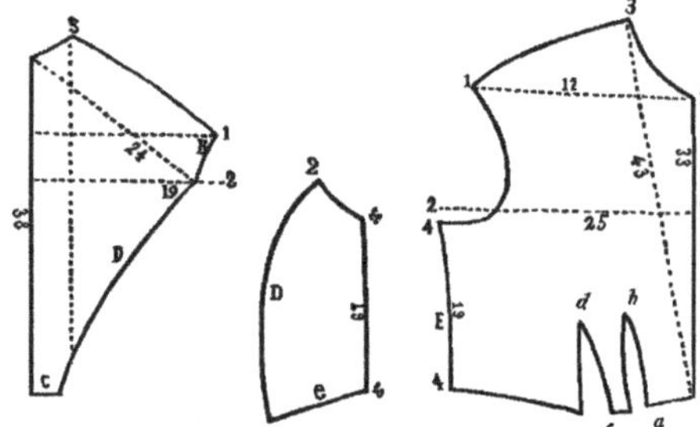

Fig. 29 *(Right.)* A drawing from Sylvia's *'Cutting by Measure', Dressmaking Lessons,* 1877

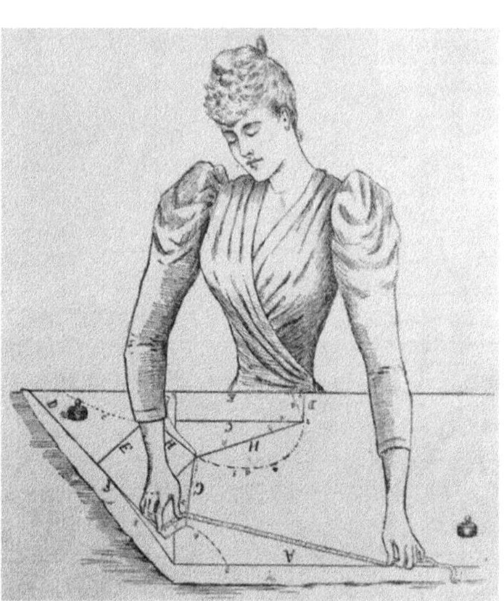

Fig. 30 *(Left.)* An illustration from *S. T. Taylor's System for Cutting Ladies' Garments,* 1890. *Courtesy of the Library of Congress*

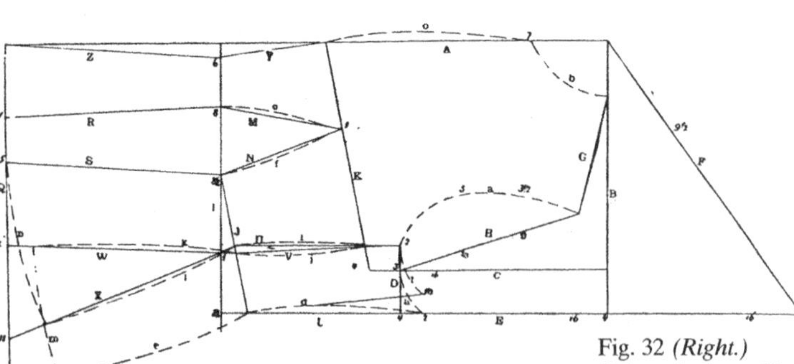

Fig. 31 Draft for an 'English Walking Jacket'. *S. T. Taylor's System for Cutting Ladies' Garments,* 1890. *Courtesy of the Library of Congress*

Fig. 32 *(Right.)* Cuirass jackets. *The Englishwoman's Domestic Magazine,* Vol. XV July 1878. *Courtesy of The Nottingham Trent University*

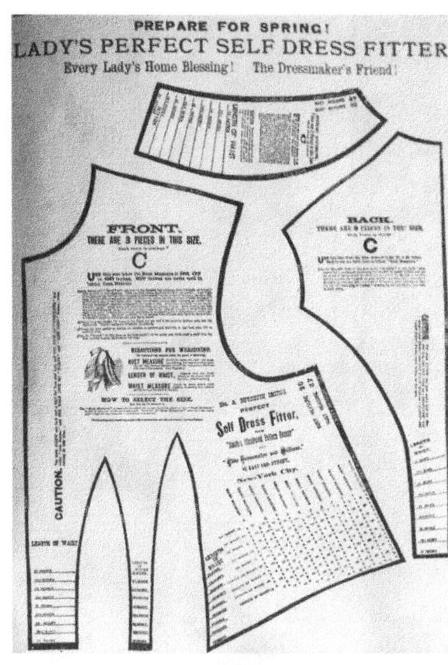


Fig. 33 *(Left.)* A cardboard template for tracing bodices in different sizes. *The Elite Dressmaker and Milliner*, Vol. 2 No. 3 October 1877. *Courtesy of the Library of Congress*

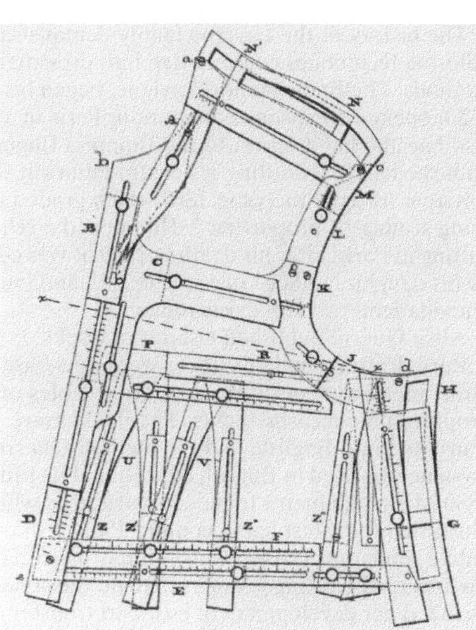

Fig. 34 *(Right.)* A dress cutting machine. *A. Mcdowell's Adjustable Pattern-Plates for Drafting Garments.* American Patent, No. 213436, 1879. *By permission of The British Library*

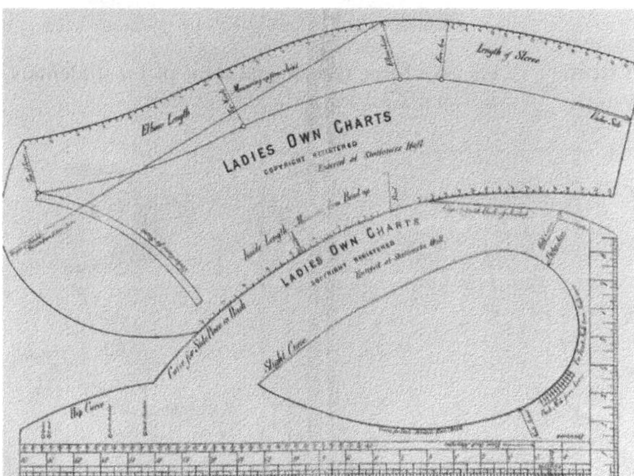


Fig. 35 A cardboard template for tracing curves and pattern shapes. The Anglo Parisien Associated School of Dress Cutting, Draping and Design, *Ladies Own Charts*, 1891. *By permission of The British Library* 1820.h.8 (8)

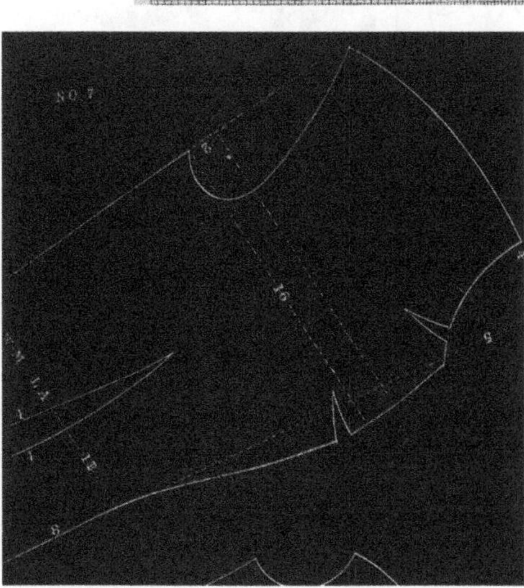

Fig. 36 *(Left.)* A tailor's insertion of bust darts. *E. Dilday's Plain and Concise method of Garment Cutting*, 1856. *Courtesy of the Library of Congress*

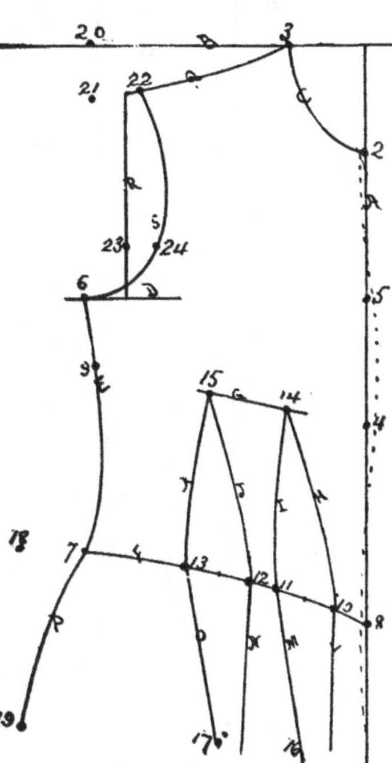

Fig. 37 *(Right.)* Drafting the dart for a 'body'. Vienna Ladies Tailoring Institute, *Artistic Ladies' Tailor System*, 1896. *Courtesy of the Library of Congress*

The history of the Lavigne family demonstrates how tailoring techniques could evolve into dressmaker methods. The French tailor, Lavigne, began his trade in 1820, opened a maison de couture in Paris in 1847 and also became habit maker to the Empress Eugenie. He published his first drafting system for tailors in 1841, and a system for couturieres in 1867 which graded patterns using scaling by proportion[26]. He opened a school of cutting in Paris; after his death in 1880, it was continued by his daughter, Alice Guerre (Fig. 38), and later by his granddaughter. It still exists today[27].

Alice Guerre published a series of books on her new pattern drafting methods; these were now based on direct measurements, but also offered tables of proportionate measurements. The books were translated into English, and the method Guerre-Lavigne was used in English educational institutes[28]. In 1880 Madame Guerre founded a magazine which illustrated the latest haute couture Paris fashions; but unlike similar magazines, which simply offered patterns, she included drafting lessons to create the styles. These included her development of bust dart transfer (Fig. 39) and pattern adaptations (Fig. 40).

Before the spread of classes in the institutes and the emergence of City & Guilds examinations in dressmaking and tailoring, many private schools were established in all parts of Britain. Some spread from America as dress cutters wished to export their systems[29].

Fig. 38 Mme Guerre and some of her students. *L'Archives de Lavigne. Courtesy of ESMOD, Paris*

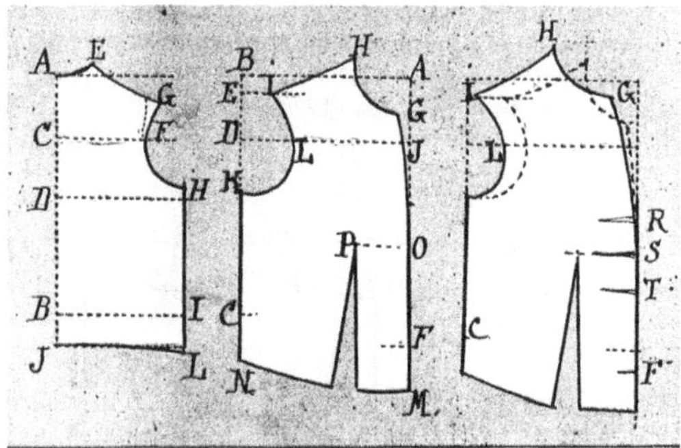

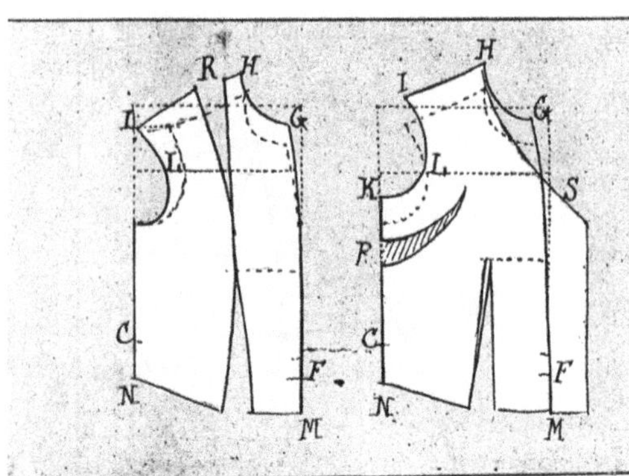

Fig. 39 Bust dart transfer. *L'Art Dans Le Costume*, Juin 1906 p. 91. *L'Archives de Lavigne. Courtesy of ESMOD, Paris*

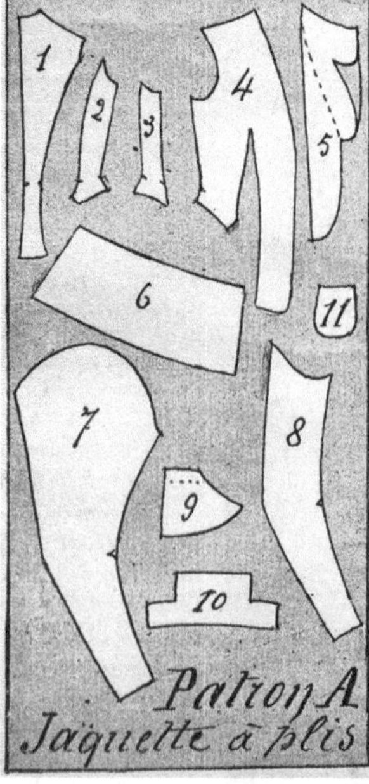

Fig. 40 A pattern adaptation of the jacket design on the right. *L'Art Dans Le costume*, Juin 1906 p. 85 and 95. *L'Archives de Lavigne. Courtesy of ESMOD, Paris*

## Magazines and Garment Patterns 1860–1910

News of fashion was supplied by the incredible number of women's magazines which proliferated during the nineteenth century[30]. They gave access to Paris styles by offering patterns for professional and home dressmakers. The early magazines offered patterns for a wide range of jackets and outerwear as well as dresses (Fig. 41) and often included pattern sheets (Fig. 42) or cut paper patterns with the magazine[31]. Ordered patterns could be supplied as 'body' linings or as paper patterns in a range of sizes. Commercial pattern companies produced their own magazines and they became huge businesses selling millions of patterns. Commercial pattern sales began in America; whilst Butterick was the first to supply *size graded* patterns in 1865, it was a Madame Demorest two years earlier who had the original idea of selling patterns commercially[32].

Fig. 41 Outerwear styles. *Harpers Bazar*, Vol. IX No. 42 October 14th 1876. *Personal Collection*

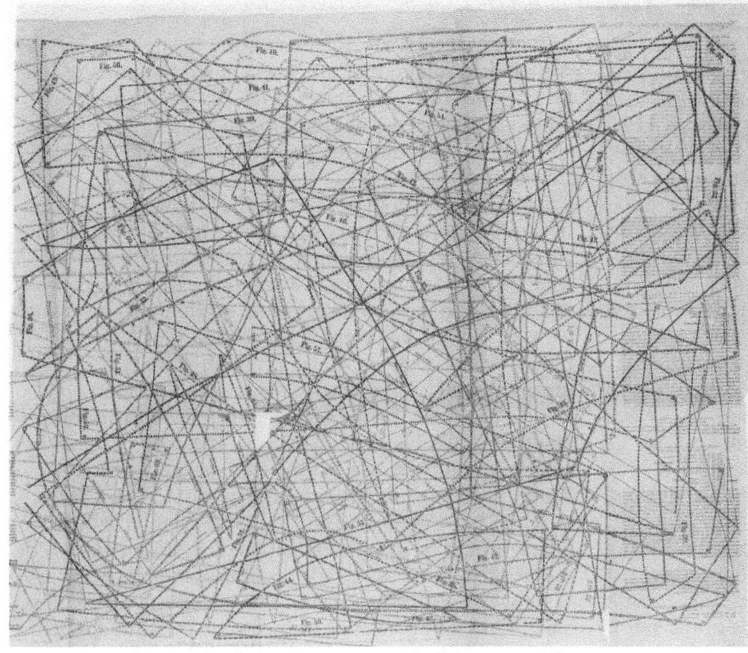

Fig. 42 A pattern sheet which includes all the garments shown above. *Harpers Bazar*, Vol. IX No. 42 October 14th 1876. *Personal Collection*

Fig. 43 The 'tailored girl'. *The Delineator*, January 1911.

Fig. 44 The new draped styles. *Butterick Fashions*, Summer 1913.

Fig. 45 Both of these images are now referred to as 'tailored' wear. *The Delineator*, March 1919.

The three images are published: *Courtesy of Butterick Co. Inc. Archives N.Y.*©

## After 1910 – A Revolution in Shape

In 1911 *The Delineator* proclaimed that 'This is the day of the "tailored" girl' and 'the woman is expected to wear her coat as the man is demanded to wear his' (Fig. 43)[33]. By 1913 the magazine was saying, 'Drape it now ... the acceptance of draped styles has been remarkably prompt' (Fig. 44)[34]. Indirectly, the work of two French designers contributed to the most significant change in the evolution of the woman's tailored jacket. Poiret dismissed the corset, and Chanel offered a casual easy-fitting sporting style. The majority of women responded to these ideas; the softer garments of the artistic and rational dress movements contributed to the changing attitudes to dress, whilst the practicalities of the 1914–18 war accelerated the active desires of women. By 1919 a softer body-skimming line became permanently established, from the tailored jacket to the dressmaker suit (Fig. 45). This became the underlying shape of body blocks for most of the twentieth century (Fig. 46).

The dressmakers' method of working from the 'inside' creating the close-fitting boned underbody, which had been used for most of the nineteenth century, disappeared in a few years. Many methods of the tailor and the dressmaker merged in this revolution in shape. The word 'tailored' became more associated with a style rather than a craft; it described jackets from very different sources. Even amongst the bespoke tailors a softer line emerged and they extended their range into dresses and other garments (Fig. 47). Many of them adopted some dressmaking practices such as working without seam allowances and adapting basic body shapes.

Below the level of haute couture, there were the bespoke tailors who specialised in women's jackets and suits. They steadily declined in numbers as they lost custom to the mass-producers making a similar, simple style of suit in an increasing level of quality. The ready-to-wear suits were easier fitting, often derived from blocks which were based on proportionate measurements and could be successfully graded (Fig. 48). There was also the styled, soft tailored suit, more responsive to changes of fashions, these were made by smaller manufacturers, dress houses and dressmakers.[35] The influence of the paper pattern industry has often been underestimated; from 1870 the popular women's magazines democratised fashion by offering patterns of modified couture styles for popular clothing. They also bought designs from some of the top couture designers. The books and magazines which they published offered tailoring skills, tools and aids (Fig. 49), both to the professional and the home dressmaker.[36]

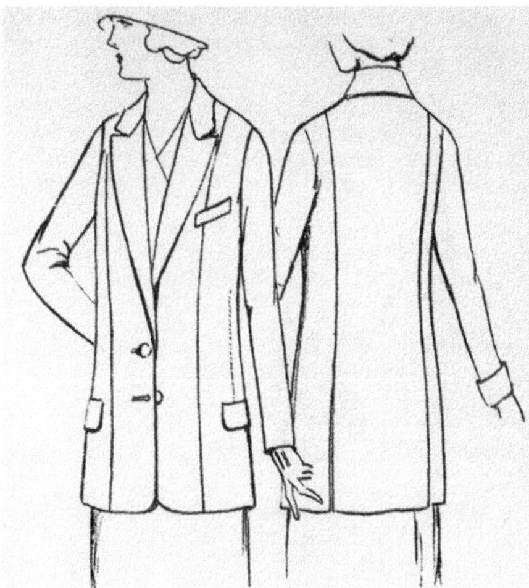

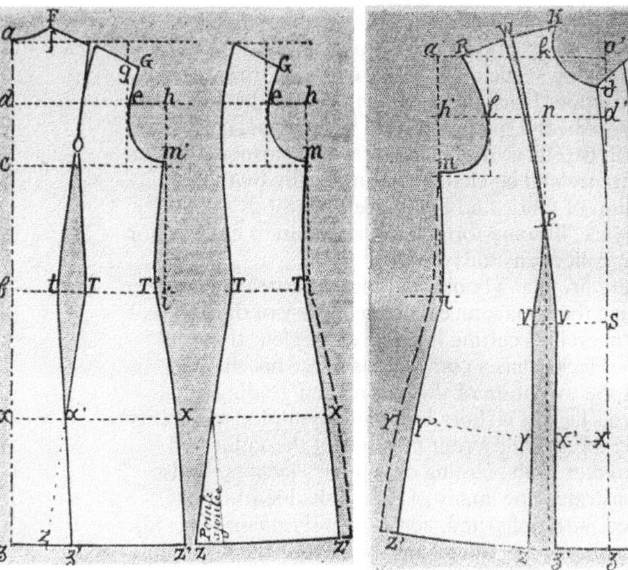


Fig. 46 Illustration and block for a 'tailored' jacket. *Manuel de Coupe*, Mme. Guerre-Lavigne, 1925. *L'Archives de Lavigne. Courtesy of ESMOD, Paris*

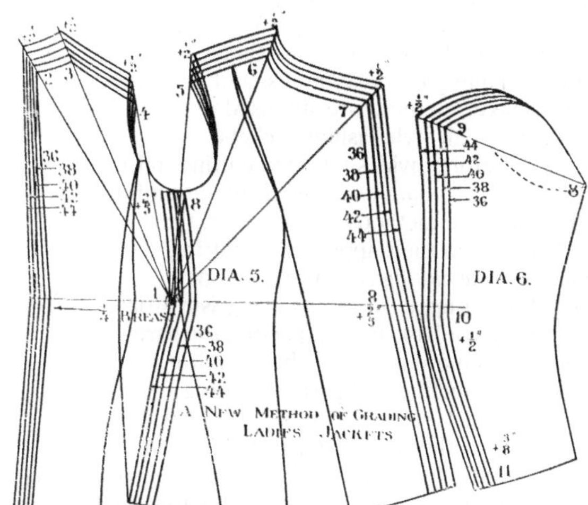


Fig. 48 *One of the many new grading techniques.* W. D. Vincent, *The Cutters' Practical Guide, Ladies' Garments. Tenth Edition*, 1924. *Courtesy of E. W. Newton*

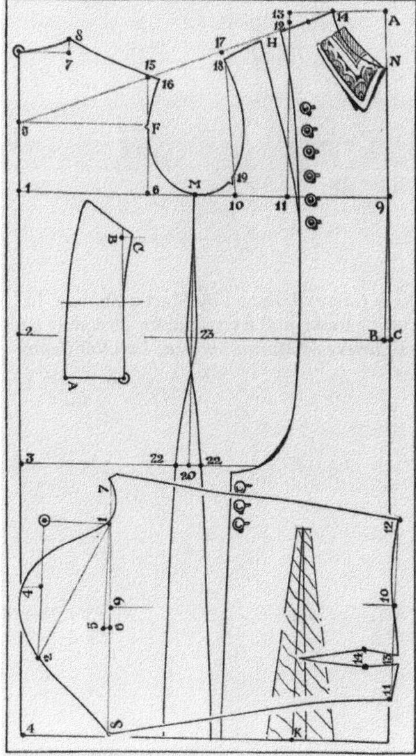

Fig. 47 The Ladies Tailor, *Ladies' Garment Cutting and Making*, 1926. *By permission of the British Library* 07742.c.26.
©EMAP Publishing (Nederland) BV

Do Your Own Tailoring
SHOWING
THE Fitwell COAT FRONT
FOUNDATION
Use a "Fitwell"—Save Cost of Tailor

Fig. 49 An advertisement for prepared canvas fronts. *Butterick Fashions*, Autumn 1913. *Courtesy of Butterick Co. Inc. Archives N.Y.*©

## Conclusion

Tailored jackets drift in and out of fashion with different emphases on shape and structure. Today, the woman's classic tailored jacket is synonymous with business and career wear. But the jacket has a wider popularity which rests on two facts: it is such a practical garment, and its appearance can be changed dramatically by the selection of fabric and by different methods of cut. Therefore, in some form, jackets remain in most major design collections today.

There are many books and journal articles which examine the social and economic history of the garment trade as well as cutting history[37]. It is clear that the tailored jacket has a complex history. This chapter about the evolution of the cutting and grading of women's jackets is short, but it has attempted to identify clearly the very different methods of the tailor and dressmaker to the cutting of women's jackets. It also demonstrates how many of their valuable practices merged, were inherited, adapted, and remain (Fig. 50). They still provide the means to produce the affordable and 'respected' ready-made tailored jacket. Whilst the ready-made engineered jacket is manufactured for the majority of the population, tailors' methods are still used by the remaining bespoke tailors, and the more flexible dressmaker methods are still used in the creation of some high style fashion jackets.

The book therefore divides 'tailored cutting' into three parts: *bespoke cutting, engineered cutting,* and *style cutting.* Although the methods may overlap, there are distinct differences in their approach to cutting. Traditional *bespoke cutting* is restricted by its techniques of make-up, *engineered cutting* is restricted by the machinery available to manufacture the garment, and *style cutting* is more adaptable because it is practised on small numbers of garments using flexible methods of manufacture with highly skilled workers.

Contemporary methods of cutting jackets are covered in each section; but there are also descriptions of some historical methods which may have been discarded, but now have a renewed value in current practices.

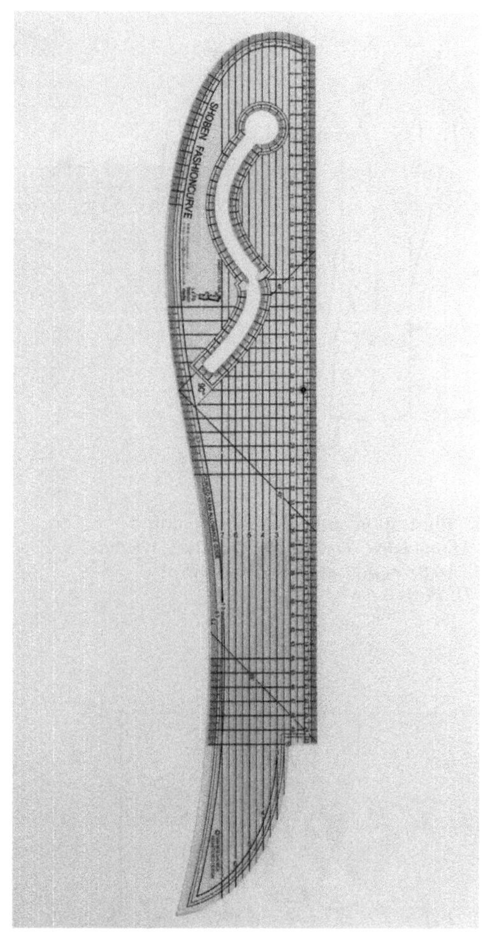


Fig. 50 *The Fashion Curve*, designed by Martin Shoben. In 2001 this type of cutting tool is still a vital aid for designing and cutting garments. *Courtesy of Martin Shoben, London Centre for Fashion Studies*

# 2 FABRICS, MEASUREMENTS AND TOOLS

# Fabrics for Jackets

Jackets of a *tailored style* can be made in almost any fabric. Most fabrics today can be mounted or fused with a light-weight interlining to give the designer the weight of fabric required. Full glossaries of fabrics can be found in many books on textiles; the edited list on the right covers light-medium to heavy fabrics that are commonly used for all types of jackets. Conventional tailoring fabrics are shown in bold type.

Jackets that are tailored to give a traditional appearance, either by bespoke or engineering methods, require or prefer certain qualities from the fabric. The principal ones are: a medium weight, a soft handle and the ability to mould under steam pressure. The latter characteristic is known as tailorability and tests have been devised to give manufacturers precise information on how the fabric will behave through the production process. The British, European and International Standards offer tests which describe the suitability of instruments for testing, weight, thickness, drape and stretch. The KES-F (Kawabata Evaluation System for Fabrics) test was devised in Japan to evaluate the 'fabric hand' based on the properties required for men's suits. The FAST (Fabric Assurance of Simple Testing) was developed in Australia; its specific aim was to give a reliable measurement of 'tailorability' in men's suitings[1].

Historically, bespoke tailoring has been associated with high quality fabrics made from wool fibre. The availability of fine wool tweeds and worsteds in England during the last century was a major factor in the scale and reputation of English tailoring during the second half of the nineteenth century and the first half of the twentieth century. Cloth made from wool remains the fabric that has the greatest 'tailorability'. However, the introduction of blends with man-made fibres, particularly nylon and polyester, has allowed yarns to be produced which give added qualities of strength and extended wear. The lack of resilience in the fabrics constructed from man-made fibres such as polyester means that the shaping has to be achieved by the cut of the pattern rather than the craft stitching and moulding. Dressmakers in the nineteenth century, who created tailoring styles but used many non-resilient silk fabrics, had to use cut to achieve a close-fitting shape. The invention of elastane fibres in 1959 by DuPont under the trade name Lycra has had a significant influence on the current women's trade; it can add a valuable stretch characteristic to close-fitting jackets.

**Linings**

The qualities required by a lining fabric are light-weight, non-shrink, with a close weave structure and a smooth surface finish. Silk or fine cottons were used originally, but by the turn of the century rayons (artificial silk) became available. Today some excellent modified rayons or rayon/polyester blends are available, but because of its lower cost, most of the middle market use polyester lining. Stretch linings are available from continental suppliers, but these are too expensive for most producers.

| LIGHT-MED. | MEDIUM | MED.-HEAVY | HEAVY |
|---|---|---|---|
| Afgalaine | **Alpaca** | **Bedford cord** | **Astrakhan** |
| Angora | Bagheera | **Bouclé** | **Beaver** |
| Bengaline | **Barathea** | **Broadcloth** | **Double** |
| Cashmere | **Bark crepe** | Burlap | Duffle |
| Chino | Brocade | **Camel hair** | Felt |
| Chintz | Butcher | Canvas | Fur fabric |
| Cire | Calico | Chenille | Loden cloth |
| Crepon | **Cavalry twill** | Cheviot | **Melton** |
| Dupion | Cloque | Corduroy | **Plush** |
| Faille | Coutil | **Donegal tweed** | Quilted |
| Foulard | **Covert** | Drill | |
| Gingham | **Crepe** | Duck | |
| Homespun | Damask | Dungaree | |
| Honan | Denim | **Duvetyn** | |
| Lame | Doeskin | **Flannel** | |
| Marocain | Faconne velvet | Fleece | |
| Matelasse | **Gabardine** | Flock | |
| Mohair | Grenadine | **Fustian** | |
| Moire | Grosgrain | **Harris tweed** | |
| Ottoman | **Haircord** | **Honeycomb** | |
| Panama | **Hopsack** | Intarsia | |
| Percale | Jacquard | Jersey double | |
| Pique | Jean | **Llama fabrics** | |
| Sateen | Knop | **Moleskin** | |
| Satin | Panne velvet | **Tapestry** | |
| Shantung | Repp | Ticking | |
| Sharkskin | Sailcloth | **Tweed** | |
| Slipper satin | **Saxony** | **Velour** | |
| Surah | **Serge** | Venetian | |
| Taffeta | **Suitings** | **Vicuna fabrics** | |
| Tussore | **Tartan** | **Whipcord** | |
| | Velvet | | |
| | Velveteen | | |
| | **Worsted** | | |

Fabrics marked in bold are the fabrics commonly or historically found in tailored jackets or coats for women.

# Interlinings

An interlining is a fabric sewn or fused inside a garment to give it shape and stability. Designers and cutters should become familiar with the wide range of interlinings that can be used. They also need to be able to cut the interlining pattern pieces that will shape the garment into the form that they have designed.

Interlinings have been used in clothing for centuries. Towards the end of the eighteenth century, when the type of formal tailoring that we recognise today emerged, there was a considerable number of very suitable fabrics available made from cotton, linen and wool. During the nineteenth century interlinings were developed especially for particular areas of a garment and it is claimed that 7000 variations existed by the middle of the century[2]. The company William Clark & Son Ltd, who currently provide the trade with a wide range of classic and contemporary interlinings, was founded in 1840.

The most important quality of an interlining for tailoring is that it should provide stability and shape to a garment without changing the inherent characteristics of its fabric, particularly its handle. Interlinings can be sewn in or fused to the garment fabric. Sew-ins are used mainly by bespoke tailors; the bulk of interlining production is in fusibles which are used by manufacturers producing engineered garments. However, a garment may be constructed using both types. Interlinings for tailored garments have to be resilient and must not shrink when dry cleaned, or in some cases when washed. Woven, non-woven and knitted fabrics are all used for interlinings. They can be further categorised into non-fusible and fusible.

### Woven Interlinings

The warp of woven interlinings is usually spun cotton, but different wefts of viscose, hair and wool are inserted depending on the resilience that is required. The structure is usually a plain weave but a few twills are available. The finishing process is important in that it can improve the qualities of handle and crease resistance and can create soft raised surfaces.

### Non-woven Interlinings

Whilst many claims are made about the quality of non-woven interlinings (and they have improved substantially since the early 1990s), they are rarely used in high quality tailored garments. Their greatest value is probably in the field of washable garments. The fibres used are mainly viscose, polyester or nylon.

Non-woven interlinings are constructed by pressing the fibres together to form sheets of fabric. There are many methods of doing this. The fibres can be parallel, cross or random laid or a combination of these methods. They are held together by applying synthetic binders by different bonding processes: foam, wet, spray, print, powder and thermal. Fleece and felt type interlinings are created by entanglement, needling or stitch bonding.

Non-woven interlinings have to be set, a process known as curing, to protect them from any further treatment which they may encounter during the manufacture or cleaning of the garment.

### Knitted Interlinings

Knitted interlinings are rarely used as non-fusibles; however, they are the base fabrics of a large proportion of fusible interlinings used in all types of manufacture. These base fabrics are warp knitted and constructed as lock-knit or weft insertion, the latter giving more stability.

### Fusible Interlining

Improvements have been made in fusing technology, the drive to reduce the costs of manufacture has led to an enormous increase in their use. They are used in some parts of most manufactured tailored garments today.

Woven, non-woven and knitted fabrics can be used as the base fabrics for fusibles. They are coated with resins consisting of polyethelene, polypropylene, polyamides, polyesters and PVCs. The resin on the back of fusible interlining becomes plastic when heated at certain temperatures. Pressure is applied (usually on large heat presses), and this allows the resin to adhere to the garment fabric. It has to bond securely to the fabric without striking through to the surface. This is a tricky process and accurate timing is needed. Once set, the interlining should not become detached or a bubbling effect occurs.

### Non-fusible Interlining

Non-fusible woven interlinings are used predominantly in bespoke tailoring. Some of these tailors still use the high quality wool/hair interlinings that have been used for many years. Although tremendous advances have been made in fusing technology, most people in the trade can recognise the 'drape' of a garment which has no fusing. Within the top ranges of manufacture it is common to find the use of fusible and non-fusible interlinings in the same garment, thereby gaining the advantages of both types. Technological developments have given interlining fabrics new stretch qualities and improvements in garment handle. For example, William Clark has developed an interlining that can be fused to the fabric during manufacture but then becomes detached in the final pressing process, giving a 'bespoke' feel to a jacket.

A range of interlinings are available in the department stores; more specialist interlinings may be purchased at:
*Rai Trimmings, 9–12 St Annes Court, Off Wardour St., London W1V 3AX.*
*William Gee Ltd.,520 Kingsland Rd., London E8 4AH.*
*McCulloch & Wallis Ltd, 25-26 Dering St., London W1R 0BH.*
*Whaleys (Bradford)Ltd., Harris Court, Great Horton, Bradford BD7 4EQ.*

Specific interlinings, their placement and the pattern shapes for jackets are shown on pages 43, 48 and 59.

# Standard Body Measurements for Jackets

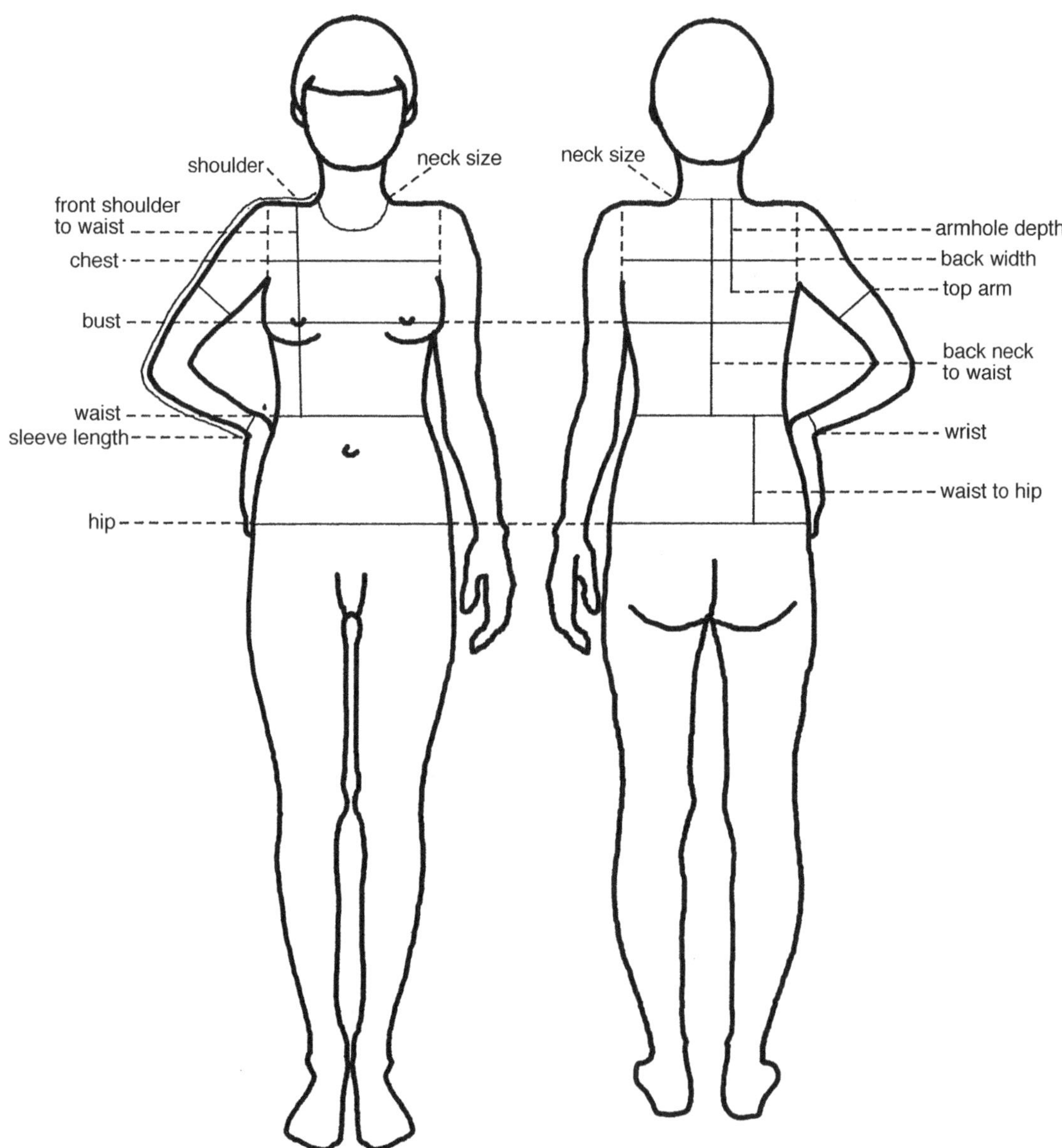


**Horizontal measurements**

**Bust**... the figure at the fullest point of bust.
**Waist**... an easy measurement round the waist.
**Hips**... the widest part of the hips approx. 21cm from the waistline.
**Back width**... the back width 15cm down from the neck bone at the centre back (armhole to armhole).
**Chest**... the chest 7cm down from the neck point at the centre front (armhole to armhole).
**Shoulder**... from the neck to the shoulder bone.
**Neck size**... the base of neck touching front collar bone.
**Dart**... standard measurement (see size charts).
**Top arm**... the biceps with the arm bent.
**Wrist**... the wrist measurement with slight ease.

**Vertical measurements**

A string tied around the waist allows the vertical measurements to be taken accurately.
**Back neck to waist**... from the neck bone at the centre back to the string tied around the waist.
**Armhole depth**... standard measurement (see size charts).
**Waist to hip**... standard measurement (see size charts).
**Sleeve length**.. from the shoulder bone over the elbow to the wristbone with the arm bent.
The measurements are taken from landmarks, control points on the body which are used for grading sizes.

The size chart on the right is based on the young High Street Fashion market in the UK.
SMALL = size 8–10 MEDIUM = size 12
LARGE = size 14–16 XLARGE = size 18

The two charts below are based on UK size coding: 10, 12, 14 etc. One chart is based on 4cm intervals, the other on 5cm to give companies a choice.

European size charts mainly uses 4cm increments. However, different countries assign different measurements to the codes. For example, for the UK codes **10, 12** (84cm and 88cm busts): Germany and Holland use the codes **36**, **38**; France and Spain **38, 40**; Italy **42**, **44**.

The data for size charts are collected by public bodies, consortiums or companies using sizing surveys. Small scale surveys are done by smaller companies targeting their type of customer. Size coding changes in different countries. For guidance in the UK, see the British Standards Instutution BS3666; for European and ISO international standards, see CEN and Winks[3].

| **UK HIGH STREET FASHION (6cm increments)** | | | | |
|---|---|---|---|---|
| SIZE SYMBOL | **S** | **M** | **L** | **XL** |
| BUST | 82 | 88 | 94 | 100 |
| WAIST | 62 | 68 | 74 | 80 |
| HIPS | 87 | 93 | 99 | 105 |
| BACK WIDTH | 32.8 | 34.4 | 36 | 37.6 |
| CHEST | 30.6 | 32.4 | 34.2 | 36 |
| SHOULDER | 11.9 | 12.3 | 12.6 | 13 |
| NECK SIZE | 35.5 | 37 | 38.5 | 40 |
| DART | 6.1 | 7 | 7.9 | 8.8 |
| TOP ARM | 26.4 | 28.4 | 30.4 | 32.4 |
| WRIST | 15.3 | 16 | 16.7 | 17.4 |
| BACK NECK TO WAIST | 39.2 | 40 | 40.8 | 41.6 |
| FR. SHOULDER–WAIST | 39 | 40 | 41 | 42 |
| WAIST TO HIP | 20.2 | 20.6 | 21 | 21.4 |
| ARMHOLE DEPTH | 20.2 | 21 | 21.8 | 22.6 |
| SLEEVE LENGTH | 57.4 | 58.4 | 59.4 | 60.4 |

| **WOMEN OF MEDIUM HEIGHT – SIZE CODING (4cm increments)** | | | | | | | |
|---|---|---|---|---|---|---|---|
| SIZE SYMBOL | **8** | **10** | **12** | **14** | **16** | **18** | **20** |
| BUST | 80 | 84 | 88 | 92 | 96 | 100 | 104 |
| WAIST | 60 | 64 | 68 | 72 | 76 | 82 | 86 |
| HIPS | 86 | 90 | 94 | 98 | 102 | 106 | 110 |
| BACK WIDTH | 32.5 | 33.5 | 34.5 | 35.5 | 36.5 | 37.5 | 38.5 |
| CHEST | 30 | 31.2 | 32.4 | 33.6 | 34.8 | 36 | 37.2 |
| SHOULDER | 11.75 | 12 | 12.25 | 12.5 | 12.75 | 13 | 13.25 |
| NECK SIZE | 35 | 36 | 37 | 38 | 39 | 40 | 41 |
| DART | 6 | 6.5 | 7 | 7.5 | 8 | 8.5 | 9 |
| TOP ARM | 26 | 27.2 | 28.4 | 29.6 | 30.8 | 32 | 33.2 |
| WRIST | 15 | 15.5 | 16 | 16.5 | 17 | 17.5 | 18 |
| BACK NECK TO WAIST | 39.5 | 40 | 40.5 | 41 | 41.5 | 42 | 42.5 |
| FRONT SHOULDER TO WAIST | 39.5 | 40 | 40.5 | 41.3 | 42.1 | 42.9 | 43.7 |
| WAIST TO HIP | 20 | 20.25 | 20.5 | 20.75 | 21 | 21.25 | 21.5 |
| ARMHOLE DEPTH | 20.2 | 20.6 | 21 | 21.4 | 21.8 | 22.2 | 22.6 |
| SLEEVE LENGTH | 57.5 | 58 | 58.5 | 59 | 59.5 | 60 | 60.5 |

| **WOMEN OF MEDIUM HEIGHT – SIZE CODING (5cm increments)** | | | | | | | |
|---|---|---|---|---|---|---|---|
| SIZE SYMBOL | **10** | **12** | **14** | **16** | **18** | **20** | **22** |
| BUST | 82 | 87 | 92 | 97 | 102 | 107 | 112 |
| WAIST | 62 | 67 | 72 | 77 | 82 | 87 | 92 |
| HIPS | 88 | 93 | 98 | 103 | 108 | 113 | 118 |
| BACK WIDTH | 33 | 34.2 | 35.4 | 36.6 | 37.8 | 39 | 40.2 |
| CHEST | 30.5 | 32 | 33.5 | 35 | 36.5 | 38 | 39.5 |
| SHOULDER | 11.9 | 12.2 | 12.5 | 12.8 | 13.1 | 13.4 | 13.7 |
| NECK SIZE | 35.6 | 36.8 | 38 | 39.2 | 40.4 | 41.6 | 42.8 |
| DART | 6.4 | 7 | 7.6 | 8.2 | 8.8 | 9.4 | 10 |
| TOP ARM | 26.4 | 28 | 29.6 | 31.2 | 32.8 | 34.4 | 36 |
| WRIST | 15.5 | 16 | 16.5 | 17 | 17.5 | 18 | 18.5 |
| BACK NECK TO WAIST | 39.5 | 40 | 40.5 | 41 | 41.5 | 42 | 42.5 |
| FRONT SHOULDER TO WAIST | 39.5 | 40 | 40.5 | 41.3 | 42.1 | 42.9 | 43.7 |
| WAIST TO HIP | 20.3 | 20.6 | 20.9 | 21.2 | 21.5 | 21.8 | 22.1 |
| ARMHOLE DEPTH | 20.5 | 21 | 21.5 | 22 | 22.5 | 23 | 23.5 |
| SLEEVE LENGTH | 57.3 | 58 | 58.7 | 59.4 | 60.1 | 60.8 | 61.5 |

# Tools

Calculator
Calico for toiles
Curved rules
Metre stick
Metric grading square
Model stands
Paper and card
Pattern hooks punch: notcher, weights
Pattern notcher
Pattern punch
Pattern weights
Pencils
Pens
Pins
Rubber
Ruler
Scissors: shears
Sellotape
Stanley knife
Tailors' chalk
Tape measure
Tracing wheel

Tailors' graduated squares. These may seem to be an anachronism but it is faster to work out fractional scales on them than using calculators.

Sewing and pressing equipment for making up toiles. This should include a sleeve board or roll, a tailor's ham for shaping, and a wooden block for pressing.

A full description of CAD (Computer Aided Design) systems for drafting and grading patterns is given on pages 67 to 71.

Equipment can be obtained from:
*Eastman Machine Co. Ltd, 118 Curtain Rd, London EC2A 3AP*
*Franks Ltd, Kent House, Market Place, London W1N 8EJ*
*Morplan, 56 Great Tichfield St. London W1P 8DX.*
*Staples Group, Lockwood Rd, Huddersfield HD1 3QW*

# Part One:

# 3 THE BESPOKE JACKET



BESPOKE CUTTING

Today, individual craftsmen and women still pursue the methods to make personal garments and private commissions, but tailoring classes run by colleges have diminished rapidly during the last two decades. People have less time to undertake time-consuming skills. There are also very few bespoke tailors of ladies' jackets today, and even fewer who are still working by only the traditional methods of the craft. It is almost impossible to do so, as some of the interlinings that were used are very difficult to obtain. However, both groups would adhere to the basic principles of moulding and shaping by using: the 'tailorability' of the fabric which allows re-shaping by stretching and shrinking it under steam and pressure; and by the use of under-stitching (pad stitching) which holds the shaping. Therefore, the finished form of the garment does not conform to the shape of the original pattern pieces. Because the advantage of bespoke tailoring is in the shaping, close-fitting jackets benefit the most from the technique.

Although basic jacket shapes can be bespoke tailored to give a couture finish, a pattern drafted specially for a bespoke tailored jacket will usually have the following main differences:

1. a more exaggerated front shoulder slope;
2. wide bust darts or bust shaping in the seams;
3. dart or seam close-fitting shaping at the waist;
4. classic collar and rever styles with an acute angled break line;
5. shaped collars;
6. shaped two-piece sleeves.

The main benefits of ladies' bespoke tailoring are its capacity to mould a personal fitted shape closely to the body and also pad out any figure defects.

# The Bespoke Jacket Block – Basic Grid

**Close-fitting with Pronounced Bust Shaping**

MEASUREMENTS REQUIRED TO DRAFT THE BLOCKS

The block can be drafted to individual measurements; however, many bespoke tailors keep a set of blocks in a range of sizes and then alter the measurement points which differ.

The block illustrated is drafted to the UK size 10. Refer to the 4cm size chart (page 31) for other standard measurements.

| **Size Code** | **10** | **12** | **14** | **16** |
|---|---|---|---|---|
| Bust | 84 | 88 | 92 | 96 |
| Waist | 64 | 68 | 72 | 76 |
| Back width | 33.5 | 34.5 | 35.5 | 36.5 |
| Shoulder | 12 | 12.25 | 12.5 | 12.75 |
| Neck size | 36 | 37 | 38 | 39 |
| Dart size | 6.5 | 7 | 7.5 | 8 |
| Wrist | 15.5 | 16 | 16.5 | 17 |
| Back neck to waist | 40 | 40.5 | 41 | 41.5 |
| Waist to hip | 20.25 | 20.5 | 20.75 | 21 |
| Armhole depth | 20.6 | 21 | 21.4 | 21.8 |

No seam allowances included.

Square down and across from 0.

**0–1** 1.75cm.
**1–2** Neck to waist plus 1cm; square across.
**1–3** Finished length; square across.
**2–4** Waist to hip; square across.
**1–5** Armhole depth plus 3cm; square across.
**1–6** $^1/_2$ armhole depth plus 3cm; square out.
**1–7** $^1/_4$ armhole depth minus 2cm; square out.
**5–8** $^1/_2$ back width plus lcm; square up to 9 and 10.
**0–11** $^1/_5$ neck size plus 0.25cm; draw neck curve.
**11–12** Shoulder length plus l.5cm. This measurement includes shoulder ease of 0.5cm.
**2–13** 2cm.
**13–14** 1.25cm; square down to 15.
**5–16** $^1/_2$ bust plus 8cm; square down to 17 and l8.
**18–19** 1cm.
**16–20** Square up the measurement 0–5 (add 0.3cm for each size above l4.
**16–21** $^1/_3$ measurement 5–16 plus $^1/_2$ dart measurement; square up.
**16–22** $^1/_2$ the measurement 16–21.
**20–23** $^1/_5$ neck size plus 1.25cm.
**23–24** Dart measurement; join 23 and 24 to 22 to create a dart.
**22–25** The measurement 22–23.
**10–26** 2cm; square across.
**25–27** Shoulder measurement plus 1cm. Draw in the shoulder line with a slight curve.
**21–28** $^1/_4$ measurement 16–20 minus 1cm; join 27–28. Square down from 22 to 29 on the waistline and 30 on the hipline.
**21–31** $^1/_2$ the measurement 8–21; square down to 32 on the waistline, 33 on the hipline, 34 on the hemline. Join 34–19 with a curve.
**8–35** $^1/_2$ measurement 5–8; square down to 36 on the waistline, 37 on the hipline, and 38 on the hemline.
**28–39** $^1/_3$ measurement 27–28.

Draw armhole as shown in diagram touching points 12, 9, 31, 28, 27; the curves also touching points: 2.8cm from 8, and 2cm from 21. (Add 1mm for each size up.)

SLEEVE

Draft a two-piece sleeve (page 38).

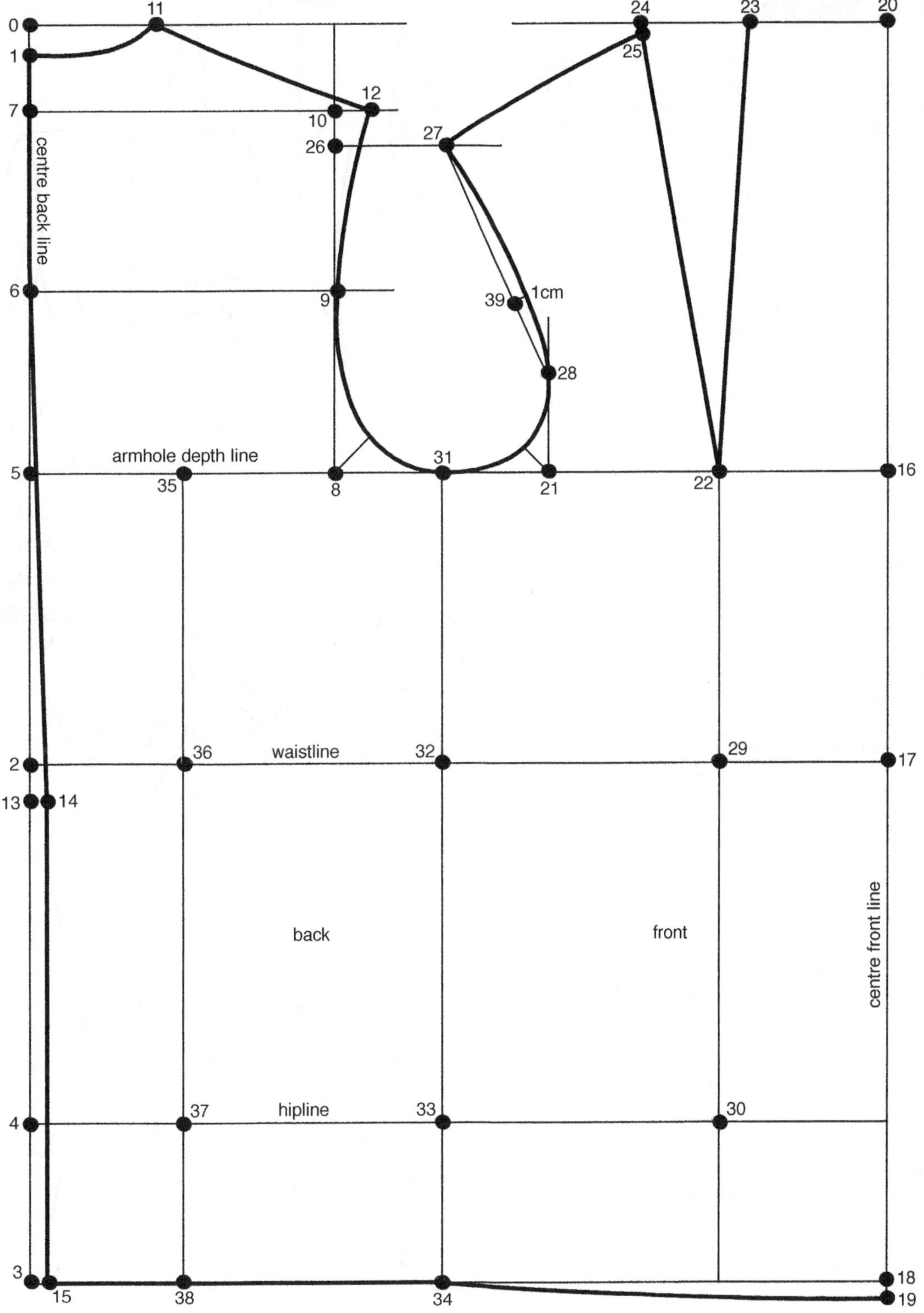
0
1
7
6
5
2
13
14
4
3
15
11
12
10
26
9
8
35
36
37
38
27
39
1cm
28
31
32
33
34
21
24
25
23
20
22
29
30
16
17
18
19
centre back line
armhole depth line
waistline
hipline
back
front
centre front line

# Waist Shaping

There are many different positions for waist shaping, and more can be taken out for a very close fit. The diagrams show some basic waist shaping (11.75cm) which demonstrates the different amounts that are taken on the back and front sections of the figure.

STANDARD WAIST SHAPING
Mark points 16, 17, 18, 19, 20, 22, 23, 25, 29, 30, 31, 32, 33, 34, 35, 36, 37, 38.

**Side seam**
**32–40** 2.5cm.
**34–41** 0.5cm. Draw in front side seam with curves from point 31, through points 40, 33 and 41.
**32–42** 1.5cm.
**33–43** 1cm.
**34–44** 1.5cm. Draw in back side seam with curves from point 31, through points 42, 43 and 44.

**Back dart**
**37–45** 7cm. Draw in 2.5cm dart at point 36.

**Front dart**
**22–46** 2.5cm.
**30–47** 5cm. Draw in 4cm dart at point 29.
The example shows bust dart transferred to shoulder. Mark point 48 at the centre shoulder. Join 22–48. Cut up the line and close the original bust dart. (After any adaptation the dart is shortened 2.5cm).

WAIST SHAPING IN PANELS
When drawing panels, always draw the first panel line to the waist, then take out the darting as shown.
The example shows slight flare at the hem.
Mark points 20, 22, 23, 25, 31.

**Side seam**
Draw side seam as above, but add an extra 1cm flare at points 41 and 44.

**Front panel lines**
Draw in curved front panel line to waist passing through point 22. Mark points 49, 50.
**50–51** 2.5cm.
**51–52** 1.25cm; square down to 53.
Add 1cm flare to point 53. Mark points 54, 55.
Draw front panel line, through points 49, 22, 50, 54.
Cut along the panel line and close the bust dart.
Draw in side front panel line through points 49, 22, 51 and 55.
Draw in a 1.5cm dart in the side panel.

**Back panel lines**
Draw in curved back panel line to waist.
Mark points 56, 57.
**57–58** 2.5cm.
**58–59** 1.25cm. Square down to 60.
Add 1.5cm flare to point 60. Mark points 61, 62.
Draw in back panel line through points 56, 57, 61.
Draw side back panel line through points 56, 58, 62.

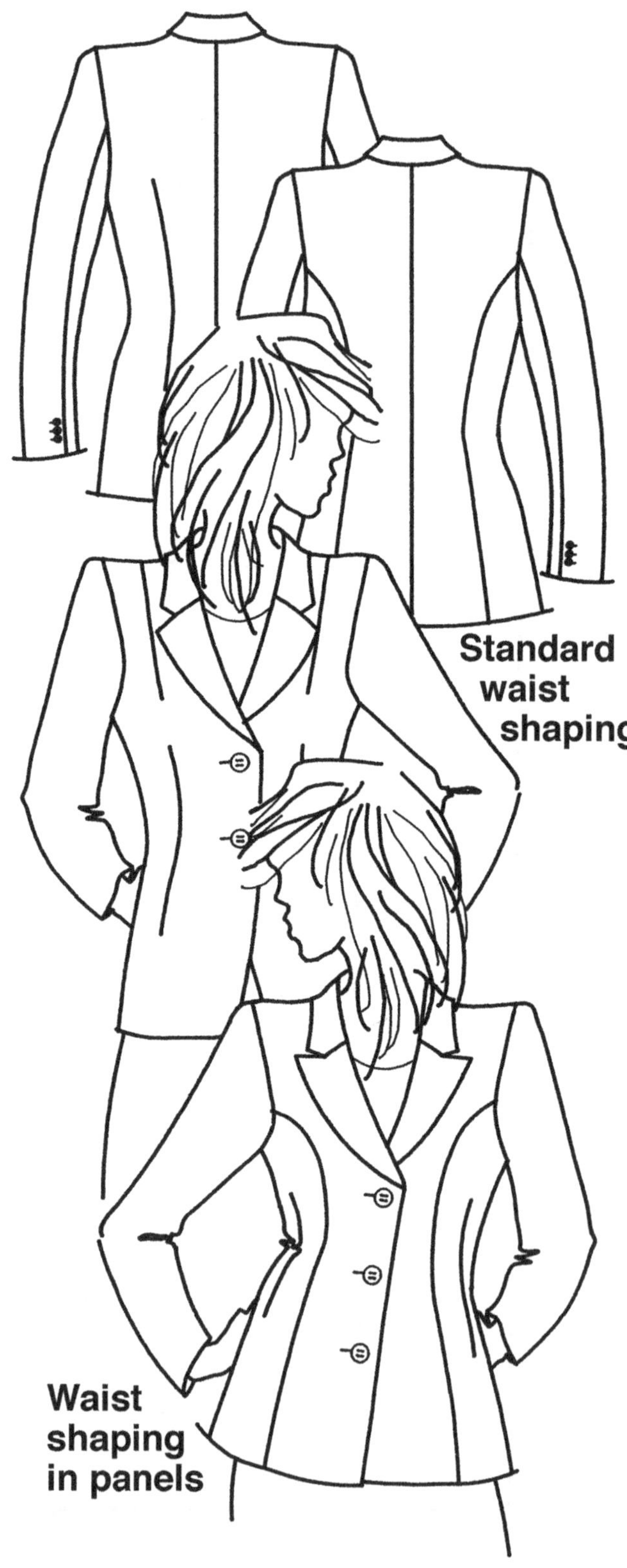

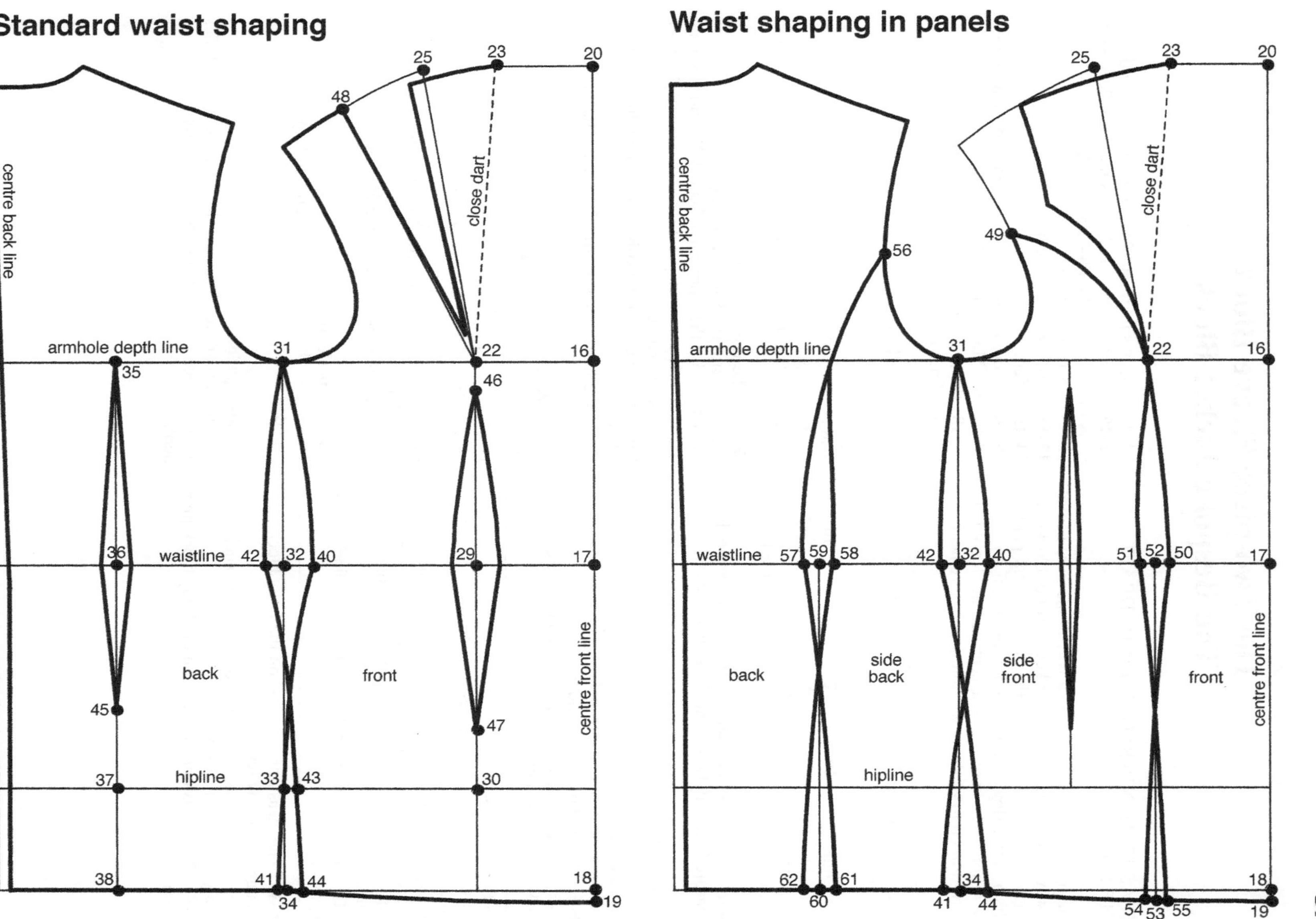
Standard waist shaping
Waist shaping in panels
centre back line
armhole depth line
waistline
hipline
back
side back
side front
front
centre front line
close dart

# The Two-piece Sleeve Block
# The Bespoke Jacket Block

MEASUREMENTS REQUIRED TO DRAFT THE BLOCK

The block can be drafted to individual measurements; however, many bespoke tailors keep a set of blocks in a range of sizes and then alter the measurement points which differ. However, it is important that if an alteration to the body armhole is made, the sleeve must be re-drafted to fit the new armhole measurement.

The block illustrated is drafted for the UK size 10. Refer to the 4cm size chart (page 31) for other standard measurements.

| **Size Code** | **10** | **12** | **14** | **16** |
|---|---|---|---|---|
| Sleeve length | 58 | 58.5 | 59 | 59.5 |
| Wrist size | 15.5 | 16 | 16.5 | 17 |
| Armhole (scye) | measure the armhole of the block. | | | |

**Note** It is important that the curve of the armhole is measured accurately; see the diagram opposite.

No seam allowances included.

**Sleeve draft**

Square down and across from 0.

**0–1** $^1/_3$ armhole measurement.

**1–2** $^1/_2$ measurement 0–1 minus 1cm; square across.

**0–3** $^1/_4$ measurement 0–1.

---

**On the body block**

Mark points A at the underarm point, B and C at the shoulder points.

Mark points D and E at the base of lines which are squared up to touch the armhole lines.

**D–F** The measurement 0–2 on the sleeve block; mark F *pitch point.*

**E–G** The measurement 0–3 on the sleeve block; mark G *pitch point.*

---

**3–4** The measurement G–C on the body block (straight line) plus 1cm.

**4–5** The measurement F–B on the body block (straight line) plus 0.7cm.

**0–6** The measurement A–E on the body block plus 0.3cm.

**0–7** 1.5cm; square out 2cm both ways to 8 and 9.

**1–10** Sleeve length plus 2.5cm; square out 2cm both ways to 11 and 12. Join 8–11 and 9–12.

**10–13** 2.5cm; square out.

**13–14** wrist size minus 1cm.

**14–15** 2.5cm.

**8–16** $^1/_2$ measurement 8–11; square out to mark the elbow line. Mark points 17 on the line 9–12.

**6–18** the measurement A–F on the body block (straight line) plus 1cm.

Join 18–15. Join 6–9.

Join 5–14 and 18–15. Mark points 19 and 20 on the elbow line.

**Top sleeve outline**

**4–21** $^1/_2$ measurement 4–5.

Divide the line 4–3 into 3 sections; mark points 22 and 23.

Draw in the top sleeve head:

from 4–5 raise the back curve 1.5cm at 21;

from 4–3 raise the front curve 2cm at 22, and 1.5cm at 23. (Add 0.1cm to each point for each size up). Join 3–8 with a slight curve.

Curve the line 8–11 inwards 2cm at point 16 on the elbow line.

Curve the line 5–14 outwards 2.25cm at 20. Join 11–14.

**Under sleeve outline**

**6–24** $^1/_3$ measurement 6–18.

**6–25** $^1/_2$ measurement 6–9.

Draw in under sleeve:

from 6–18 hollow the curve 1cm at 24.

from 6–9 hollow the curve 0.5cm at 25.

Curve the line 9–12 inwards 2cm at point 17 on the elbow line.

Curve the line 15–18 outwards 2.75cm at 19. Join 12–15.

**Ease at the sleeve head**

The ease in the sleeve head is drafted to give a full rounded sleeve head.

**Shoulder padding**

The block is drafted for a soft shoulder line and includes an allowance for a shoulder pad of approx. 0.75cm depth.

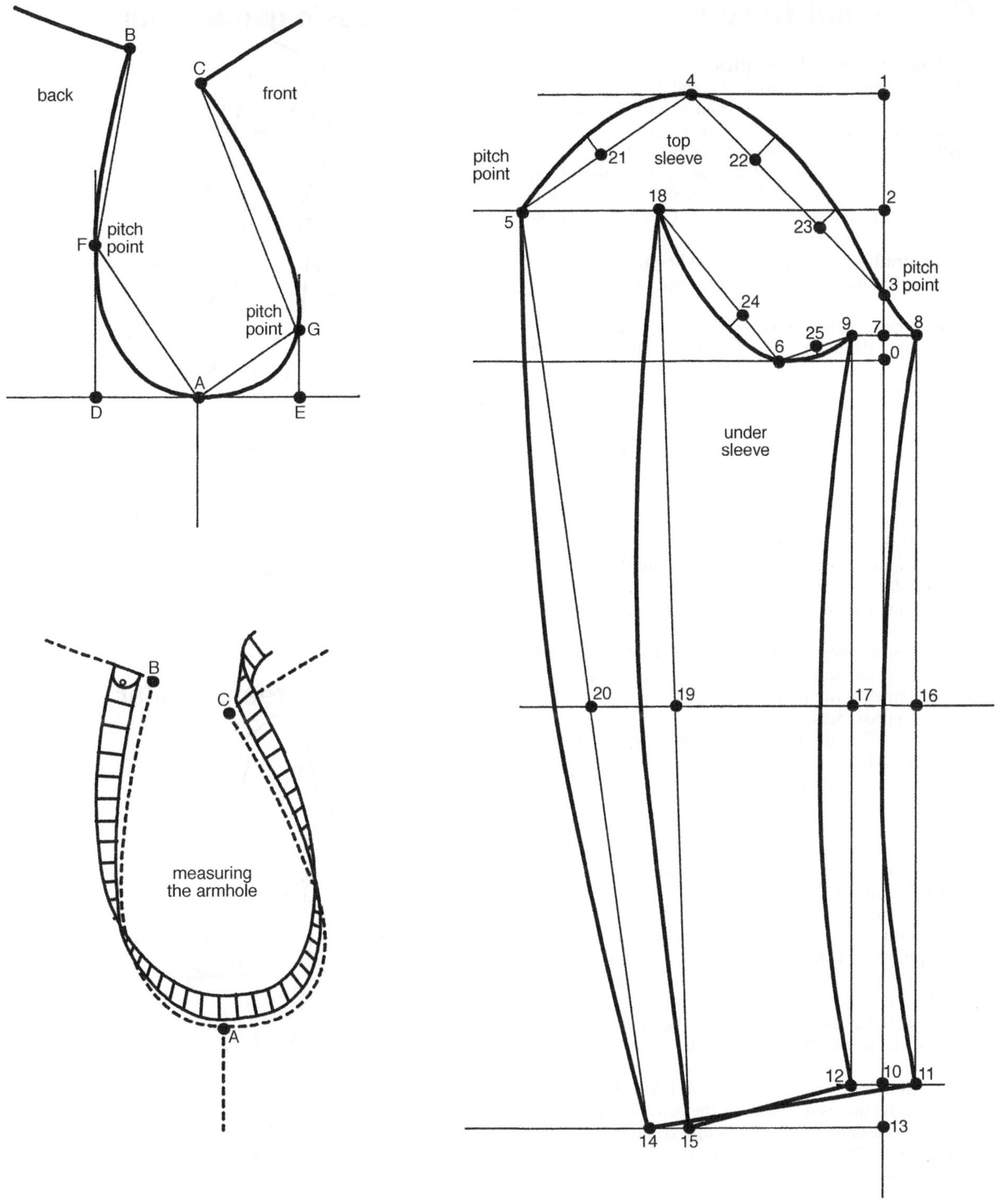
back
front
B
C
F
pitch point
pitch point
G
A
D
E
measuring the armhole
pitch point
top sleeve
under sleeve
pitch point
1
2
3
4
5
6
7
8
9
0
10
11
12
13
14
15
16
17
18
19
20
21
22
23
24
25

# Collars and Revers

## 1 Classic gents collar

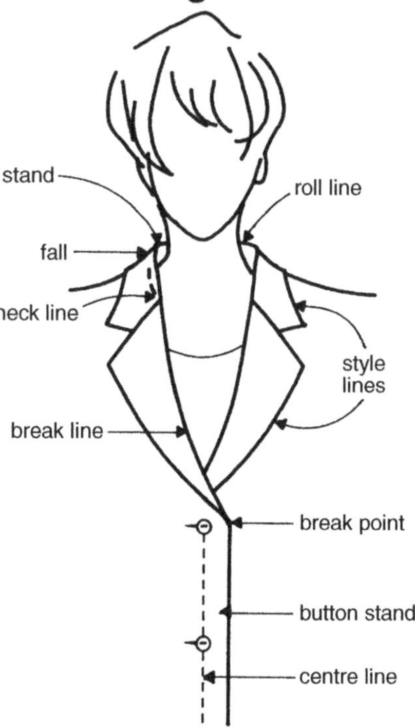


**Collars – General Principles**
TERMS used when constructing collars.

*Neckline* the line where collar is joined to neck.
*Style Line* outer edge of collar or rever.
*Roll Line* the line where the collar rolls over.
*Stand* rise of the collar from neckline to roll line.
*Fall* depth of collar from roll line to style line.
*Break Point* where the rever turns back to form lapel.
*Break Line* line along which lapel rolls back.

**Before drafting a collar** lower neckline if required, mark buttonline, buttonholes, buttonstand.

**Note** When drafting a pattern for a bespoke tailored jacket, only the undercollar is drafted. The topcollar is cut after the under collar has been shaped and the first fitting has been made. The facing is also cut after the first fitting.

1. CLASSIC GENTS COLLAR (TAILORED)

**Body section**

Trace round the jacket front. Mark buttonholes.
Add buttonstand to the centre front line: 1.5cm–2cm.
Example shows a cut away front.
Mark point 0 at the break point opposite the top buttonhole.
Mark point 1 at shoulder point. Extend shoulder line.

**1–2** 2cm: join 0–2.
**1–3** approx. 5cm; draw line parallel to the break line.
**1–4** approx. 4cm; draw in neckline and rever.

Mark point 5 at the rever point.

**1–6** approx. 5cm.

Mark point 7 on the hemline approx. 6.5cm from the centre front line.
Draw in the facing line with a curve as shown.

**Collar**

Extend the break line approx. 9cm.

**2–8** back neck measurement plus 1cm.
**8–9** 2.5cm; ensure that 2–9 is the same length as 2–8.
**9–10** 2.5cm; join 10–4.
**9–11** 4.5cm.

Mark point 12 at the collar point on the rever.
Mark point 13 at the break line.
Draw in the outer edge of the collar to point 14.
Join 12–14.
Trace off the under collar; include the line 9–2–13.
Redraw the line with a curve for the collar roll line.

2. CLASSIC REEFER COLLAR (TAILORED)

The construction is the same as the gents collar, but the neckline is usually lowered at 4 approx. 1cm.
The outline of the rever is also changed, see diagram.
Example shows the front with a straight edge.

## 2 Classic reefer collar

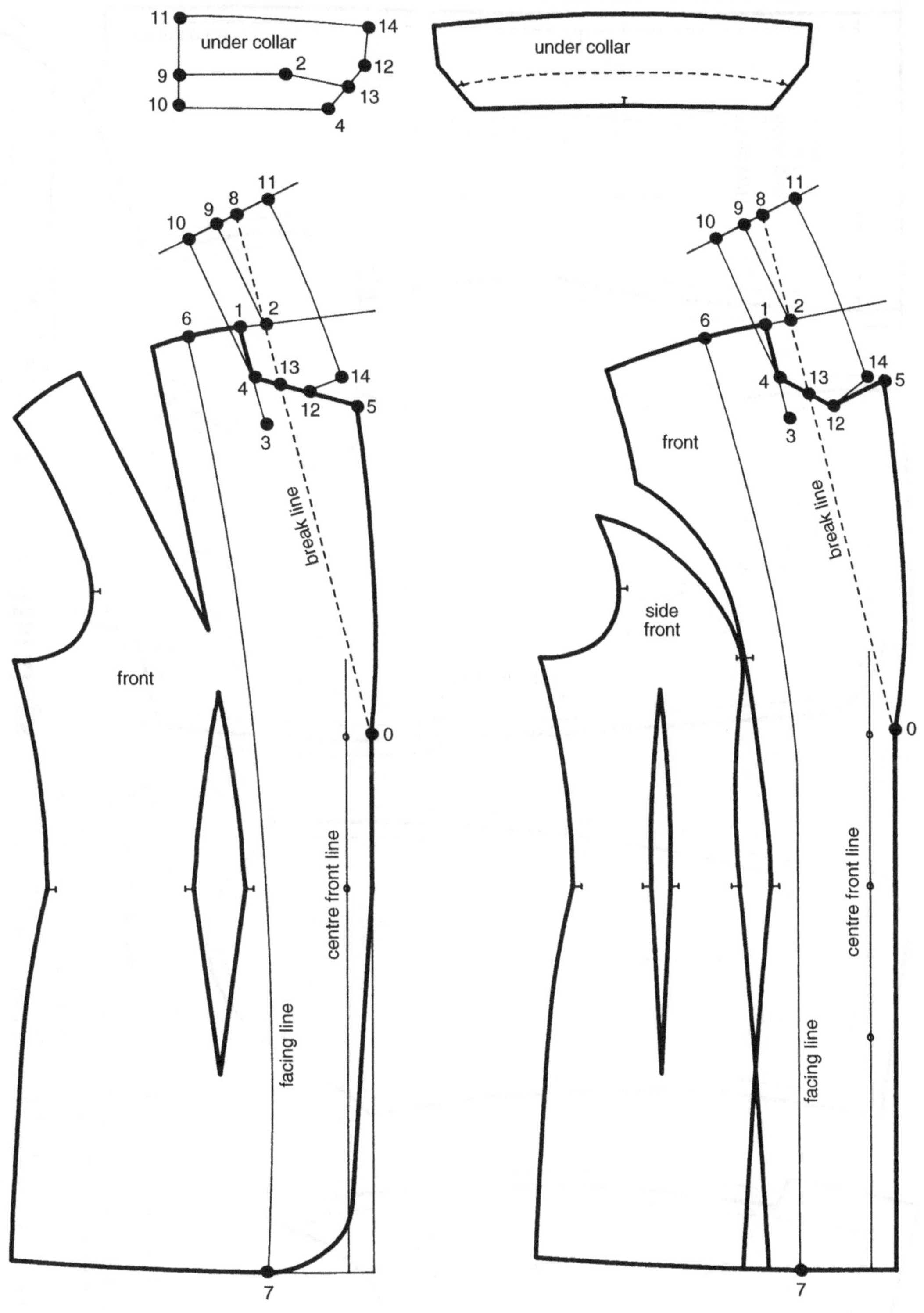


## 1 Classic gents collar

## 2 Classic reefer collar

# Seam Allowances, Inlays and Pattern Markings

The following pieces of pattern are cut for the first fitting: the back and front sections, the top and under sleeves and the under collar.
The following seam and hem allowances are used:

| | |
|---|---|
| all seams | 1.5cm (except for any special seams, e.g. welt); |
| hems | 3.5–4cm; cuff vents 3.5cm × 8cm. |

Darts are not cut out at this stage.
Inlays are extra allowances of 1.5cm added for alterations made at the first fitting. Their positions are marked on the diagram.

**Marking the pattern**

The pattern should be marked with: style number, piece name, size, number to cut, fabric type and grain line.

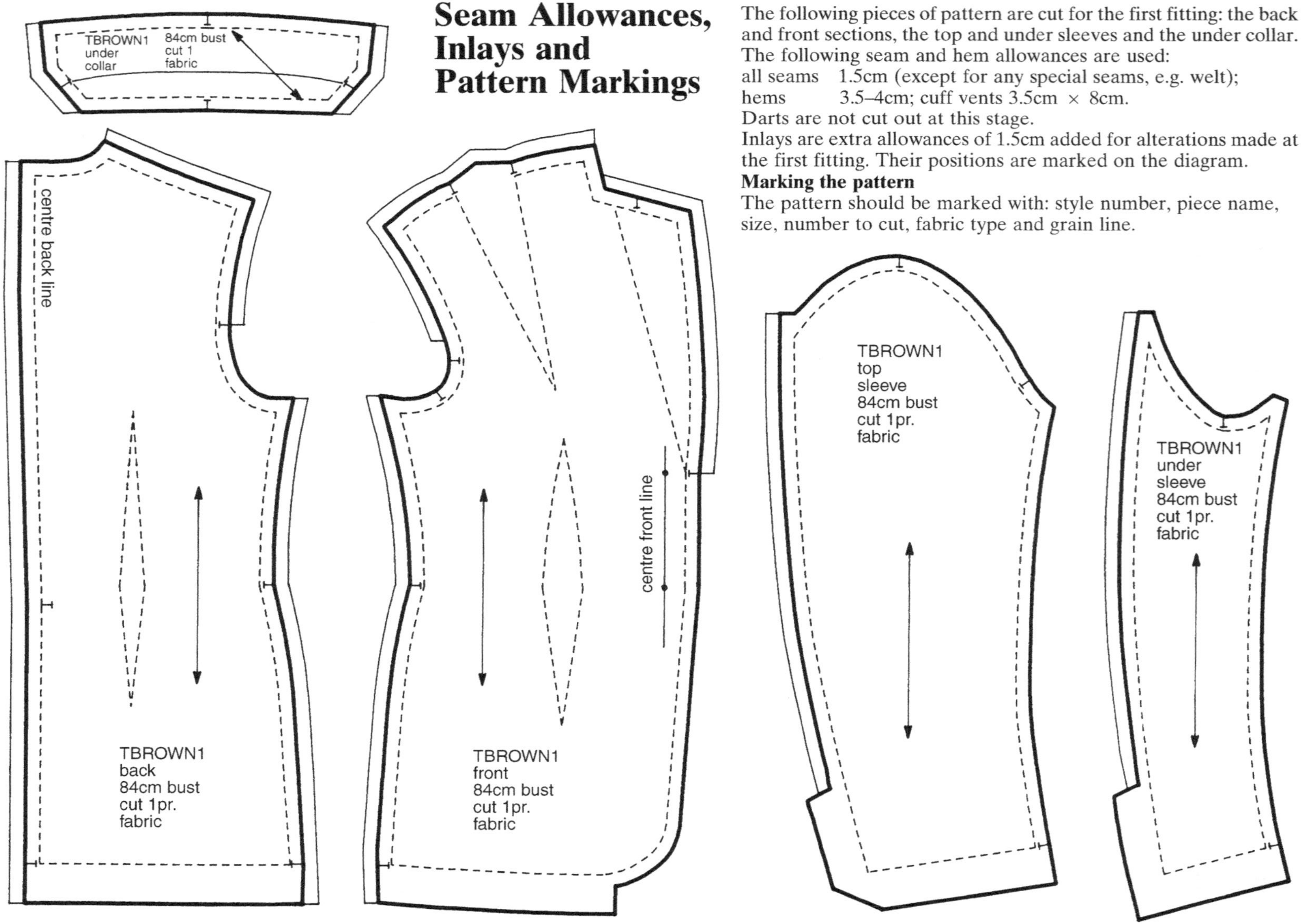

TBROWN1 under collar 84cm bust cut 1 fabric

centre back line

TBROWN1 back 84cm bust cut 1pr. fabric

centre front line

TBROWN1 front 84cm bust cut 1pr. fabric

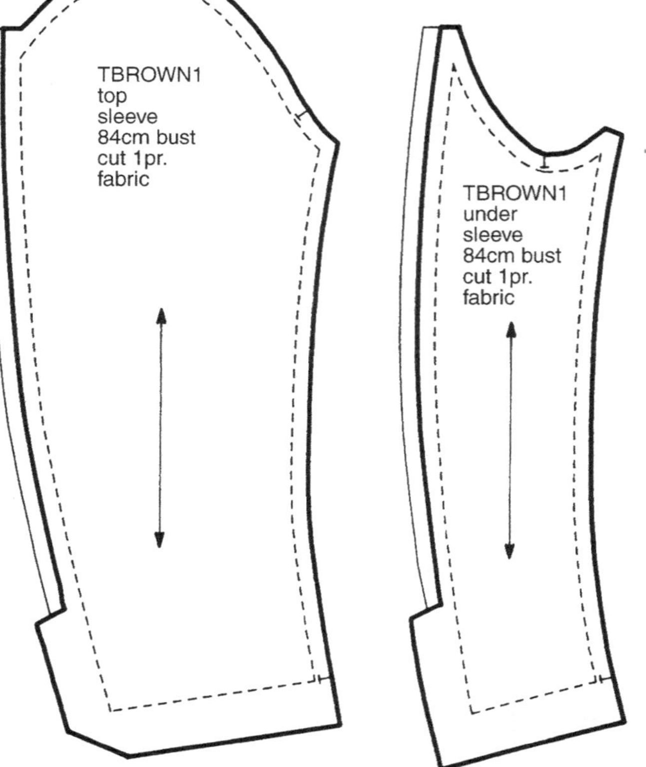

# Interlinings

BEFORE THE FITTING
Whilst some bespoke tailors use a mixture of fusible and non-fusible interlinings, the selections illustrated here are for classic bespoke tailoring and are therefore all non-fusibles (see page 29). Some of these are now quite difficult to obtain.

***All the interlinings must be fully shrunk before use.***

Interlinings **A** and **B** are cut using the garment pieces.

**A** Light-weight worsted and hair canvas; gives stability and softness to the front body section.

**B** Strong canvas (french); for the under collar.

Tack the front canvas to the garment with large tacking stitches, pad stitch and shape the undercollar, see diagram. The garment pieces are then tacked together in preparation for fitting the garment.

AFTER THE FITTING
Separate the garment pieces. Complete all alterations to the jacket pieces and cut away the surplus inlays. Complete all the alterations to the garment pattern. Cut the remainder of the interlinings.

**C** Medium-weight linen canvas; gives stability in the chest area. Cut the chest piece on the bias with no seam allowance. Any shoulder dart is closed.

**D** Light-weight linen; used in any pocket flaps or welts and to reinforce any pocket openings.

Bias strips of the linen are used at the jacket hem, the sleeve hem and vents. To cut the sleeve interlining, overlap the forearm seam. It can also be used at the front and head of the top sleeve.

**E** Fleecy domette or a padded roll; used at the sleeve head.

**F** Narrow linen or twilled cotton stay tape; used along the revers, front edge and underarm. If this is not available, narrow strips of linen can be substituted.

**G** Shoulder pad: approx. 0.7cm depth.

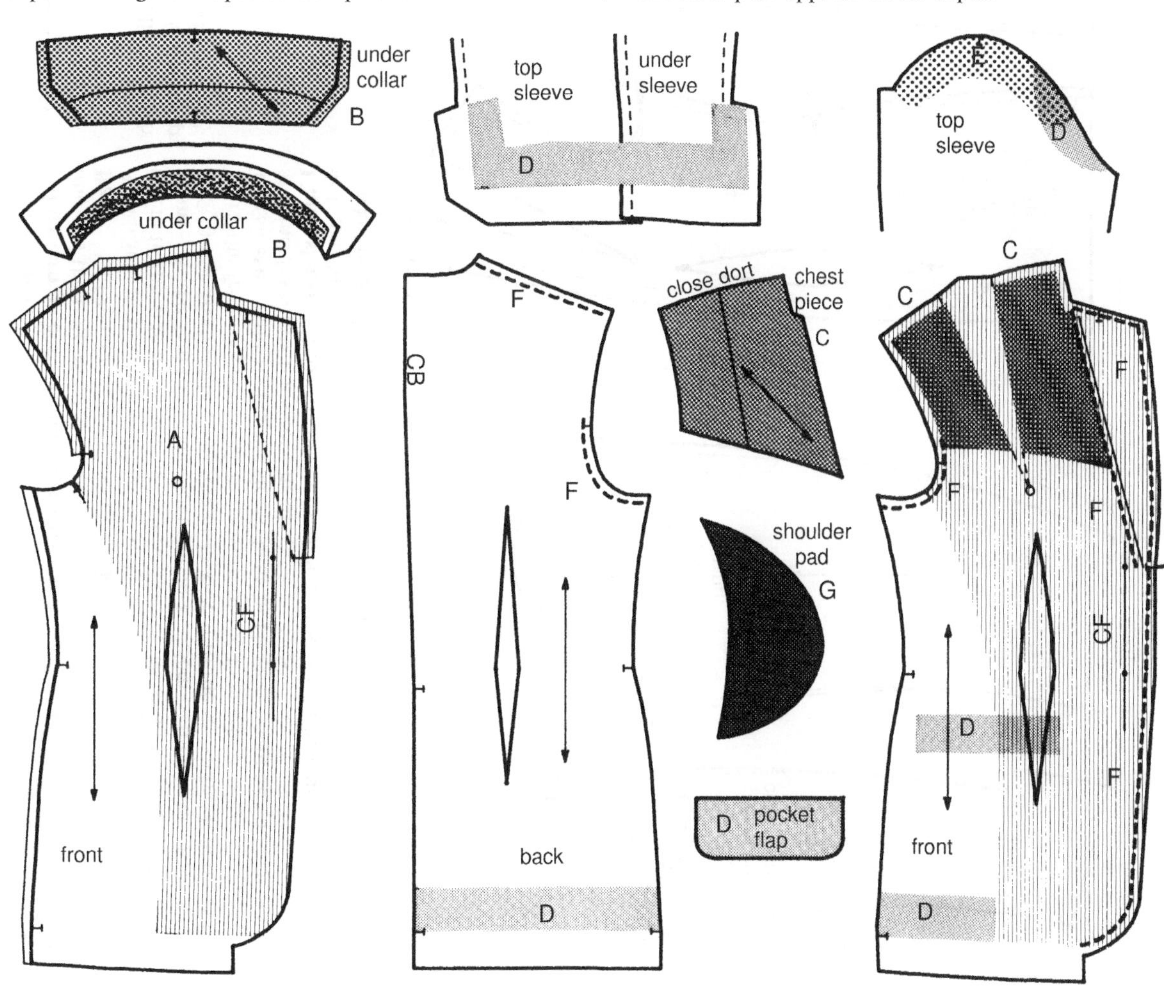

# The Facing, Top Collar and Lining

**The Facing**
Use the corrected pattern. Trace off the facing: add 0.5cm around the rever edge from A–B. Add seam allowance to the facing line.
Place the grain line of the facing parallel with the rever.

**Top Collar**
Cut a piece of fabric on the straight grain larger than the under collar. Stretch outer edge, shrink the middle area slightly, stretch the inside edge. Cut out top collar from the shaped fabric under collar. Add 0.5cm to the style line C–D.

**The Lining**
Use the corrected pattern. Cut out the lining pieces adding ease at the following places.The lining should never pull the garment out of shape or cause wrinkles.

**All pattern pieces** Lining hems are cut halfway between the hem turn up line and the bottom edge.

**Back** Add 2cm pleat to the centre back from the neck to the waistline at A. Add 0.3cm to the shoulder line at B, 0.3cm to the top armhole seam at C, 0.4cm to the side seam line at D, 0.2cm to the waist and hipline at E.

**Front** Add 0.3cm to the shoulder line at F, 0.3cm to the top armhole seam at C, 0.4cm to the side seam line at D, 0.2cm to the waist and hipline at E. Mark the front edge line 1.5cm forward of the facing line at G.

**Top sleeve** Add 1cm at the sleeve head at H. Add 1.5cm up and 0.3cm out at I and J; redraw the sleeve head.

**Under sleeve** Raise the underarm 1.5cm at K. Add 1.5cm up and 0.2cm out at L and M; redraw underarm seam.

**Pocket bags** Lining can be used for the whole, or one side of a pocket bag.

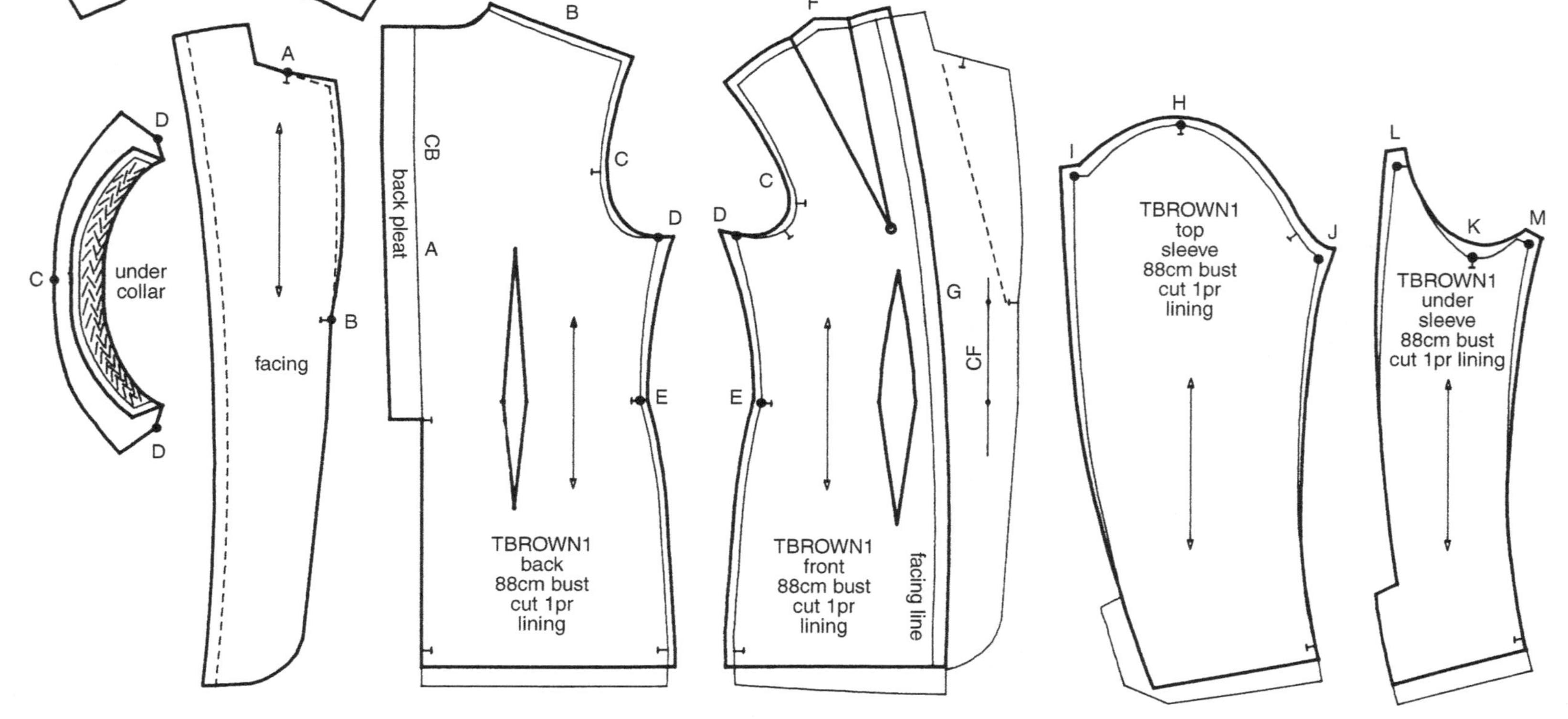

# Reshaping the Garment Pieces

The value of the practice of bespoke tailoring is that it allows the tailor to reshape the garment into a three dimensional form closer in shape to the customer's body. Fabric will re-form in a way that two dimensional patterns will not. This reshaping is done by understitching or stretching and shrinking the fabric. Whilst this is not a book about tailoring sewing methods, it is concerned with pattern shape. Therefore, some examples of these changes are described below.

1. Once the front canvas is firmly attached, the front shoulder is stretched slightly at A, to give shape over the front shoulder bone.
2. The bust area B, is created by shaping the fabric and canvas over a rounded pad to create a smooth dome shape.
3. The rever is curled outwards by pad stitching C, which holds the curl of the rever permanently.
4. When the front and back darts are completed, the 'surplus' fabric at the side seams D, is shrunk away before it is machined.
5. Some tailors reshape the fabric to the rever shape before cutting the rever out. This practice avoids placing the facing off the grain.
6. The elbow area of the top sleeve is shrunk E, and the front seam of the top and the under sleeve is stretched at F. This allows shaped sleeves to hang without twisting when seamed.
7. More fullness can be inserted into the sleeve head because it is shrunk away.

To accomplish some of these practices requires skill and can be time consuming. This means that the bespoke tailored garment is usually expensive. Engineered garments in mass production are usually cut with an easier fitting profile and straighter sleeves, and use methods of cutting to provide any shaping (see pages 52–57).

Books on bespoke tailoring methods of construction are listed in the references[1], page 120.

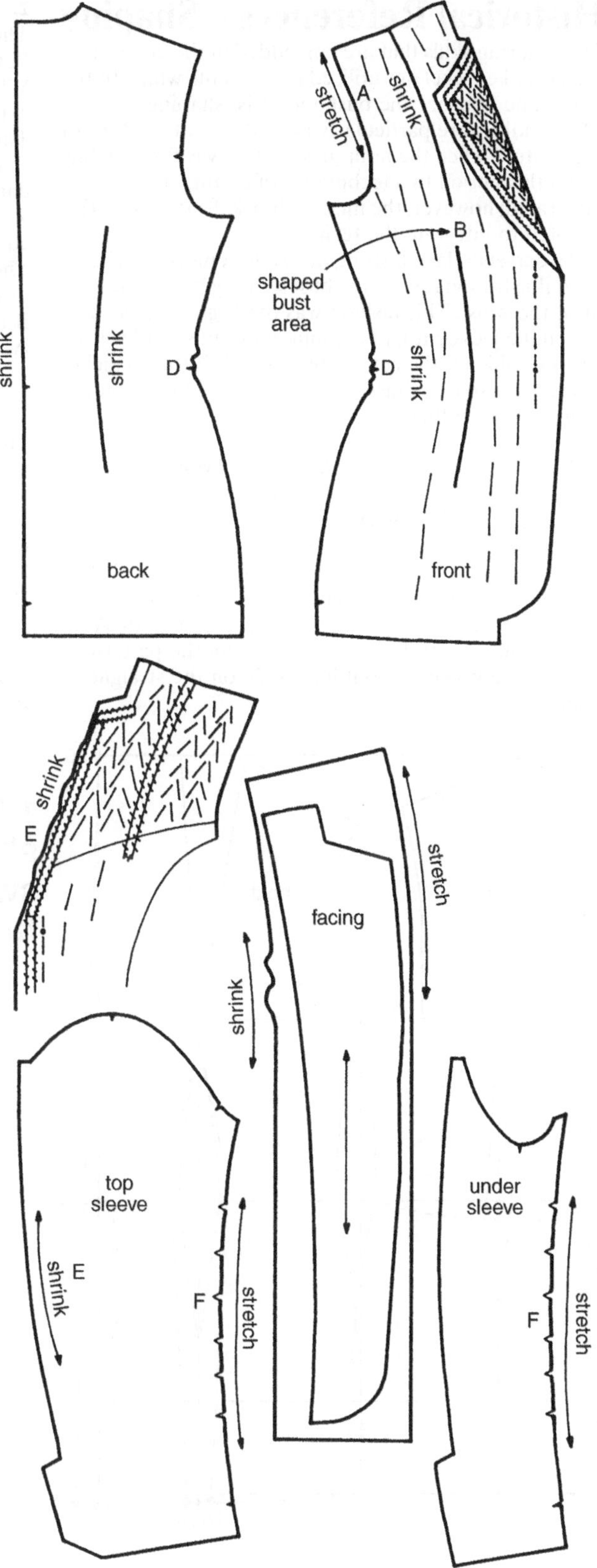

# Historical References – Shaping

The tailoring skills that are embedded in the creation of the bespoke jacket are utilised in garments which fit the figure and enhance the bust and waist shaping.
These skills were particularly in evidence at the turn of the century when the hour glass figure was fashionable. From this period two techniques of cutting are illustrated; however, the modern block draft (page 34) is adapted to integrate the techniques.

As corsets relaxed, straighter styles emerged. The third illustration retains the bust shaping but relaxes the fit of the waist. This fashion was the *beginning* of the masculine jacket; it had a minimum of bust and waist darting, which is the cut of the woman's business jacket today. This style is illustrated and drafted in Chapter 4, Engineered Cutting.

**1. Extra Bust Shaping – Swinging the Front Edge**
Mark points 17, 19, 20 from the original draft with standard waist shaping (page 37).
19–A 2cm: join A–20. Mark B at the waistline.
Widen the front waist dart by the measurement B–17.
Mark point C on the hem line of the front dart.
C–D and C–E are each half the measurement 19–A.
Draw in new front dart as shown. Swing the pattern to place the new centre front line A–20 on the straight grain.

**2. Waist Shaping – Very Close-fitting**
The diagram shows an adaptation of Waist Shaping in Panels (page 30) which increases the shaping (14cm).
When an extra close fit is required, it is wise to create extra panels in the garment as shown in the diagram.
The diagram shows an example of the amounts of shaping taken on the panel, and the distribution of the darting. The side seam is moved forward approx. 2.5cm.
The diagram also shows how increased flare can be added at the hip line to emphasise the tight waist.
The centre front line can also be shaped, but it must be drawn to create a good line with the rever.
It is essential that this type of edge is taped.
An example of separating some of the panels is shown.

**3. Waist Shaping – Easy-fitting**
This diagram illustrates the inclusion of a side panel and a reduced amount of darting at the waist (9 cm).
Mark points 2, 8, 21. 2–A 1.25cm
8–B 2cm; square up to C and down D on the waistline.
D–E 2.5cm; square down from centre of the dart to F.
Draw panel seams; add 1.25cm flare to each seam at F.
21–G 2cm; square up to H, down to I and J.
I–K 1cm. I–L 1.75cm. J–M 0.75cm. J–N 1.5cm.
Draw front panel seams as shown.
Reduce front dart to 2.5cm at O.

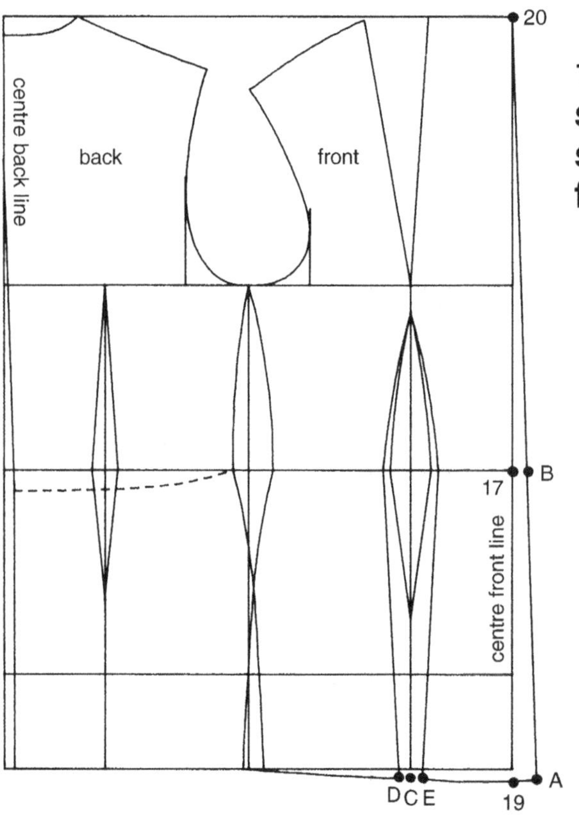


**1 Extra bust shaping – swinging the front edge**

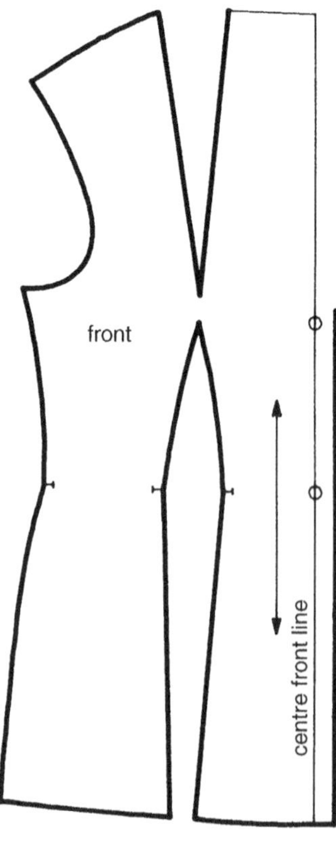

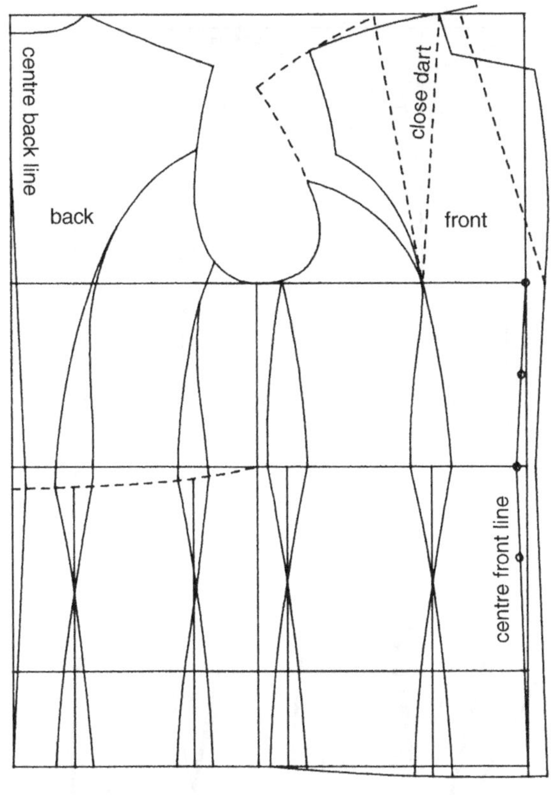


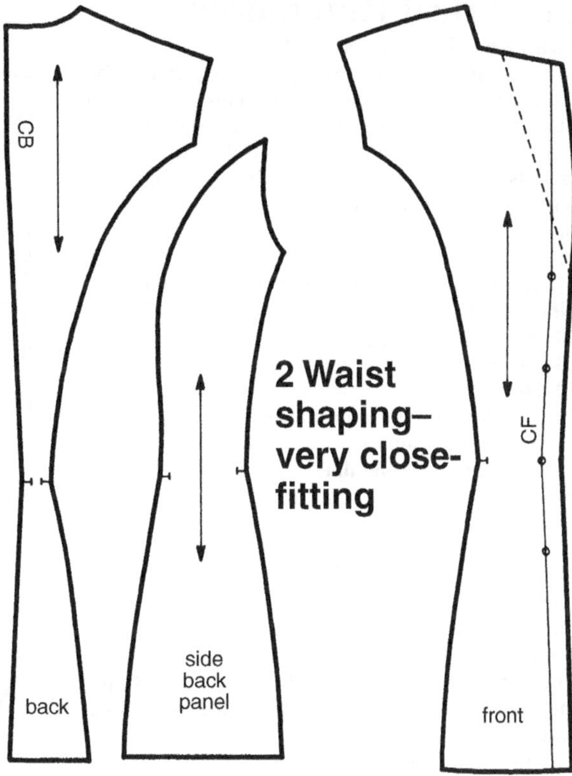


**2 Waist shaping– very close-fitting**

## 3 Waist shaping–easy-fitting

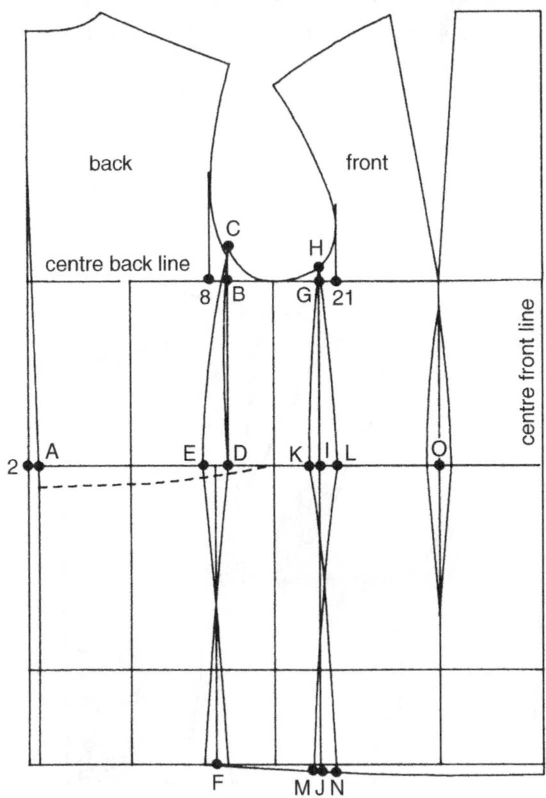


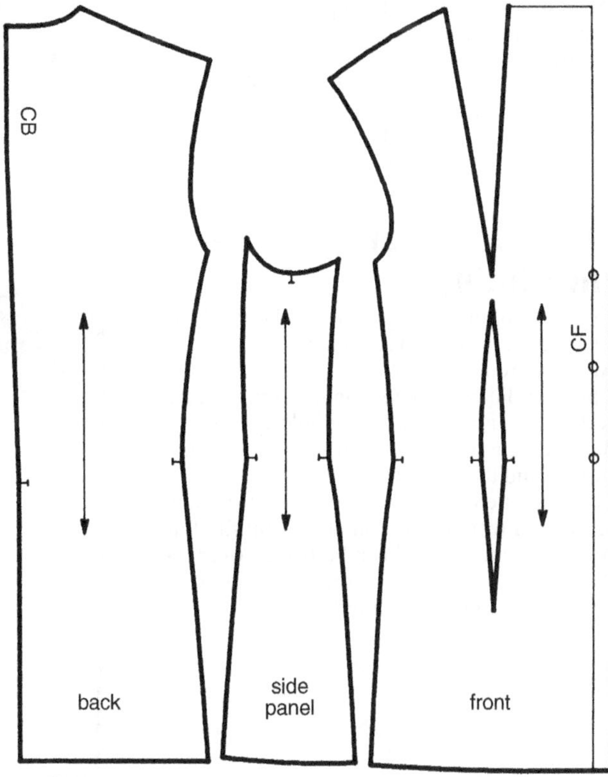

# Historical References

**Extra Bust Shaping - Neck Darts**

Many of the drafts for women's wear, drafted by men tailors, included neck darts. This gave added bust shaping to drafts already well provided. However, this technique is a useful addition for jackets where there is very little bust shaping. The dart is hidden under the rever and therefore provides a very clear chest area.

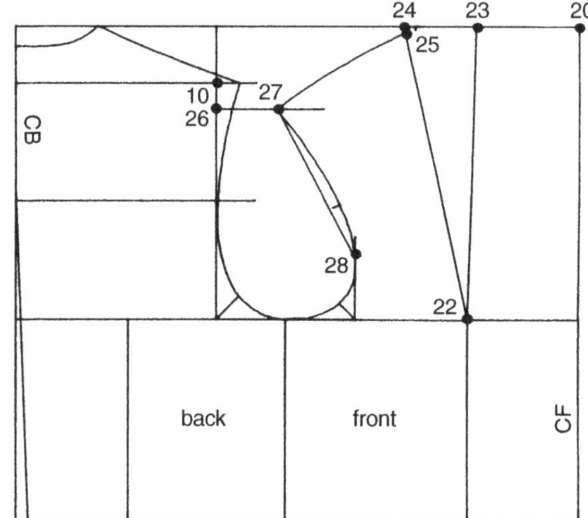


Make the following alterations to the original block draft (page 34). Mark points 20, 22, 28.

**20–23** $^1/_5$ neck size plus 1.5cm.
**23–24** dart measurement.
**10–26** 2.25cm.
**26–27** the shoulder measurement plus 1cm.
Draw in front armhole.

**Creating the neckline dart**

Add buttonstand and mark break point.
Extend the shoulder line.
**23–A** 2cm; draw in break line.
Draw in neckline from 23–B parallel with break line.
Draw in the outline of the rever. Mark the collar position C.
The dart can be inserted midway between B and the break line or midway between the break line and collar point C.
The first example is illustrated.
Mark D at centre of the dart.
Join D–22. D–E $^1/_2$ the measurement D–22.
Draw in a 1cm dart at D to point E.
Draw in the facing line.

**Facing**

Trace off the facing. Extend the dart to the edge of the facing; close the dart.
Draft any collar from the facing pattern because this has the neck dart closed.

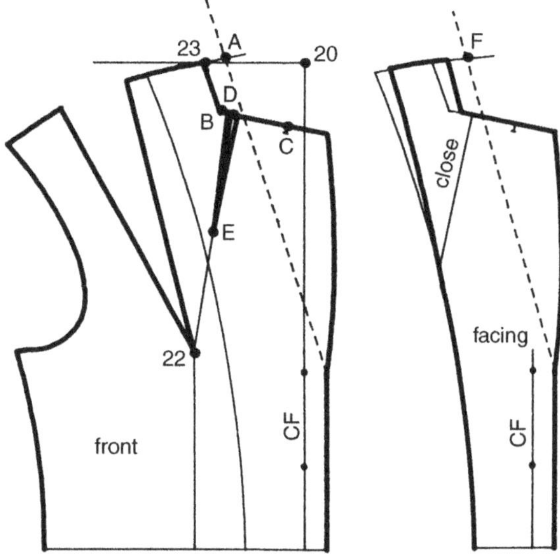


# Historical References – Interlining

Examples of interlinings that can be used to create a more structured jacket.

**A.** The front canvas can be cut on the cross, but a piece of linen on the straight grain must be added to reinforce the buttonholes.

**B.** Medium weight linen; used at the back neck and around the armholes.

**C.** Domette or felt; the front armhole linen can be padded with felt or domette to fill the bust hollow. A circular pad can be placed over the bust. The domette at the armhole and bust is sometimes quilted onto the lining.

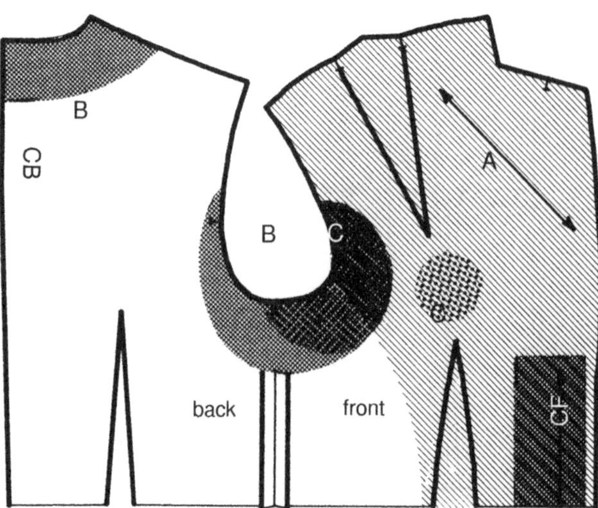

# Part Two:

# 4 THE ENGINEERED JACKET



ENGINEERED CUTTING

Most of the shape of the bespoke tailored jacket is achieved by the steaming, stretching and shrinking of the cloth garment pieces. The shape of the engineered tailored jacket has to be achieved almost entirely by the cut of the pattern. The block which is offered to demonstrate the process of engineering a jacket, is an easy-fitting block. This is a very popular shape; it is not very structured, it is comfortable, does not require a great deal of body shaping, and will fit a wide range of figures that fall within a size code. The main features are:

1. the wide back which will drape;
2. the side panel and front dart for subtle shaping;
3. the wide soft shoulder and straight full sleeve which will drape;
4. the dart from neck to break point to allow the front ease to be held by machined tape;
5. the separate collar and stand, the cut providing the shape.

The engineered jacket has evolved from the ready-to-wear trade which used both tailoring and dressmakimg techniques. However, it has been further systemised to maximise and control the production in order to offer good quality at an affordable price.

**Note** Other books cover the cutting and manufacture of tailored jackets; see the references[1] on page 119.

# Engineered Classic Jacket Block – Basic Grid

**Semi-fitting with Reduced Bust Shaping**

MEASUREMENTS REQUIRED TO DRAFT THE BLOCKS

The block illustrated is drafted to the UK size 10. Refer to the 4cm size chart (page 31 for other standard measurements).

| **Size Code** | **10** | **12** | **14** | **16** |
|---|---|---|---|---|
| Bust | 84 | 88 | 92 | 96 |
| Back width | 33.5 | 34.5 | 35.5 | 36.5 |
| Shoulder | 12 | 12.25 | 12.5 | 12.75 |
| Neck size | 36 | 37 | 38 | 39 |
| Wrist | 15.5 | 16 | 16.5 | 17 |
| Back neck to waist | 40 | 40.5 | 41 | 41.5 |
| Waist to hip | 20.25 | 20.5 | 20.75 | 21 |
| Armhole depth | 20.6 | 21 | 21.4 | 21.8 |

No seam allowances included.

**Basic body sections**

There is 0.75cm ease in the back shoulder.

Square down and across from 0.

**0–1** Armhole depth plus 3cm; square out.

**0–2** $^1/_2$ measurement 0–1 plus 1cm; square across.

**0–3** Back neck to waist plus 2cm; square across.

**3–4** Waist to hip length; square across.

**4–5** 12cm; square across.

**3–6** 1.25cm; square down to 7; join 6–2 to complete back seam line.

**0–8** $^1/_5$ neck size plus 1.2cm; square up.

**8–9** 2.75cm; draw back neck curve.

**1–10** $^1/_2$ across back plus 2.5cm; square up to 11 and 12.

**12–13** $^1/_{10}$ measurement 0–1 minus 0.2cm; square out approx. 6.5cm.

**9–14** Draw in shoulder line with a hollowed curve to touch the line from 13, shoulder measurement plus 1.5cm.

**10–15** 2.5cm (add 0.1cm for each size up); square out 1cm to 16.

**1–17** $^1/_2$ bust plus 8.5cm; square up to 18, down to 19 and 20.

**20–21** 1cm; square out approx. 3cm.

**19** The position of the waist buttonhole.

**22** The position of the top buttonhole.

**22–23** 2cm; square down to 24 on the waistline, 25 on the hemline.

**1–26** $^1/_2$ measurement 1–17 minus 1cm; square down to 27 and 28. Join 21–28 with a curve.

**17–29** $^1/_3$ measurement 1–17 plus 2.5cm.

**17–30** $^1/_2$ measurement 17–29 plus 0.5cm; square down to 31 and 32.

**30–33** 1.5cm.

**29–34** $^1/_3$ measurement 17–18 minus 1cm.

**29–35** Measurement 10–15; square out 0.7cm to 36.

**18–37** 1.25cm; square across.

**37–38** Measurement 17–30 plus 2cm; join 38–33.

**38–39** 3cm; join 39–33.

**14–40** 1.75cm; square out approx. 12cm.

Draw in front shoulder line 38–41 with a curve to touch the line from 40, shoulder measurement plus 0.75cm.

Draw in back armscye shape to touch points 14, 11, 16, 26, 36, 34, 41.

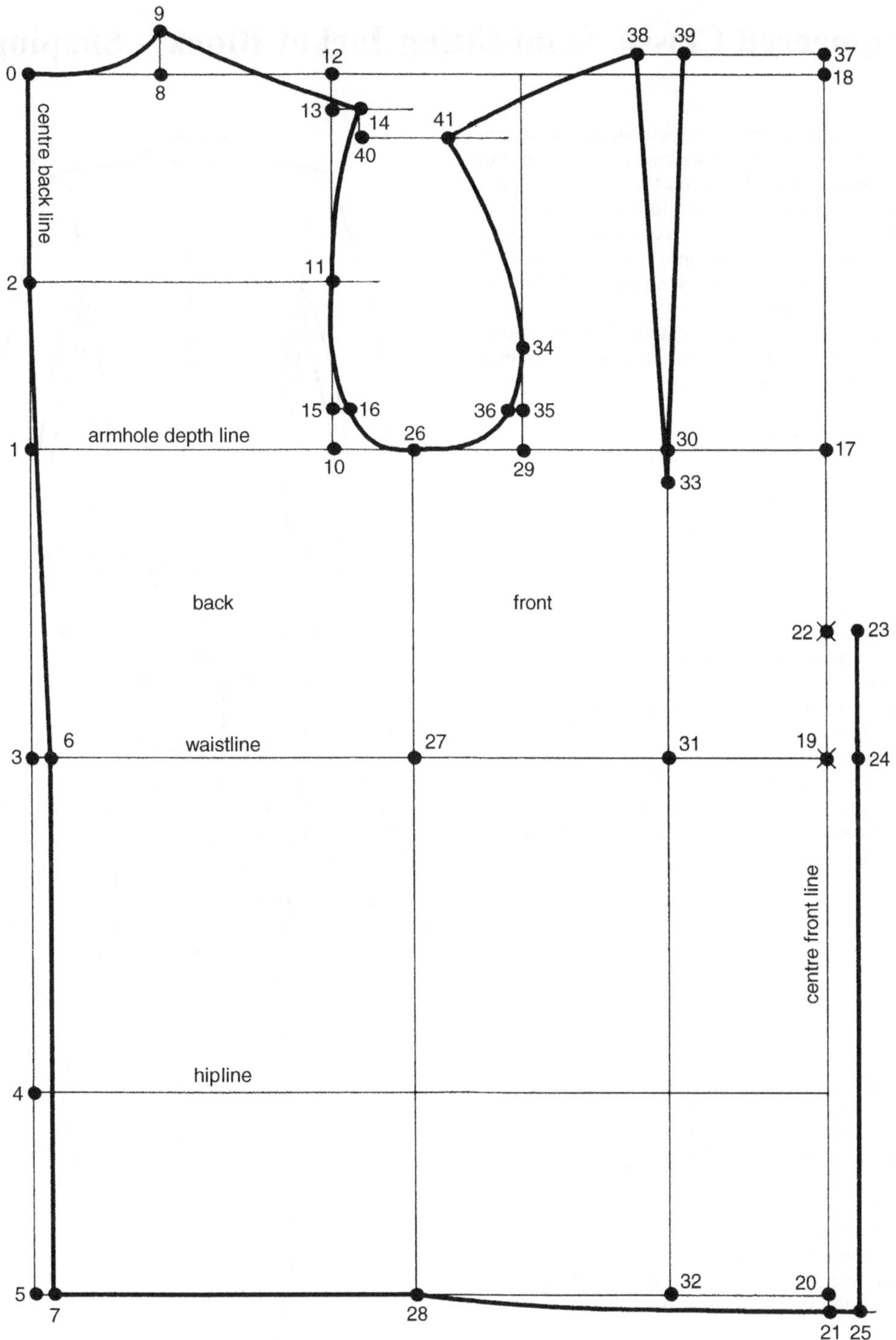

0
9
8
12
13
14
40
41
38
39
37
18
centre back line
2
11
34
15
16
36
35
1
armhole depth line
10
26
29
30
33
17
back
front
22
23
3
6
waistline
27
31
19
24
centre front line
4
hipline
5
7
28
32
20
21
25

# Engineered Classic Semi-fitting Jacket Block – Shaping

**Special Note** The shaping for this classic block is semi-fitting with a 'draped' easy-fitting back. The amount of waist suppression is 9cm. To retain the overall shape and balance of the jacket this should be retained or modified only slightly. The placings of the panels can be varied to almost any new positions, but the amount of suppression for the front and back should be balanced as shown in this example.

Jackets that are to fit closely around the figure have to be cut quite differently with less ease and more bust dart shaping (see pages 34 and 78).

**Side panel and front dart shaping**
From point 16 square up 0.5cm and out 0.25cm to 42.
Square down from 42 to 43.
**43–44** 4.75cm; square down to 45.
**45–46** 3cm; draw in back seam line. Curve line inwards from 16–44 and outwards from 44–46 as shown.
**46–47** 1cm. Draw in side panel back seam line through points 42, 43 and 47 curving outwards as shown.
Join 21–47 with a slight curve.
Square down from point 36 to 48 on the waistline and 49 on the hemline.
**49–50** 2cm. Draw in side panel front seam line. Draw the line straight from 36–48 and curving the line outwards from 48–50 as shown.
**31–51** 6.5cm; square out 1.5cm to 52.
**52–53** Draw in pocket line 15cm length.
Draw in front dart waist shaping 1.5cm at 31 and 1cm at 51 on the pocket line.
**48–54** 1.5cm.
Mark point 55 on the pocket line where it crosses the line 48–50.
**55–56** 1cm.
**49–57** 1.5cm. Draw in front seam line in two sections: curve line 36–54 inwards, 54–55 and 56–57 and outwards as shown.

**Front shaping**
Straight front: use the front edge line 23–25.
Shaped front: Join 24–21 at front edge line.
Curve the lower front edge at 21 as required.

**Front darting**
Cut along the pocketline.
Cut out the front dart at waist.
Cut along the line 33–38. Close the dart 38–39 at the neck point to open up the front waist dart.

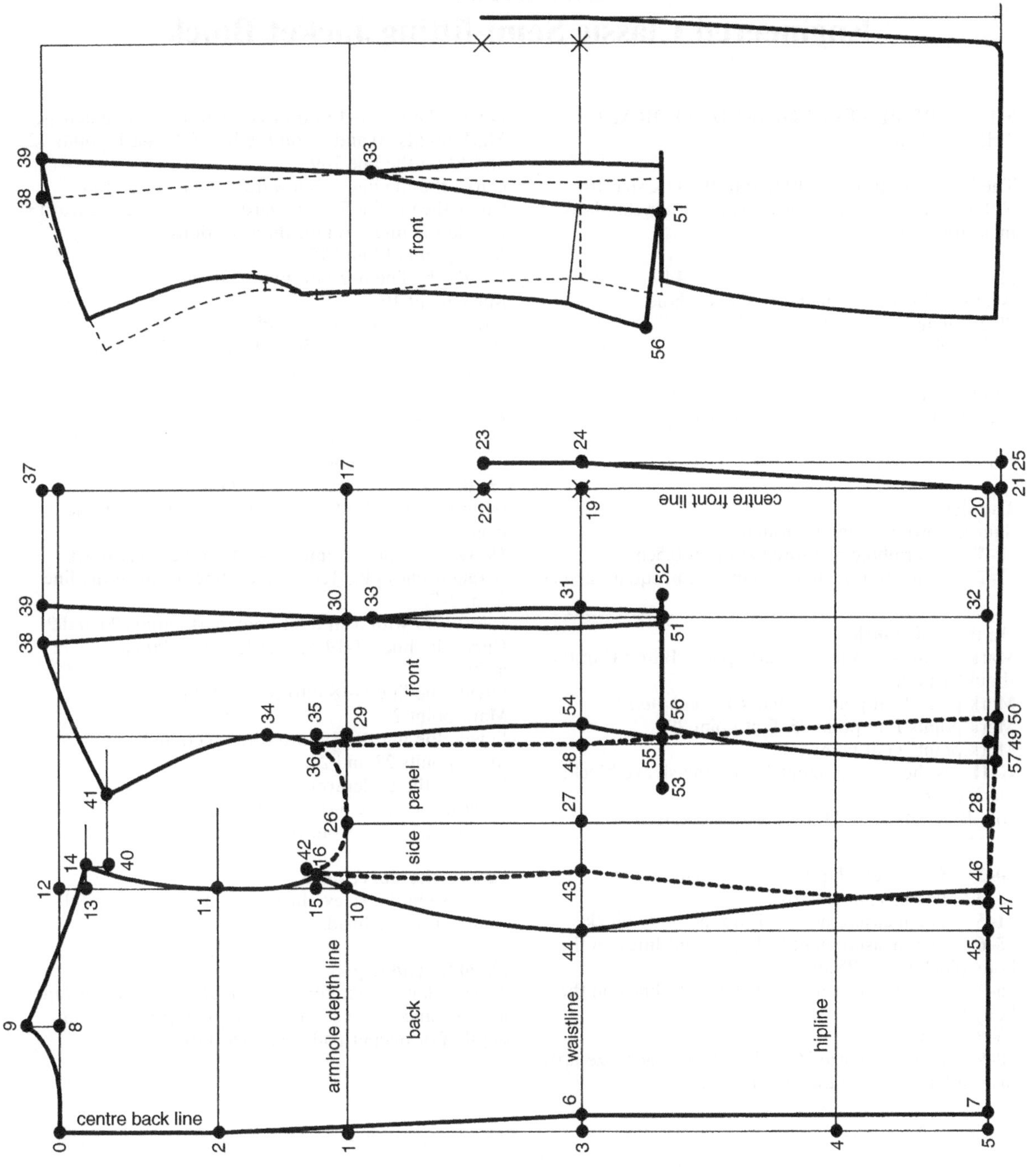
centre back line
armhole depth line
waistline
hipline
back
side
panel
front
centre front line
front

# The Sleeve
# Engineered Classic Semi-fitting Jacket Block

MEASUREMENTS REQUIRED TO DRAFT THE BLOCKS

The block illustrated is drafted to the UK size 10. Refer to the size chart (page 31) for other standard measurements.

| **Size Code** | **10** | **12** | **14** | **16** |
|---|---|---|---|---|
| Armhole (scye) | measure the armhole | | | |
| Sleeve length | 58 | 58.5 | 59 | 59.5 |
| Wrist size | 15.5 | 16 | 16.5 | 17 |

**Note** It is important that the curve of the armhole is measured accurately; see the diagram opposite.

No seam allowances included.

### Top sleeve

Square down and across from 0.

**0–1** $^1/_3$ armhole measurement plus 0.5cm.

**1–2** $^1/_2$ measurement 0–1 minus 1cm; square across.

---

**On the body block**

Mark points A at the underarm point, B and C at the shoulder points.
Mark point D at point 36; mark D *pitch point.*
Mark points E at point 35, F at point 29.
Mark points G at point 10.
**G–H** is the measurement 1–2 on the sleeve block; mark H *pitch point.*
Join B–H, H–A, A–D, D–C with straight lines.

---

**0–3** Sleeve length plus 2.5cm; square across.

**3–4** 1.5cm; square across.

**1–5** The measurement F–E on the body block.

**5–6** The measurement C–D (straight line) on the body block plus 1.25cm.

**6–7** The measurement B–H (straight line) on the body block plus 0.75cm.

**3–8** 2cm; join 5–8.

**8–9** 15.5cm for size 36, (add 0.25 for each size up); draw a line to touch the line from 4.

Divide the line 1–4 into three sections; square across.
Mark points 10 and 11 on the line 5–8; mark points 12 and 13 on the line 7–9.
Curve the the line 5–8 inwards 1cm at 10 and 11.
Curve the the line 7–9 outwards 1.5cm at 12; 1.3cm at 13.
Divide the line 5–6 into three sections.
Mark points 14 and 15.
Divide the line 6–7 into two sections.
Mark point 16.
Draw in the top sleeve head.
Raise the curve 5–6 2.5cm at 14 and 1.2cm at 15.
Raise the curve 6–7 2cm at 16.

### Under sleeve

**8–17** $^2/_3$ the measurement 8–9 minus 1cm; draw the line to touch the line from 4.

**5–18** The measurement A–D on the body block (straight line) plus 0.3cm; draw a line to touch the line from 1.

**18–19** The measurement A–H on the body block (straight line) plus 1cm; draw a line to touch the line from 2–7.

Join 17–19 with a straight line; mark points 20 and 21.
Curve the line 17–19 outwards 2cm at 20 and 1.7cm at 21.
Divide the line 5–18 into two sections.
Mark point 22.
Divide the line 18–19 into three sections.
Mark points 23 and 24.
Draw in the underarm curves for all sizes.
Hollow the curve 5–18 0.7cm at 22.
Hollow the curve from 18–19 1cm at 23 and 0.7cm at 24.

### Ease at the sleeve head

The ease in the sleeve head is drafted to give a full rounded sleeve head.

### Shoulder padding

The block is drafted for a soft shoulder line and includes an allowance for a shoulder pad of approx. 0.75cm depth. For deeper pads see page 110.

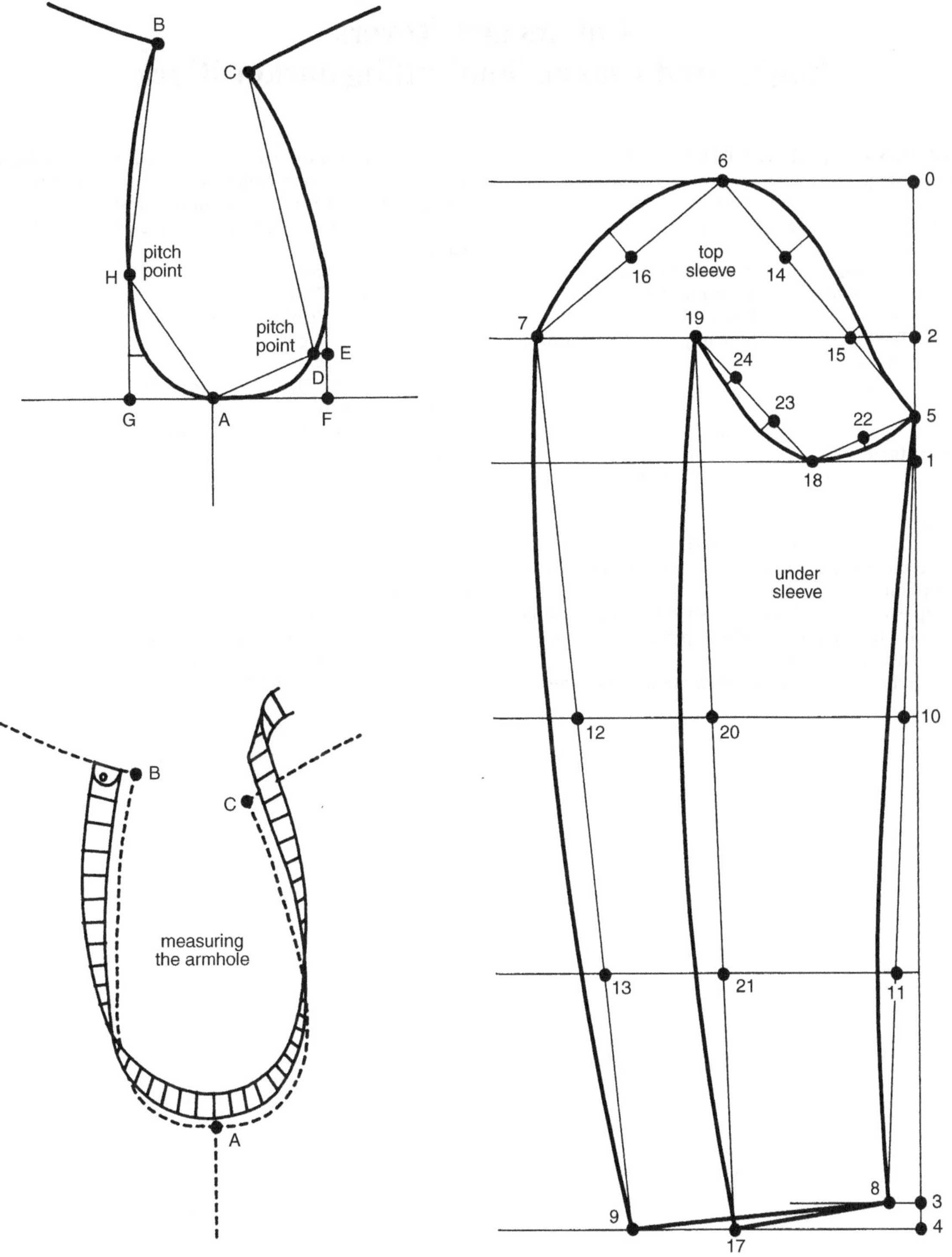
B
C
pitch point
H
pitch point
E
D
G
A
F
B
C
measuring the armhole
A
6
0
top sleeve
16
14
7
19
2
24
15
23
22
5
18
1
under sleeve
12
20
10
13
21
11
8
3
9
17
4

# Collars and Revers
# Engineered Classic Semi-fitting Jacket Block

### LOW REVER AND GENTS COLLAR

**Front – stage one**

Mark points 19, 24, 25 and 39.

From point 39 square down 2.5cm and out 0.25cm to point A.

Draw in the shape of the rever from A to 24.

Extend the shoulder line from point 39.

**39–B** 2cm; join B–24. Mark point C on the rever.

**B–D** Back neck measurement plus 0.25cm: square across both ways.

**D–E** 2.25cm.

**D–F** Collar depth; (example is 4.75cm).

Draw in the style line of the collar F, G, H.

**Collar stand**

Trace off the collar stand A, E, D, B, C.

**E–I** is the back neck measurement.

**Collar**

Trace off collar, C, B, D, F, G, H.

Divide the line C–D into four sections: square up from each point.

Cut up each line and open the style line the required amount. The example for this depth of collar is 0.35cm at the style line of each cut.

*If the collar depth is deeper, then the style line must be opened more to allow it to sit lower around the shoulders.*

Trace around the new collar shape for the under collar.

The under collar is often cut on the cross.

The top collar has 0.3cm added to the edge from F–H.

**Facing**

On the front section:

**24–J** Approx. 7cm.

**25–K** Approx. 8cm; join J–K.

Join A–J with a slight curve.

Trace off facing.

Add 0.5cm to the facing edge from H–24.

**Front – stage two**

Cut down the line from C–24; open 1.5cm dart at neckline.

**24–L** 9cm; shorten dart to point L.

### HIGH REVER AND REEFER COLLAR

The diagram shows the same method of drafting for a jacket with a straight front, higher button fastening and reefer collar and rever.

Mark points 22 and 23.

After the construction of the collar and facing, construct the dart on the front section but make the distance to the base of the dart 23–M 6cm.

# Collars and revers

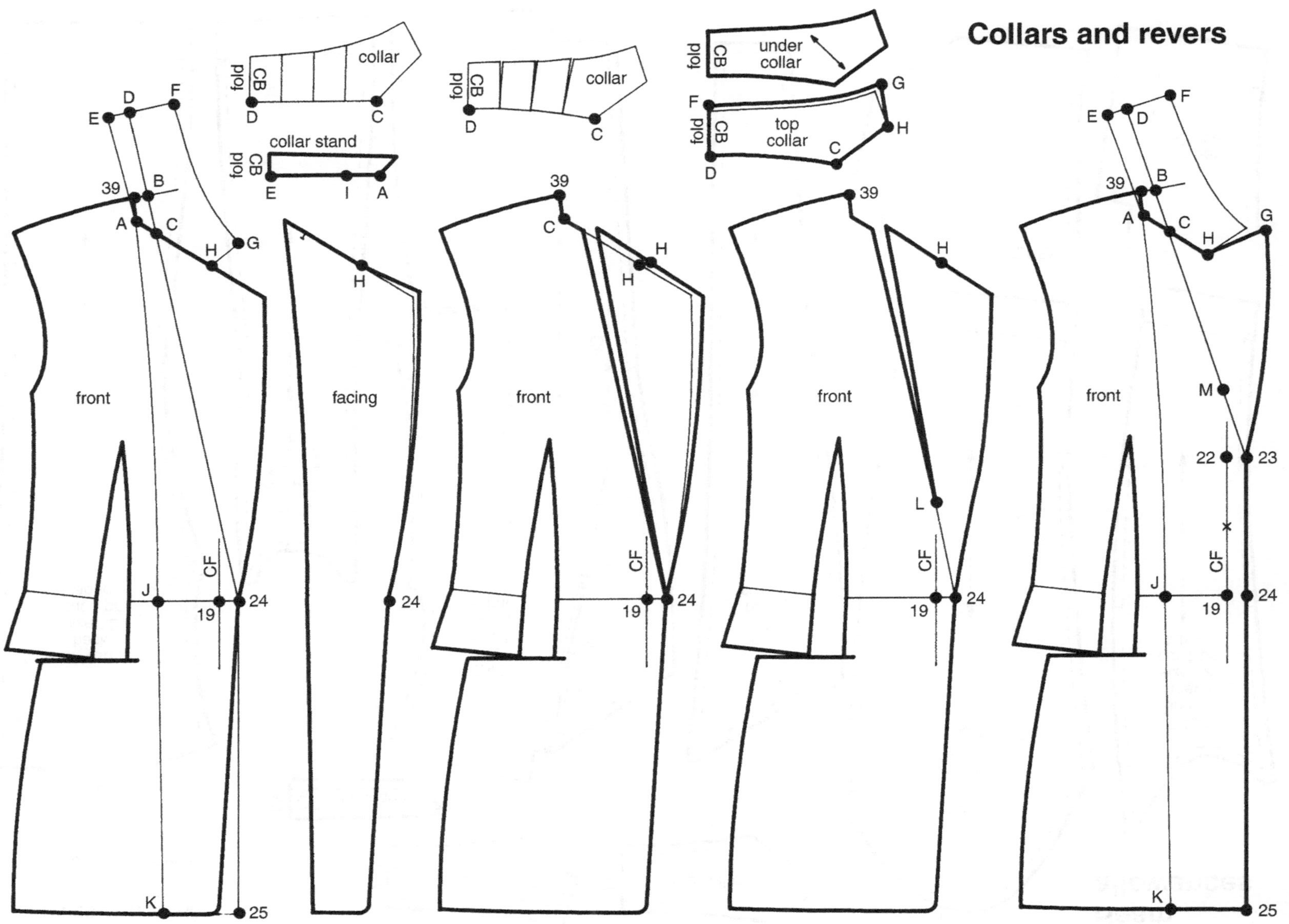

## Seam allowances

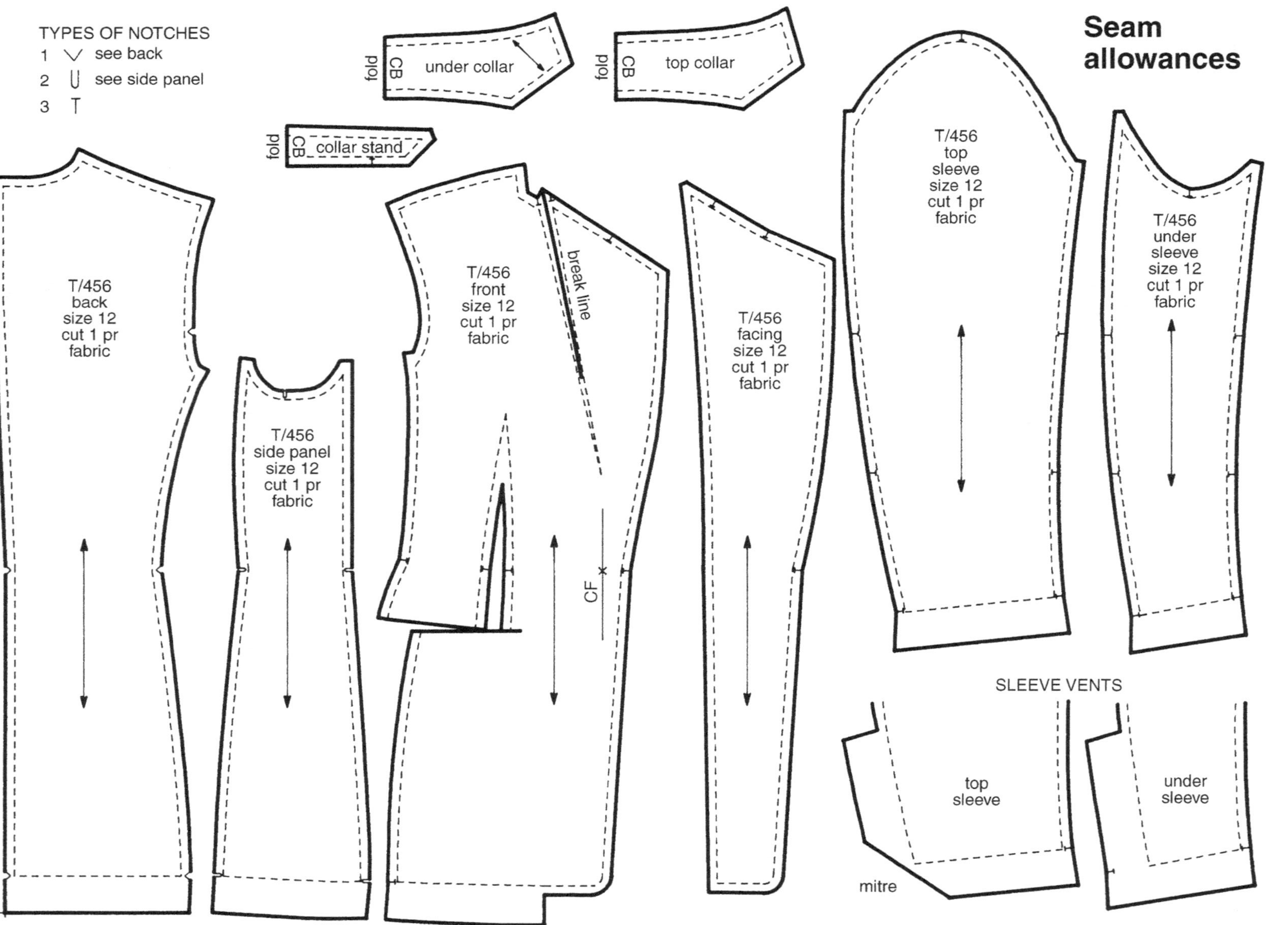

# Completing the Patterns – Seam Allowances and Interlinings
# Engineered Classic Semi-fitting Jacket Block

## ADDING SEAM AND HEM ALLOWANCES

The standard seam allowance measurement is 1cm as shown. Enclosed seams (the collar or rever) can be reduced to 0.5cm, but 1cm seams may be trimmed during the making up. High quality garments may have 1.5cm seams on the back and side seams. Fancy seams such as welt seams will also vary in size.

Where two curved seams are to be matched (armhole and sleeve), the seam allowance is squared off to give accurate matching points. This has to be carefully measured to give accurate smooth lines.

Hem allowances on the coat body and sleeve are approx. 4cm. Sleeve vent extensions 3.5cm.

## NOTCHES

Card patterns usually have the V or U notch for pencil or chalk markings. Computer patterns have the T notch.

## MARKING THE PATTERN

The pattern should be marked with: style number, piece name, size, number to cut, fabric type and grainline.

## THE INTERLINING PATTERNS

The selection of interlinings is crucial in establishing the form of a garment. The diagram below is an example of the type (see page 29), pattern shapes and placements of interlinings for a jacket with a 'soft' handle.

**A** Light-weight knitted fusible to give stability and softness to the front body section. Used also on the top collar.

**B** Very light-weight knitted fusible on the sleeve and rever; also used on the back and side panel hems. Sometimes added to the top of sleeve head on fabrics without 'body'.

**C** Sew-in medium-weight linen used in a chest piece to give stability yet flexibility.

**D** Fusible collar felt on undercollar and stand.

**E** Light-weight linen used at the front of the top sleeve.

Narrow strips of light-weight linen are used to stabilise seams – shoulder, armhole and rever dart.

**F** Felt shaped piece at the sleeve head to give a 'roll'.

**G** Shoulder pad, approx 0.7cm depth.

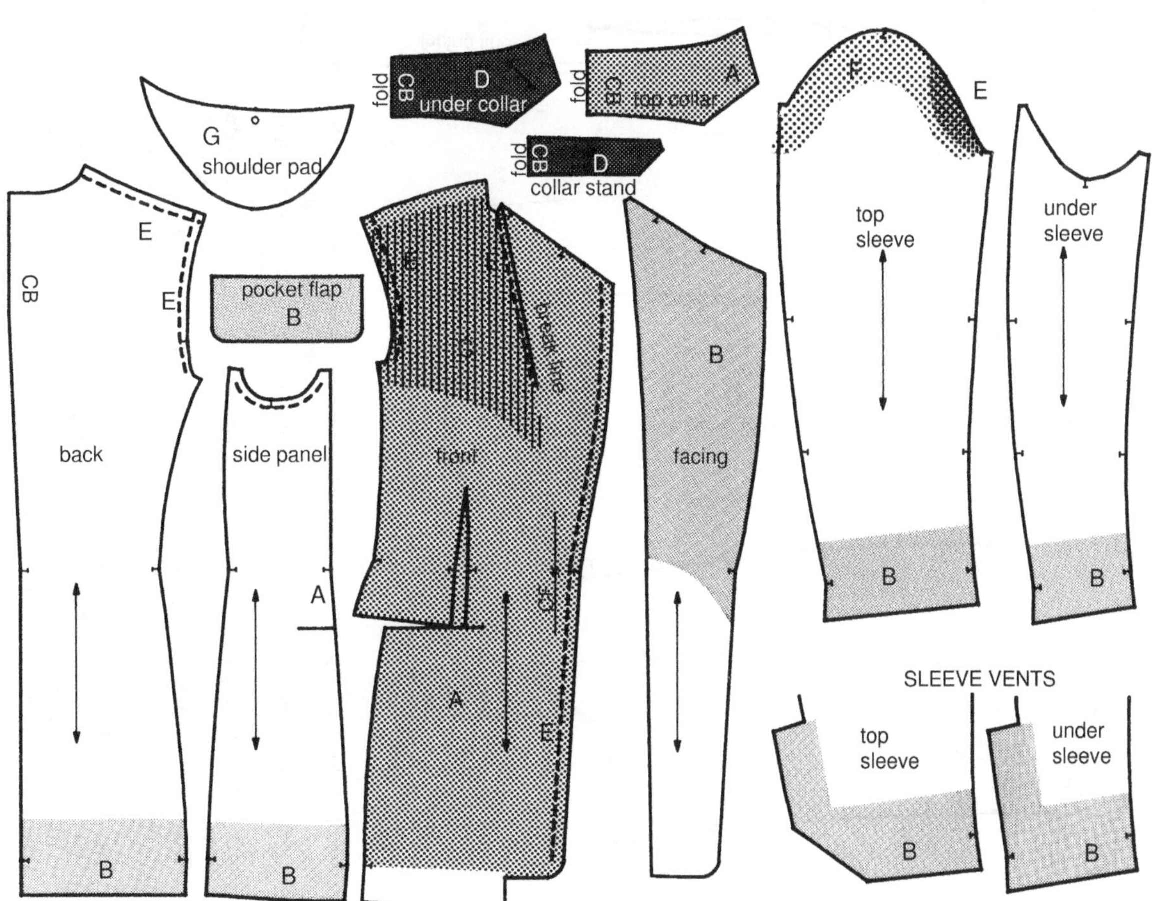

# Completing the Patterns – Linings Engineered Classic Semi-fitting Jacket Block

Lining patterns should always include ease. The lining should never pull the garment out of shape and cause wrinkles. The ease may have to be increased; this depends on the amount of spread or stretch in the garment fabric.

**All pattern pieces** Lining hems are cut along the hem turn up line.
**Back** Add 2cm pleat to the centre back from the neck to the waistline at A.
Add 0.2cm to the shoulder line at B, and 0.2cm to the panel seam from C–D.

**Side panel** Add 0.2cm to each panel seam at E–F and G–H.
**Front** Draw a line from the side seam I–J; cut along the line. Close the waist dart to its original position on the basic draft and create a bust dart on the side seam. Shorten the bust dart 1.5cm. Extend front dart 1cm below pocket line.
Add 0.2cm to the shoulder line at K, 0.2cm to the panel seam at L, and 0.5cm at the waist at M. Mark the front edge line 1cm forward of the facing line at N.
**Top sleeve** Add 0.5cm at the sleeve head at O. Add 1.5cm up and 0.2cm out at P and Q; redraw the sleeve head.
**Under sleeve** Raise the underarm 1.5cm at R. Add 1.5cm up and 0.2cm out at S and T; redraw underarm seam.
**Pocket bags** Lining can be used for the whole or one side of a pocket bag.

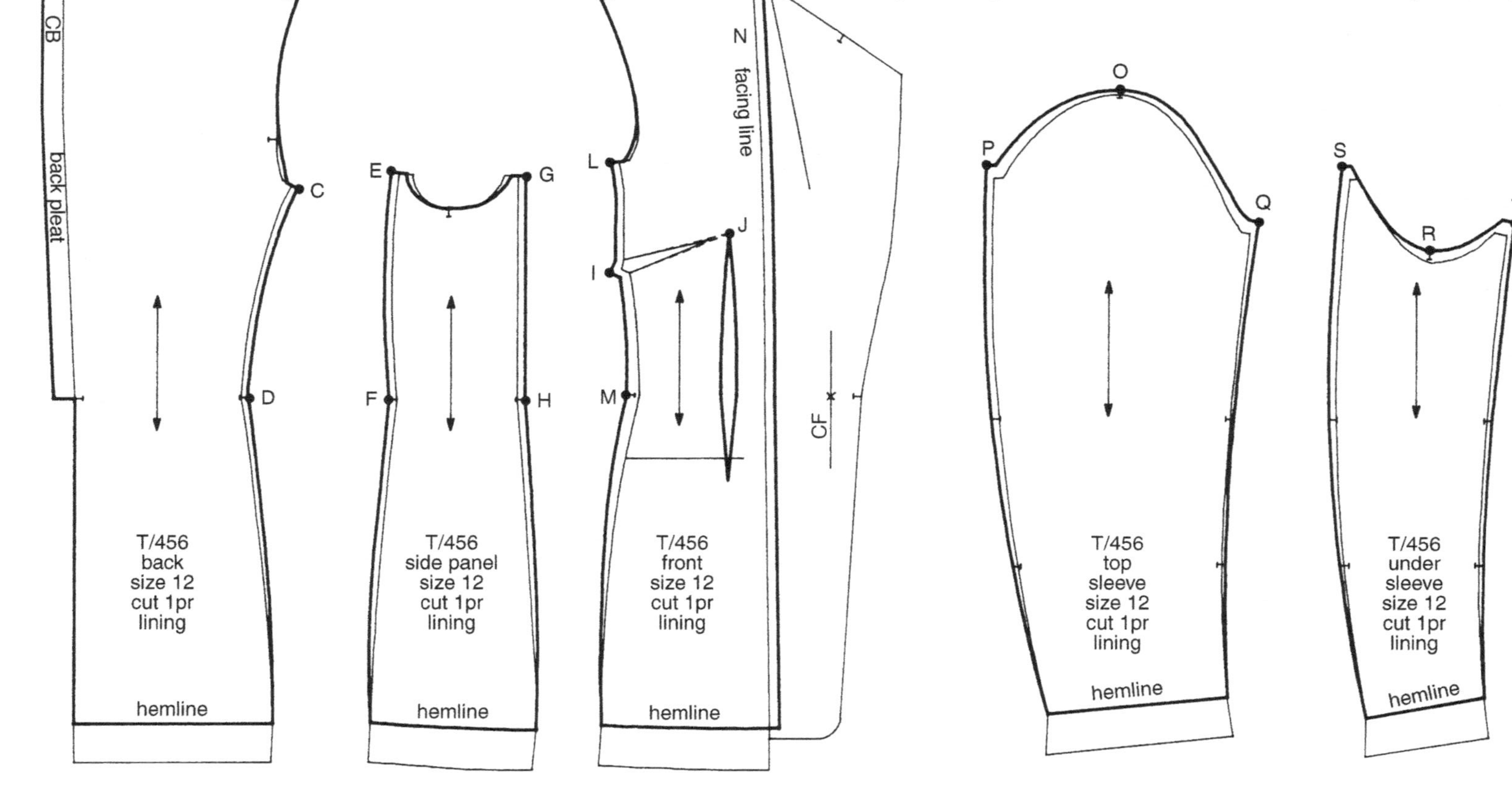

# Grading the Engineered Jacket Block

(4cm size chart, page 31.)

The grading movements can be done manually or by computer (see pages 70 and 71). First, stacking points have to be identified, which makes it easy to check the grades (e.g. on armhole depth line: centre back and centre front; underarm point on the sleeves). Vertical and horizontal movements are made with reference to the stack points.

**Back**

**1** Stack point – zero grade.
**2** Measure 0.2cm hor.
**3** Measure 0.4cm hor.
**4** Measure 0.4cm hor. 0.2cm vert.
**5** Measure 0.4cm hor. 0.5cm vert.
**6** Measure 0.25cm hor. 0.5cm vert.
**7, 8** Measure 1cm vert.
**9** Measure 0.25cm hor. 1cm vert.
**10** Measure 0.25cm hor.
**11** Zero grade.

**Front**

**12** Stack point – zero grade.
**13, 14** Zero grade.
**15, 16** Measure 0.25cm hor.
**17** Measure 0.25cm hor. 1cm vert.
**18, 19** Measure 1cm vert.
**20** Measure 0.1cm hor. 0.7cm vert.
**21** Measure 0.13cm hor. 0.7cm vert.
**22** Measure 0.4cm hor. 0.55cm vert.
**23, 24** Measure 0.4cm hor. 0.33cm vert.
**25** Measure 0.33cm hor.

**Under Sleeve**

**26** Stack point – zero grade.
**27** Measure 0.1cm hor. 0.25cm vert.
**28** Measure 0.25cm vert.
**29** Zero grade.
**30** Measure 0.25cm hor. 0.3cm vert.

**Top Sleeve**

**31** Stack point – zero grade.
**32** Measure 0.1cm hor. 0.25cm vert.
**33** Measure 0.25cm vert.
**34** Zero grade.
**35** Measure 0.25cm hor.
**36** Measure 0.5cm hor. 0.25cm vert.

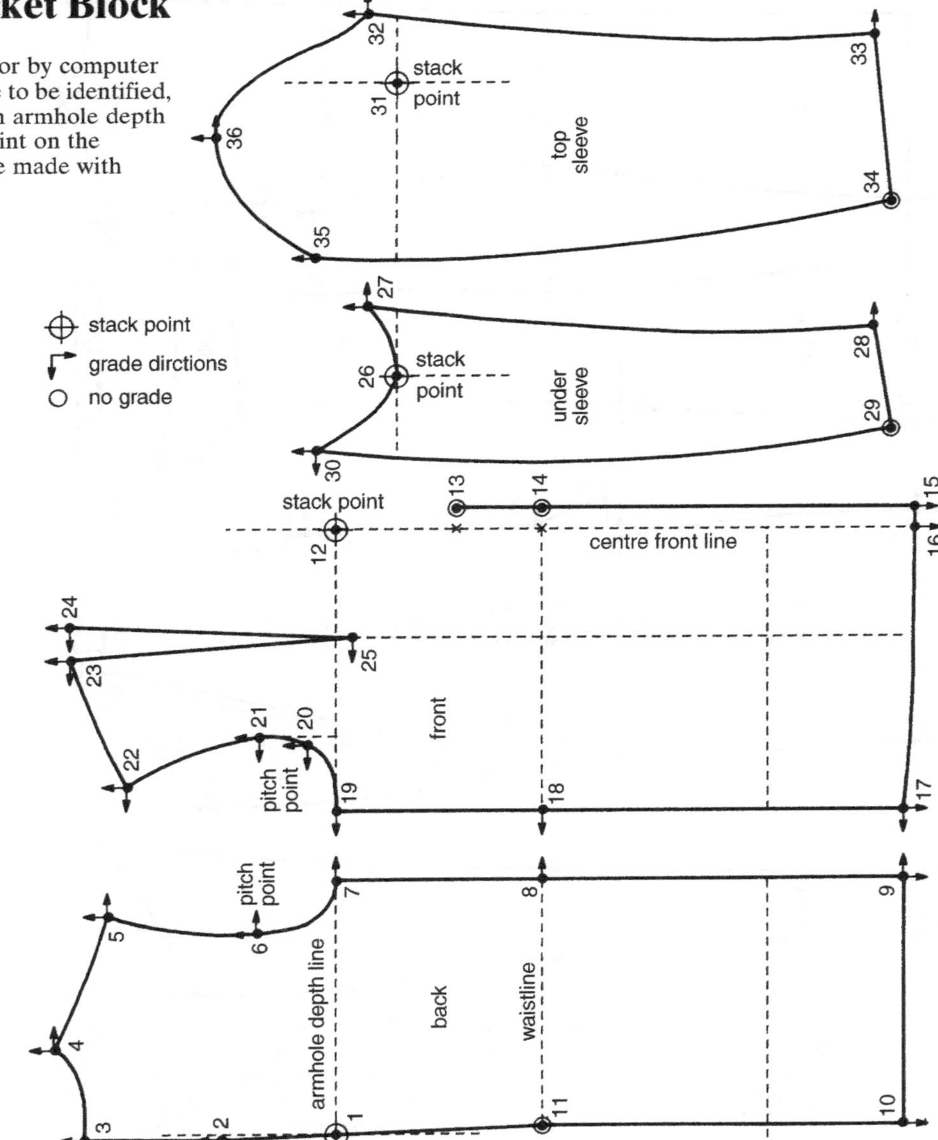

# Grading the Semi-fitted Jacket

(4cm size chart, page 31.)

The front dart has been moved and included in the waist dart; this has shifted the angle of the side seam. To ensure that the side seams of the graded sizes are parallel, the grade directions on points 30 to 36 have to be calculated with reference to the new angle of the waistline, pocket line and armhole depth line.

**Back**

**1** Stack point – zero grade.
**2** Measure 0.2cm hor.
**3** Measure 0.4cm hor.
**4** Measure 0.4cm hor. 0.2cm vert.
**5** Measure 0.4cm hor. 0.5cm vert.
**6** Measure 0.25cm hor. 0.5cm vert.
**7** Measure 0.1cm hor. 0.5cm vert.
**8** Measure 0.5cm vert.
**9** Measure 0.25cm hor. 0.5cm vert.
**10** Measure 0.25cm hor.
**11** Zero grade.

**Side Panel**

**12** Stack point – zero grade.
**13** Measure 0.1cm hor. 0.3cm vert.
**14, 15** Measure 0.3cm vert.
**16** Measure 0.25cm hor. 0.3cm vert.
**17** Measure 0.25cm hor. 0.5cm vert.
**18** Measure 0.5cm vert.
**19** Measure 0.1cm hor. 0.5cm vert.

**Front**

**20** Stack point – zero grade.
**21** Zero grade.
**22, 23** Measure 0.25cm hor.
**24** Measure 0.27cm hor. 0.7cm vert.
**25** Measure 0.7cm vert.
**26, 27, 28, 29** Measure 0.33cm vert.
**30, 31** Measure 0.33cm vert; along the lines 30–33 and 31–32.
**32, 33** Measure 0.7cm vert; along the lines 31–32 and 30–33.
**34** Measure 0.1cm hor. 0.7cm vert; square from the line A–B.
**35** Measure 0.13cm hor. 0.7cm vert; square from line A–B.
**36** Measure 0.4cm hor. 0.55cm vert; square from line A–B.
**37, 38, 39, 40** Measure 0.4cm hor. 0.33cm vert.
**41, 42** Measure 0.4cm hor.
**43** Zero grade.

**Facing**

All the facing grade points are the same as the front except for point C. Measure 0.25cm hor.

**Collar and Stand**

All grades as point D. Measure 0.25cm vert.

The diagram shows the extra grades required at the new points when the block is further adapted. However, many grades remain the same. If CAD grading is used, these points can be copied from the block, other patterns or from grade rule libraries (see page 71).

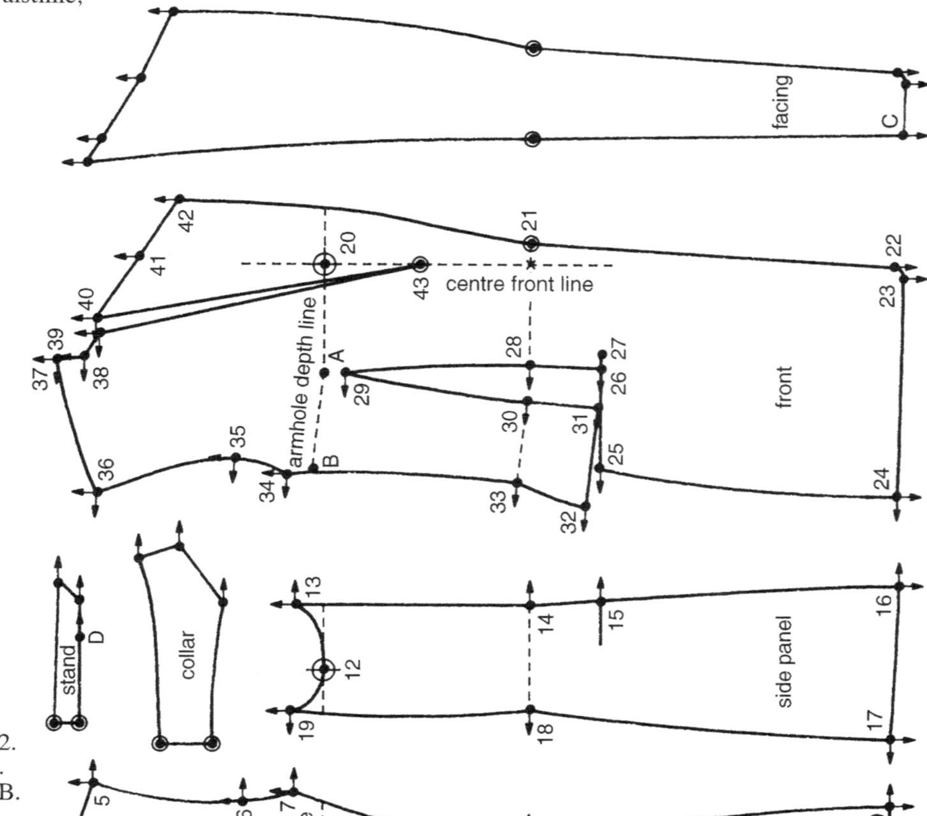

# Part Two:

# 5 THE ENGINEERED PROCESS OF MANUFACTURE

# The Engineered Process of Manufacture

Because the tailored jacket is a complex garment with many parts in different fabrics, the engineered manufacturing process has to be precise. The machinery and tooling up for this precision can be costly. The process is usually undertaken by companies who have large orders for garments that are based on a basic shape that is then modified to provide alternative styling. The process is now dominated by computers.

There is no point in making clothes if you cannot sell them. A manufacturer has to make a considerable investment in machinery to produce a fully engineered garment. This means that it has to be sold in considerable quantities to make it profitable and to allow the manufacturer to offer quality at a reasonable price. However, to sell the garment the manufacturer has also to offer a fashionable but not extreme cut, a relevant sizing system and to offer some degree of choice.

The manufacturer offering the engineered tailored jacket will be producing for a targeted rather than speculative market; therefore market research plays a significant part in the early stages of design and the sourcing of materials. This is combined with technological research in liaison with fabric and machinery suppliers. Communications by the internet are becoming vital in the process, and the preliminary costings and material sourcing underpin the initial inputs into PDM (Production data management) systems which control the whole production process of the garment. This process can be described in the following stages:

Design and marketing;
Production data management;
Pattern creation and modification;
Sizing and grading;
Marker-making, cutting and fusing;
Making-up and pressing.

# Design and Marketing

Technological advances during the 1990s have produced revolutionary changes in design and marketing procedures. The greatest change has been communication. The internet provides a link between all sectors of the chain; it links fabric and trimming suppliers, the garment manufacturers and the retailers. Many of these are likely to be in different countries. The large retailers now demand a fast reaction to their orders and also to changes in direction.

Retailers make many decisons from virtual fabrics and virtual garments created by 2D and 3D textile and drape programs. Woven, knitted or printed fabrics can be realised on screen and printed by inkjet printers onto fabrics for instant sampling.

Collections can be visualised by mapping fabrics onto sketches and photographs (see the jacket image *right*), thus creating virtual models and reducing the amount of samples needed each season. Professional catalogues can be created in-house and retailers can produce virtual store displays which help them to select the way they display merchandise.

*Draping a jacket image with fabric, from the graph.assyst program*

*Photograph by permission of assyst bullmer*

It is now possible to access virtual models online through the internet and see them from all angles as they rotate in real time. Particular areas of the garment can be identified for further detailed examination.

The garment image can be re-mapped with any of the different fabrics shown on the screen. This increases the possibility of individual customers selecting the fabric and ordering made-to-measure clothing online (see page 69).

*e-dress* – 3D presentation software

*e:marketplace* – 3D module for commercial platform

*Photographs by permission of echtzeit AG*

# Production Data Management

Management of the production cycle of an engineered garment requires accurate information that is accessable to all departments. A production data management system eliminates the repetition of identical information being processed. The data base allows authorised users to view the sketches or photographs, the fabric, the linings, interfacings, trimmings, the pattern, measurements, cost lay-plan assembly instructions, and the costing calculations. External 'cut, make and trim' facilities in other factories and other sourcing information can be accessed. The information can be constantly updated with everybody being informed instantly about modifications.

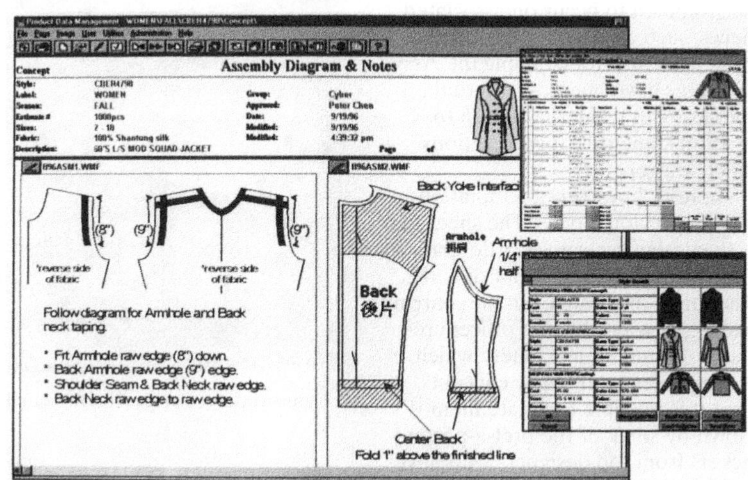


Assembly sheet from Gerber's PDM system

*Photograph by permission of Gerber Technology*

# 2D Pattern Creation and Modification by CAD

Pattern creation systems are now very sophisticated. The 'natural environment' of the work table has been reproduced by working on a digitiser with personal tools and materials. Sample calico toiles can be traced into the system and then refined to a production level, or patterns can be drafted directly on the screen. The systems are particularly adept at modifying patterns stored within the computer, and perform many standard pattern adaptations such as swinging darts, adding pleats and fullness etc. They also perform repetitive and time consuming tasks such as adding seam allowances, plotting and cutting out patterns.

The acknowledged value of the systems is that they systemise the procedure of creating an accurate pattern with many similar but slightly differing parts, such as the tailored jacket. The ability to overlay and check the parts is crucial in this process. They can also associate parts so that any modification during the development process to the outer garment can be programmed to occur on associated pieces, such as the interlining or lining. Some systems, (for example the Assyst software) have 'macros' where the operator can teach the system to perform some drafting operations which are repetitive.

There is, however, a temptation to modify previous styles. The sheer pace of the design cycle gives little space for innovative styling. It is not only the creation of the design, but the sourcing, costing, new production procedures and re-tooling of machinery which accompanies totally new concepts. That it is possible to create them is shown by some of the pret-a-porter jackets from top designers who have embraced new technology.

Silhouette 2000, Gerber's Pattern Development System

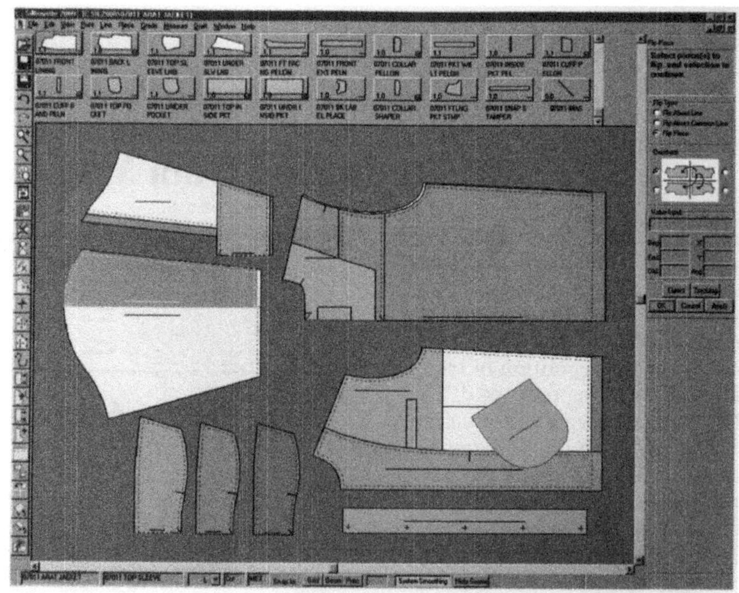

A clear overlay of pieces in Gerber's Pattern Design 2000

*Photographs by permission of Gerber Technology*

# 3D Pattern Creation and Modification by CAD

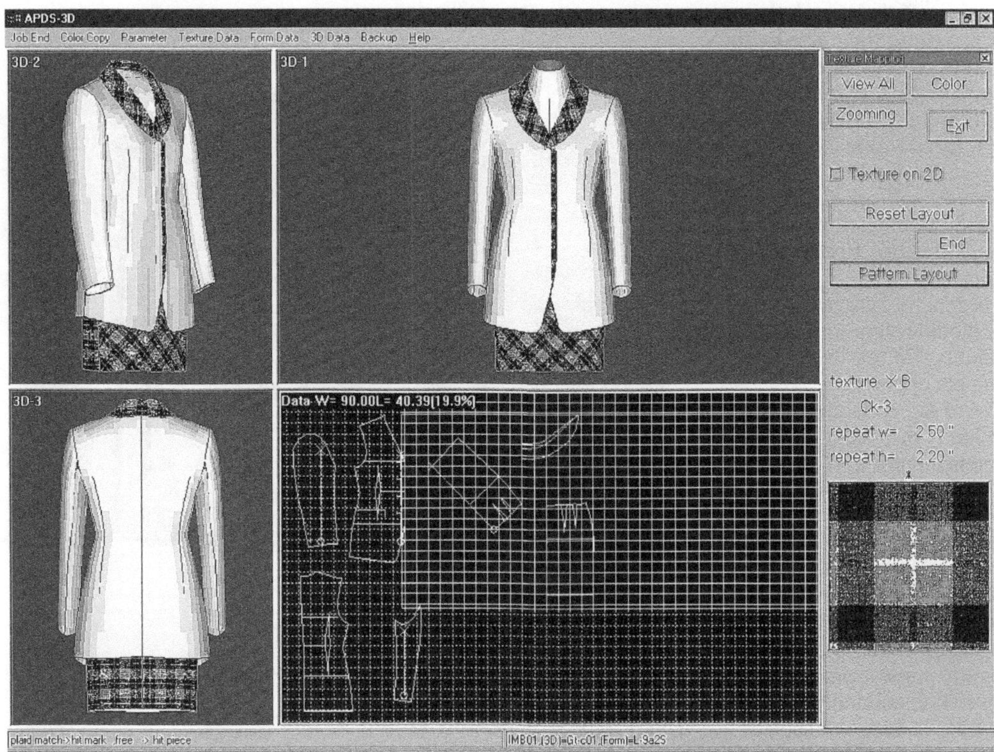


The Asahi virtual stand with garment pieces mapped to the stand, pattern pieces modified in Gerber Pattern Design 2000

*APDS-3D is a product of Asahi Ltd, licensed exclusively by Gerber Technology.*
*Photograph by permission of Gerber Technology.*

The idea of creating garment patterns in 3D directly on the virtual model stand has been an aspiration of CAD suppliers for many years. At least four suppliers are offering differing versions of 3D drape programs. Some success has been achieved in garments that closely resemble the model stand form and where the seam cutting follows the most prominent curves of the form.

Most of the suppliers claim that the principal value of their program is that the designer can see how patterns created to fit the virtual stand will look when they are mapped onto it. The software programs also demonstrate how the garment may look in different fabrics by inputting the fabric drape qualities. Far more research needs to be undertaken before these systems can cope with complex designs or can compete with fitting trials on the actual model stand or the live model.

For the engineered jacket there are possible advantages:

1. the stand can be modified to different shapes and sizes;
2. small modifications can be seen in 3D diagrammatical form to see how they may affect another section of the garment;
3. the amount and position of body ease is clear;
4. the effect of patterns such as prints or checks can be analysed.

# Sizing

People buying off-the-peg clothes generally recognise their size by the garment code. This can be confusing because many of the garments are made in different countries and their codes vary: for example a British size 12 (approx. 88cm bust) is a 38 in Germany, a 40 in France and a 44 in Italy. British interpretations of 'Eurosizing' in major British retail stores also vary.

There is general agreement that any code should relate to body measurements and not the measurements of garments. Regardless of the code number, a size chart has to provide a set of body measurements under each code. These should fit the majority of people who would buy that size (i.e. 88cm bust) of garment.

Collecting reliable data for size charts means measuring an enormous number of women in each size grouping, and this is expensive. Until recently, most sizing surveys were undertaken manually[1] but new body scanning techniques, such as the Telmat system which is illustrated here, have allowed methods to be developed which are less time consuming and less intrusive. These methods are being integrated into CAD grading programs for mass-production or providing data for made-to-measure garments. The systems also give information about the shape of the body. The price of these systems has reduced and they could give the clothing industry the opportunity to move towards mass customisation. This is particularly applicable for tailored garments. Customers could hold smart cards with their measurement data and could order custom made garments using the internet.

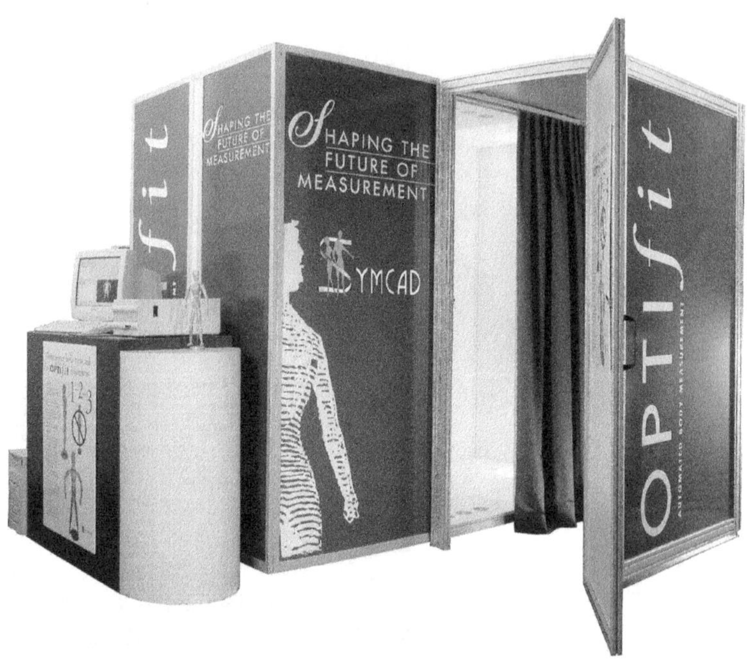


A measuring booth where body measurements are taken automatically

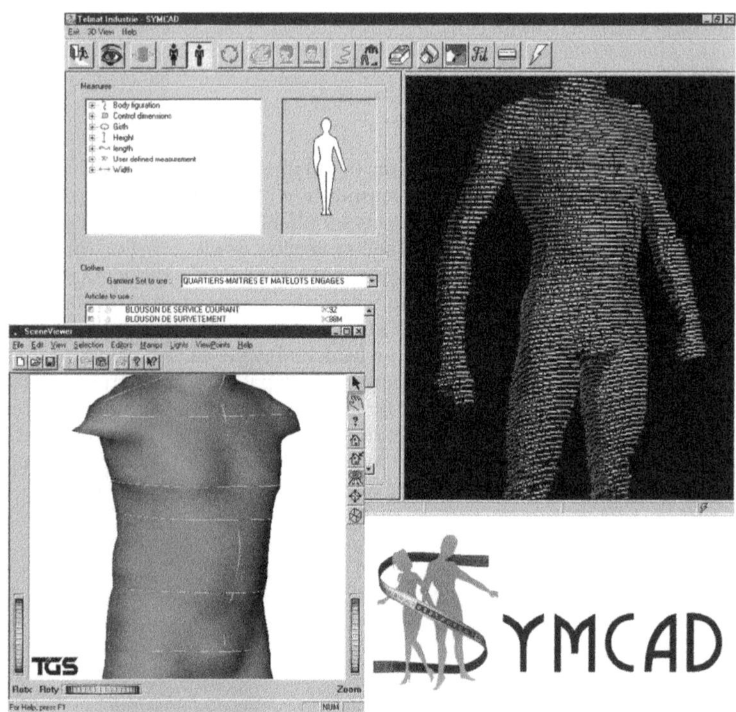


Body imaging and automatic measurement extraction

*Photographs by permission of Telmat Industrie*

# Made-to-measure

A century ago, most tailored suits were made to measure. A rapid decline began as mass produced garments, based on size intervals, increased in quality. The installation of new machinery meant that not only was consistent quality assured, but there was also a reduction in the price. Today, an increasing number of ready-to-wear companies are seriously considering a move into mass customisation (engineered ready-to-wear), for two main reasons. There is an apparent customer demand emerging for a fast made-to-measure service and new technologies have made it possible to respond to an order within seven days.

The changing mix of the population has resulted in body types becoming increasingly varied; this has created a demand for made-to-measure clothes. Mass customisation not only offers a better fit, but also offers a wider choice of styles, fabrics, linings and trimmings.

## THE PROCESS

The process begins with the customer's measurements being taken by 3D scanning systems (see page 68). These can be retained by the company or the customer on a smart card which can be continuously updated. Fabrics and styles can be selected within a store or via the internet. A 3D image of a model wearing the style can revolve in real time (see page 65). Different fabrics can be mapped onto the image for comparison.

Once the style is selected, the customer's measurements are compared to the nearest size of pattern stored in the system. A second layer of grade rules are programmed to cover most standard horizontal and vertical measurement alterations and also variations in body stance. The system automatically modifies the pattern by simply inputting the new measurements. Non-standard adjustments can be made in pattern design software. All associated lining and interlining pieces are automatically adjusted; small pieces, such as pockets and collars, rarely need any adjustments. Companies engaged on large contracts for military uniforms or corporate wear can have these pieces pre-cut and prepared.

A lay plan is constructed for the modified pattern; this is sent directly to a single-ply cutter which cuts individual garments at high speed.

## NEW SOFTWARE DEVELOPMENTS

The demand for made-to-measure software programs has led to new ways of developing the mathematics of pattern construction. 'Modulate', a new software program from OptotiTex, produces parametric model patterns. These are fully defined by a set of dimensions which can then be modified by typing in new measurements. If a point is dragged by the mouse, the system re-calculates the entire model accordingly. Assyst are also developing a new software program called 'Leonardo' based on parametrics; they describe it as 'a pattern construction system based on parameters using constraint solving technology'.

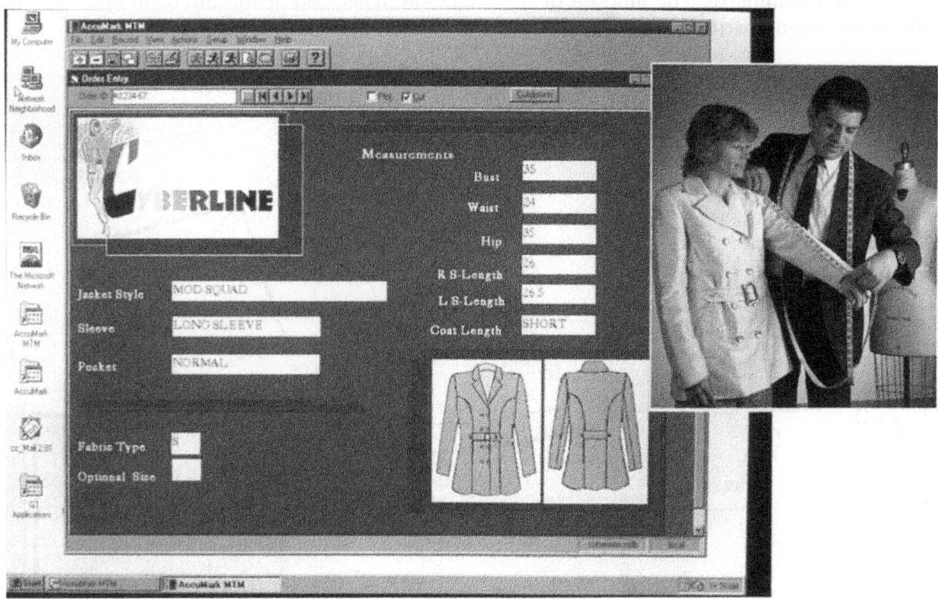


Made-to-measure software program from Gerber Technology

*Photographs by permission of Gerber Technology*

# Pattern Grading by CAD

After the sample design has been accepted and the retailer has placed an order, the garment has to be produced in a range of sizes. CADCAM clothing systems offer the means of grading patterns and most larger companies are grading patterns by CAD. The systems are faster, more consistent and accurate than manual grading, but systems are only as good as the technicians who provide the grading instructions.

Many of the companies using CADCAM systems at the present time are not using the PDS (pattern design systems) for pattern cutting. They cut their patterns for a design manually, and therefore to grade the pattern on the system the perimeter of the pattern has to be fed into the computer by digitising the contour (see illustration page 66). The pattern is placed on the digitiser and the pattern profile is entered into the computer using a cursor. The centre of the cursor's cross hairs is placed on points to be recorded. These grade points and other points define the curves or corners of the pattern.

GRADE RULES
The grading of patterns by most computer systems is based on identifying where specific points on the pattern have to be extended or reduced to create a new size. These points are moved by means of X and Y co-ordinates which tell the computer the direction of movement; measurements are also given to identify the position of the new point. Grade rules are usually calculated to 1/10th of a millimetre. The amount of movement in the X direction is written first, followed by the Y direction. For example, the movement of the shoulder point between sizes is –6mm horizontally and 5mm vertically. The GRADE RULE can be written in 1/10th millimetre (e.g. –60 50) or in centimetres (e.g. –0.60 0.50cm). A GRADE RULE is the instruction across a range of sizes. Inconsistent grades between sizes can be registered.

Grade rules can be calculated from size chart, from nested block patterns or from previous patterns. Many companies copy grades which have worked on other patterns. Grade rules can be placed individually on pattern points or accessed from grade rule libraries.

CALCULATING A GRADE RULE
Manually graded 'nests' of blocks can be used. The nest is 'stacked' on one point, usually on the armhole depth line. The direction of the X and Y co-ordinates are registered from this point. Each graded point on the nest (these are beginnings and ends of lines and specific points, i.e. special control points or notches), is measured as shown below. The measurements are checked with the grading increments on the size charts. (It is possible to calculate many points directly from size charts or garment specifications.) The X Y measurement between each size is the grade rule. The same grade rule can be used at any point which requires the same grade. One grade rule is written as zero (00.0 00.0); it is used where no grade is required. Grade rules can be copied from other patterns. Patterns with grade rules attached can be modified, and these grades will be retained on the new style.

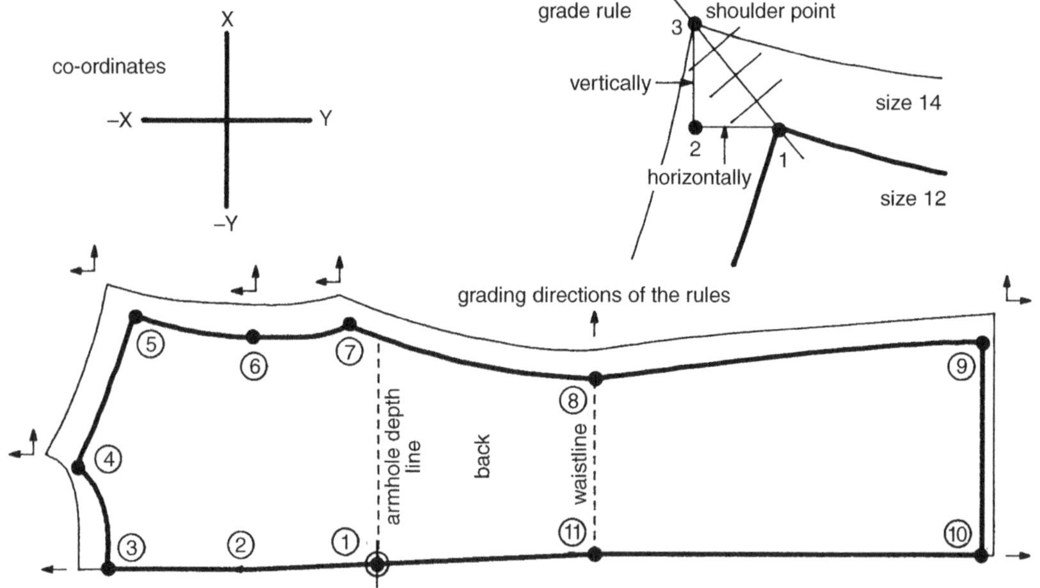

GRADE RULE LIBRARIES

A grade rule library is compiled of numbered grade rules used at the grade points. When the number is applied to a point, it operates the grade. Records can be kept of the grade rule numbers and positions for each style by means of simple diagrams.

Once the rules for a block are entered, any pattern adapted from the block can also be graded by the same method. However, few patterns are as simple as the block shape. This means that new grade rules have to be calculated by the grader and these rules added to the grade rule library.

RULE TABLE EDITOR STORAGE AREA: C: WINIFRED NOTATION: METRIC
NAME: LIBW2 GRADE METHOD: SMALL–LARGE INCRMTL
COMMENT:
POINT ATTRIBUTE:

| RULE NUMBER: | | 1 | | 2 | | 3 | |
|---|---|---|---|---|---|---|---|
| BREAKS | | X | Y | X | Y | X | Y |
| 34 | 38 | 0.00 | 0.00 | –0.80 | 0.00 | –0.80 | 25.00 |
| 38 | 42 | 0.00 | 0.00 | –0.80 | 0.00 | –0.80 | 25.00 |
| 42 | 46 | 0.00 | 0.00 | –0.80 | 0.00 | –0.80 | 25.00 |

Grade rule library – Gerber Technology

GRADING THE PATTERN

Pattern pieces constructed in the PDS pattern cutting software or digitised into the system are brought to the screen in sequence. Each grade point is identified with a screen cursor and the grade rule can be entered.

If a pattern is adapted from a block, or a previous pattern has been modified, then new points will be generated and extra grade rules will be required. These rules have to be added to the new points or added to the rule library.

When the grade points have been added, an instruction to grade the piece is given. This order will generate a nest of grades over the range of sizes, using the grade rules attached to the piece or from rules stored in the grade rule library. The patterns can be drawn out on a plotter for checking, or sent directly through the system for lay planning and cutting.

GRADING TECHNIQUES

Sophisticated grading techniques are now included in many programs. Perpendicular grading calculates the grades with reference to the angle of another line; tangent grading techniques control points along a line or the length of the line itself. If a pattern is split, the system will grade the new seam lines proportionally. If a line is altered on a pattern, it is possible for it to be modified automatically through all the grades. 'Walking' graded pieces allow seams to be checked for fit along the making up lines.

A number of companies are developing systems based on parametrics. Any sizes are based on the measurements made to construct the pattern. Any new sizes are generated not through point movements, but through measurement changes.

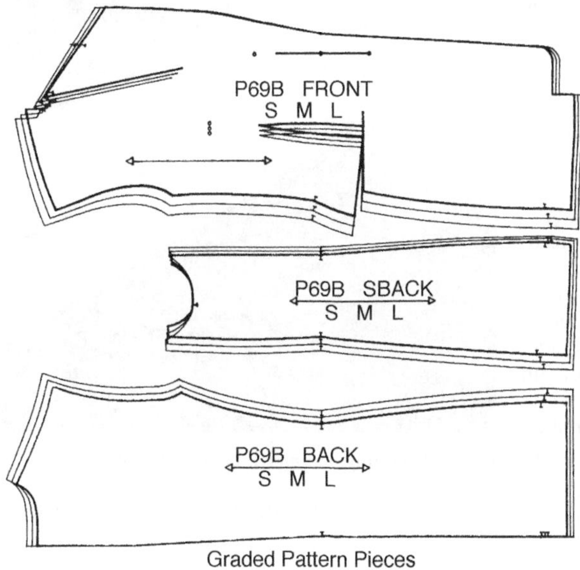


Graded Pattern Pieces

# Marker Making and Cutting by CAD

The principal reason that most companies buy a CAD system is for marker making, which offers accuracy, speed and fabric utilisation. Most companies producing engineered garments now use them.

The first stage is the creation of 'models' which are created from stored pattern pieces. A model is the group of pattern pieces from a style, which have to be cut in a particular fabric. For example, different models will be required for the outer jacket fabric, for the lining and for the different interlinings.

To create the lay plan, information about the patterns and the fabric has to be given.

1. Piece names, sizes.
2. Number of pieces.
3. Fabric constraints (single or double-ply, face-to-face, nap).
4. Any blocking of areas.
5. Any buffering around pieces.
6. Matching of checks, patterns.

The pattern pieces can then be placed manually into lay plans (markers). Markers can be assembled automatically. The system will try different ways of placing the pieces in the lay until the best fabric utilisation is achieved. The markers can be plotted out or cut automatically on high speed, deep-ply cutters for mass production or on single-ply cutters for custom made garments.

Cut Order Planning software controls every stage of the cutting process, giving precise instructions to the spreader and the cutter. Its greatest value is in the savings in fabric quantities and labour costs. The software can examine and select marker combinations to complete an order. One order may require several lays. The distribution of the number of garments and sizes in each lay is crucial to the fabric utilisation figures.

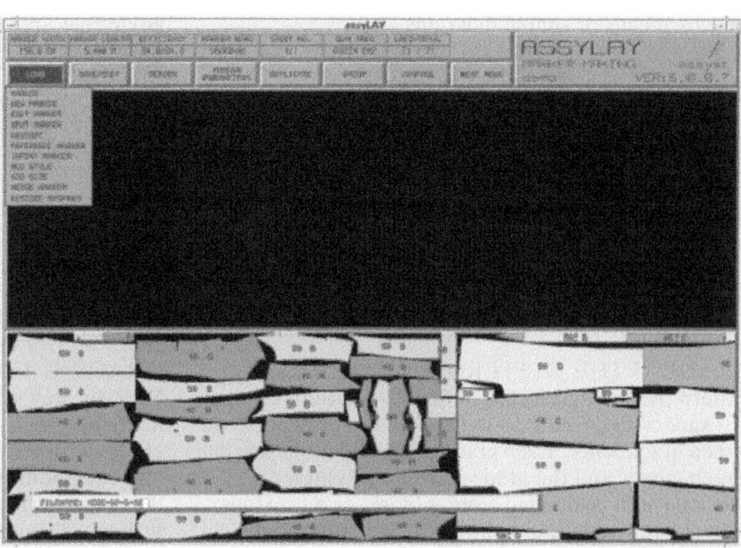


Marker making from the *lay.assyst* program

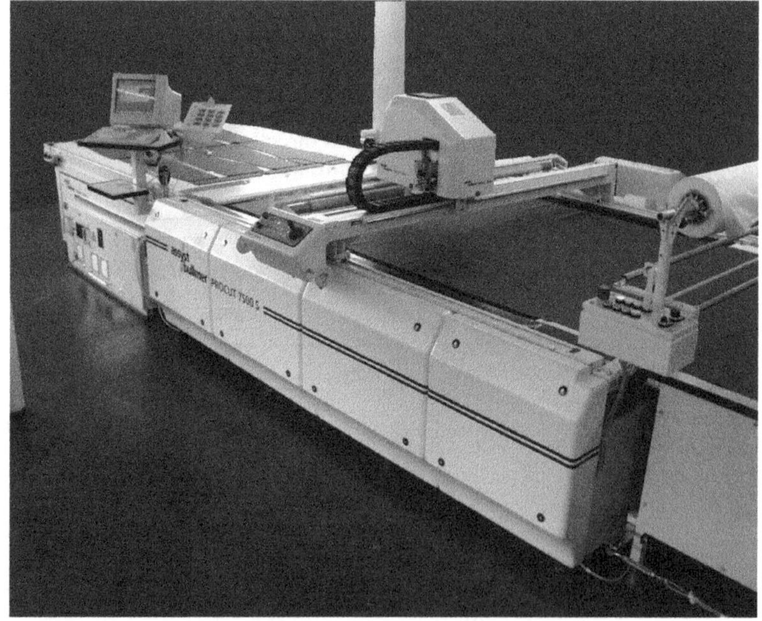

Deep-ply cutting: *bullmer* Procut knife cutter

*Photographs by permission of assyst bullmer*

# Fusing

Most mass-produced garments have both large areas of the garment (e.g. fronts), and small areas (e.g. pockets and collars) fused to the interlining. Also stay tapes at the break line and revers are often fused.

Many types of fusing presses are available, from small manually operated presses to large automatic presses which feed, fuse and stack garment pieces in a continuous conveyer belt operation. The fusing pressure is applied by large silicone heated rollers, and the temperature settings can be controlled and adjusted for different fabrics.

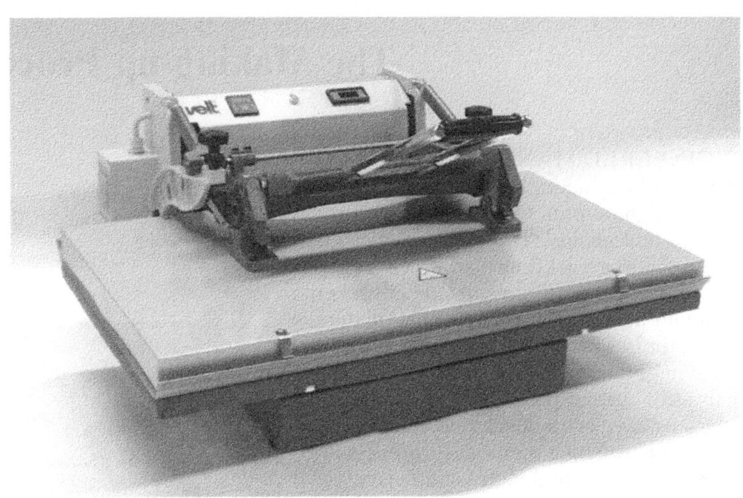


Manual press for small garment pieces

Automatic continuous press for large garment pieces

*Photographs by permission of Veit GmbH & Co.*

# The Making-up Process

ENGINEERED MANUFACTURE
The aim of engineered manufacture is to achieve high outputs whilst maintaining a high and constant quality. The production can be systemised to a workflow plan which takes care of the logistical requirements and ensures the minimum handling of garments and materials. This optimises the throughput time and control of the material stocks and can give real time analysis of current production. Software programs have been developed which can calculate alternative methods of process in order to optimise and increase efficiency.

THE MAKING-UP PROCESS
The interlined fabric shell of the garment is made up. The lining is attached to the facing and top collar. The two separate sections are then machined together along the outer edges and 'bagged out' by pulling the garment through to the right side using an opening in the sleeve lining. To accomplish this process all the pattern pieces have to be engineered perfectly.

The most important piece of machinery in this process is the sewing machine. This has many variations, foot and template additions, and is incorporated into systems which operate complex tasks. Some are illustrated here and on the opposite page.

Most of the machines have computers; microcontrol systems automatically control operations which previously needed very skilled operators to perform them. The controls can determine the differential feed of fabric, thereby controlling the ease that is so important in tailored garments.

Simple seams and darts can be stitched automatically. For curved seams a guide rail corresponds to the seam contour and a microcontrol system programs the beginning and the end of the seam, any stitch interruptions, the stitch length and sewing speed. This allows perfect seams to be produced.

Straight or slanted tailored welt, bound or flap pockets can be produced to a consistent high quality on special pocket units. No mechanical adjustments are necessary to adapt the unit to different pockets or materials. The pocket shape can be programmed and called up by means of the graphic display panel. Special devices are available which can match the check on the pocket to the check of the garment.

Identical lapels can be produced by using templates. It is also possible to realise a perfect fit by the distribution of the necessary fullness. The seam can also be trimmed as it is sewn.

The complex operation of inserting sleeves, where the correct amount of ease is crucial to the appearance of the sleeve head, has been automated. Machines can be programmed using a 'teach-in' procedure, which is mirrored to the other sleeve and can be converted to other sizes according to the size grades.

*The text and photographs are published by permission of Durkopp Adler AG*

# Pressing

Pressing technology is a vital part of the engineering process. Pressing has to be accurately controlled at the different stages of underpressing during the garment's construction. To achieve a perfect final appearance, a multiform press with plates and clamps can give the form and finish required for an engineered garment of quality.

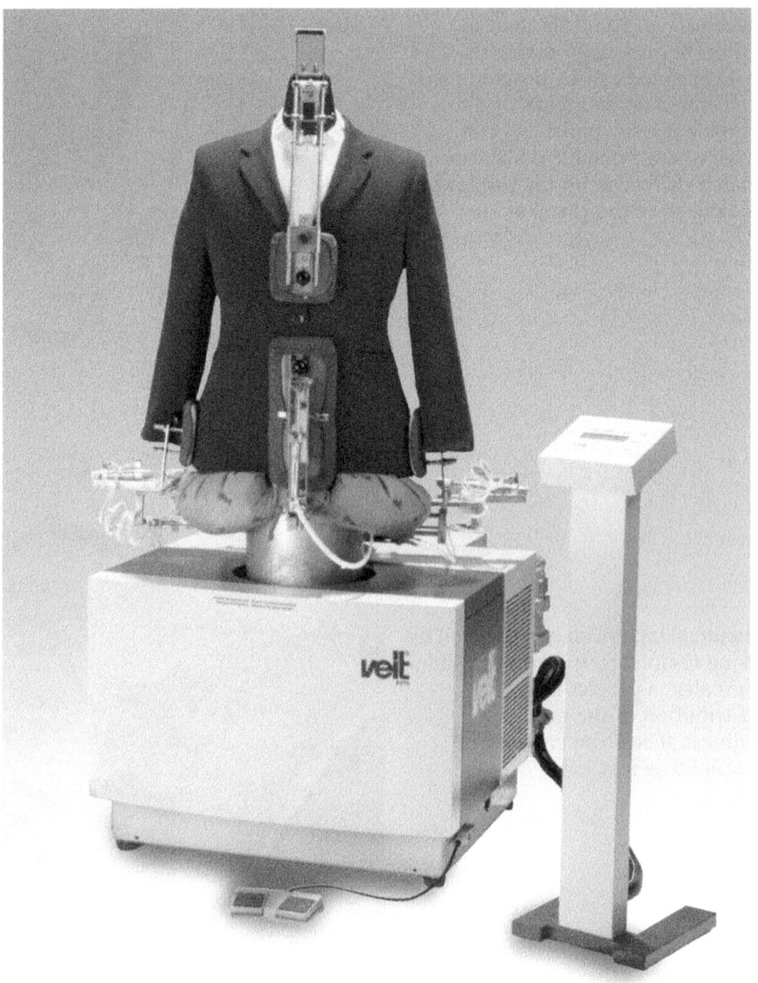


Multiform press for giving a final pressing-off

*Photograph by permission of Veit GmbH & Co.*

# Part Three:

# 6 STYLE CUTTING – BLOCK VARIATIONS



In October 1913, Vogue pronounced that 'tailored suits have been gradually undergoing a distinct change. The stiff, much stitched and sharply pressed suit has vanished completely and in its place are far more becoming suits showing a soft finish. The materials are only partly the cause of this, for the styles also have their influence'. The style 'tailleur' was adopted by the French couturières and dressmakers who interpreted it using a freedom of cutting and construction methods. This tradition of soft tailoring or style cutting remains today through many of the designer collections or designer workrooms supplying made-to-measure styling. Some of the techniques used require a high level of manual skills or are time consuming, thus the jackets will remain high cost garments. However, there are many techniques of cutting and manufacture which could be adapted for the mass market. For example: extensions of fashion shape by seaming and sleeve cutting; alternative making up processes; innovative detailing in collar and pocket design; the use of decorative techniques.

Original styling in this market has to rely on good pattern cutting to create the shape, and it is critical that the correct blocks are selected. The major choice is whether to modify a tailoring block, or to start from a dress block and add extra overgarment ease. The latter course is often selected for more extreme styles, and for designs which incorporate sleeves adapted from the one-piece sleeve block.

# Style Cutting: Close-fitting Jackets
# Adapting the Bespoke Jacket Block

**Closing the neck angle**
It is possible to use the bespoke jacket block for many softer but fitted styles; the most important modification is the reduction of the neck angle. This allows the block to be used for button-to-the-neck styles and for convertible collars. It also prevents a sagging of revers which are not taped.
Make the following alterations to the original block draft for the bespoke jacket and waist shaping (pages 34 and 36).
Mark points 10, 12, 20, 22, 28, 31.

**20–23** $^1/_5$ neck size minus 0.25cm.
**23–24** Dart measurement; join 23 and 24 to 22 to create a dart.
**22–25** The measurement 22–23.
**10–26** 1.75cm; square out approx. 7cm.
**25–27** Shoulder measurement plus 1cm. Draw in the shoulder line with a slight curve.
Draw in front armhole through points 12, 31, 28, 27.
Create the armhole curve as shown on page 34.
**20–20a** $^1/_5$ neck size plus 0.5cm; draw in front neck curve.

# Style Cutting: Close-fitting Jackets
# Adapting a Dress Block for Jacket Cutting

It is possible to modify a dress block for style jacket cutting. The dress block is often used when creating styles in softer fabrics or using soft 'dressmaker' methods of assembly. The dress block used in this example is from *Metric Pattern Cutting* by the author, but a standard dress block from any source can be used. This is particularly useful for personal cutting where a dress block has been personally developed and fitted to a figure shape.

**Body Sections**
Trace round the body section of the dress block.
Draw a new waistline 0.5cm below the original line.
Draw a new armhole line 2.5cm below the existing armhole line.
Cut up the side seam and open 3cm; draw a new side seam line in the centre.
Mark point A at the underarm point.

**Back**
Widen the neck 0.25cm and raise the shoulder seam 0.5cm at B.
Raise the shoulder seam 0.75cm; extend the shoulder seam 1cm at C.
Add 1cm to the back width at D.
Move any waist dart line back 0.5cm.

**Front**
Widen the neck 0.25cm and raise the neck 0.5cm at E.
Widen the neck 0.25cm and raise the shoulder seam 0.5cm at F.
Raise the shoulder seam 0.75cm; extend the shoulder seam 1cm at G.
Add 1cm to the front armhole at H.
Redraw the new armhole line as shown.
Move the bust dart point and the waist dart line back 0.5cm at I.

**Notes**
The alteration to the shoulder line allows for a shoulder pad of approx. 0.5cm in depth.
The waist shaping used for the bespoke jacket can be used (page 36).

**Sleeves**
A new sleeve must be drafted for the new armhole shape.
Although a classic two-piece sleeve can be used with a modified dress block, sleeves based on the one-piece sleeve block (page 82) are usually the most compatible with adapted dress blocks.

## Adapting the bespoke jacket block

## Adapting a dress block for jacket cutting

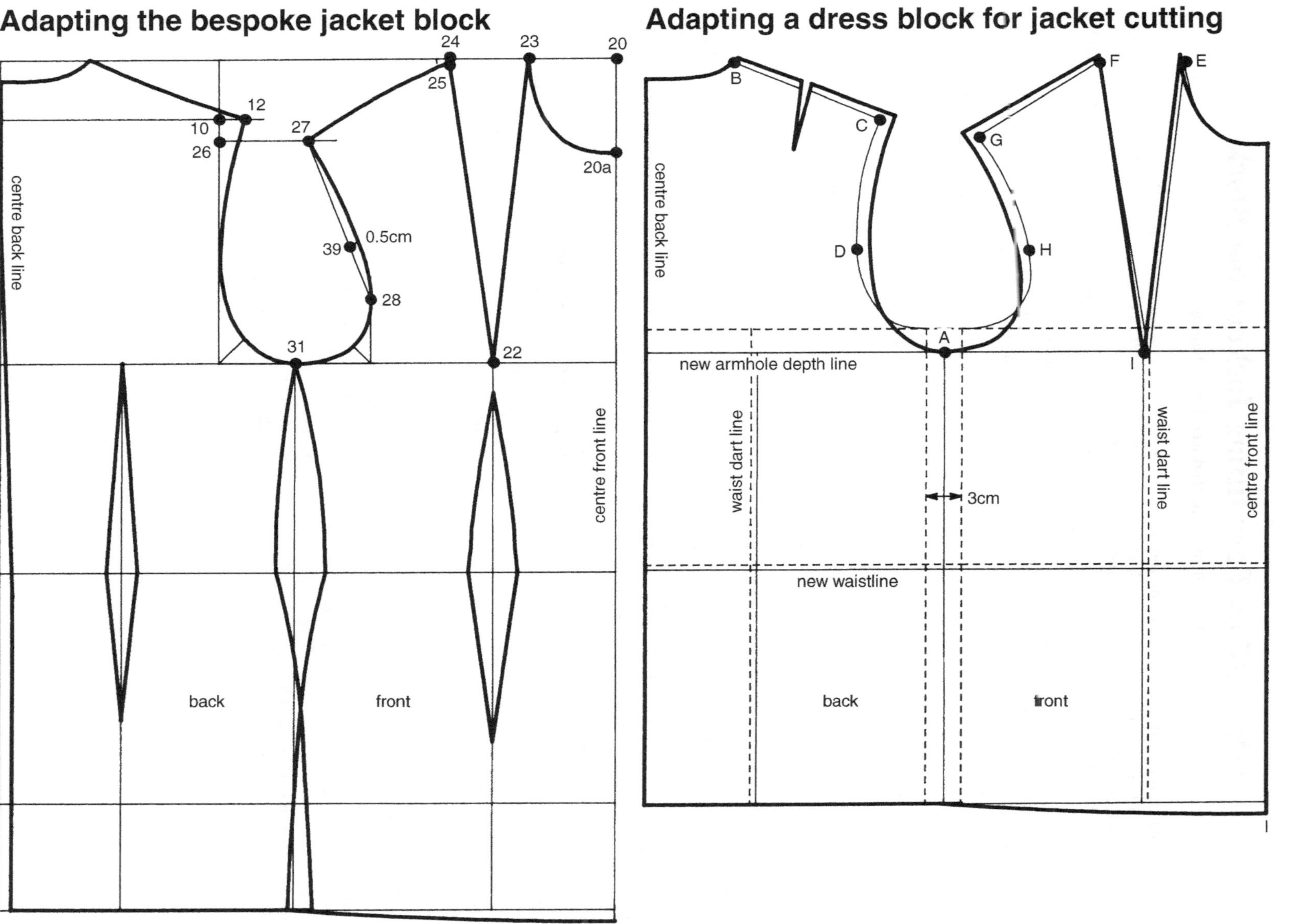

# Style Cutting: Easy-fitting Jacket/Coat Block

## Easy-fitting with Reduced Bust Shaping

Easier fitting jackets with less bust shaping require a different type of block, which gives a straighter basic shape. This block also has the reduction of the neck angle which allows the block to be used for button-to-the-neck styles and convertible collars and prevents the sagging of revers which are not taped.

The block can also be used for coats of a similar shape. The waist shaping can be varied.

MEASUREMENTS REQUIRED TO DRAFT THE BLOCKS

The block illustrated is drafted to the UK size 10. Refer to the 4cm size chart (page 31) for other standard measurements.

| **Size Code** | **10** | **12** | **14** | **16** |
|---|---|---|---|---|
| Bust | 84 | 88 | 92 | 96 |
| Waist | 64 | 68 | 72 | 76 |
| Back width | 33.5 | 34.5 | 35.5 | 36.5 |
| Shoulder | 12 | 12.25 | 12.5 | 12.75 |
| Neck size | 36 | 37 | 38 | 39 |
| Reduced dart size | 3.25 | 3.5 | 3.75 | 4 |
| Wrist | 15.5 | 16 | 16.5 | 17 |
| Back neck to waist | 40 | 40.5 | 41 | 41.5 |
| Waist to hip | 20.25 | 20.5 | 20.75 | 21 |
| Armhole depth | 20.6 | 21 | 21.4 | 21.8 |

No seam allowances included.

Square down and across from 0.

**0–1** 1.75cm.
**1–2** Neck to waist plus 1cm; square across.
**1–3** Finished length; square across.
**2–4** Waist to hip; square across.
**1–5** Armhole depth plus 4cm; square across.
**1–6** $^1/_2$ armhole depth plus 3.5cm; square out.
**1–7** $^1/_4$ armhole depth minus 2cm; square out.
**5–8** $^1/_2$ back width plus 2cm; square up to 9 and 10.
**0–11** $^1/_5$ neck size plus 0.25cm; draw neck curve.
**11–12** Shoulder length plus 2cm. This measurement includes shoulder ease of 0.5cm.
**2–13** 2cm.
**13–14** 1.25cm; square down to 15.
**5–16** $^1/_2$ bust plus 10cm; square down to 17 and 18.
**18–19** 1cm.
**16–20** Square up the measurement 0–5 (add 0.3cm for each size above 14). Square out.
**16–21** $^1/_3$ measurement 5–16 plus reduced dart measurement minus 0.5cm; square up.
**16–22** $^1/_2$ the measurement 16–21.
**20–23** $^1/_5$ neck size.
**23–24** Reduced dart measurement; join 23 and 24 to 22 to create a dart. Ensure 22–23 is equal to 22–24.
**10–25** 1.8cm; square across.
**24–26** Shoulder measurement plus 1.5cm. Draw in the shoulder line.
**20–27** $^1/_5$ neck measurement plus 0.5cm.
**21–28** $^1/_4$ measurement 16–20 minus 1cm; join 26–28.
Square down from 22 to 29 on the waistline and 30 on the hipline.
**21–31** $^1/_2$ the measurement 8–21; square down to 32 on the waistline, 33 on the hemline.
**8–34** $^1/_2$ measurement 5–8 plus 1cm; square down to 35 on the waistline, 36 on the hipline, and 37 on the hemline.
**28–38** $^1/_2$ measurement 26–28.
Draw armhole as shown in diagram touching points 12, 9, 31, 28, 26; the curves also touching points: 2.8cm from 8, and 2.3cm from 21. (Add 1mm for each size up).

**Semi-fitted Waist Shaping**

Note that the amount of shaping can be varied.
**22–39** 2.5cm.
**30–40** 5cm. Draw in the 2.5cm front waist dart.
**36–41** 8cm. Draw in the 1.5 back waist dart.
**32–42** 1cm.
**32–43** 1.75cm.
**33–44** 1.5cm.
**33–45** 0.5cm.
Draw in the back side seam 31, 42, 44.
Draw in the front side seam 31, 43, 45.

**Sleeves**

A one-piece or two-piece sleeve can be drafted for this block. See pages 82 and 84.

## Easy-fitting jacket/coat block

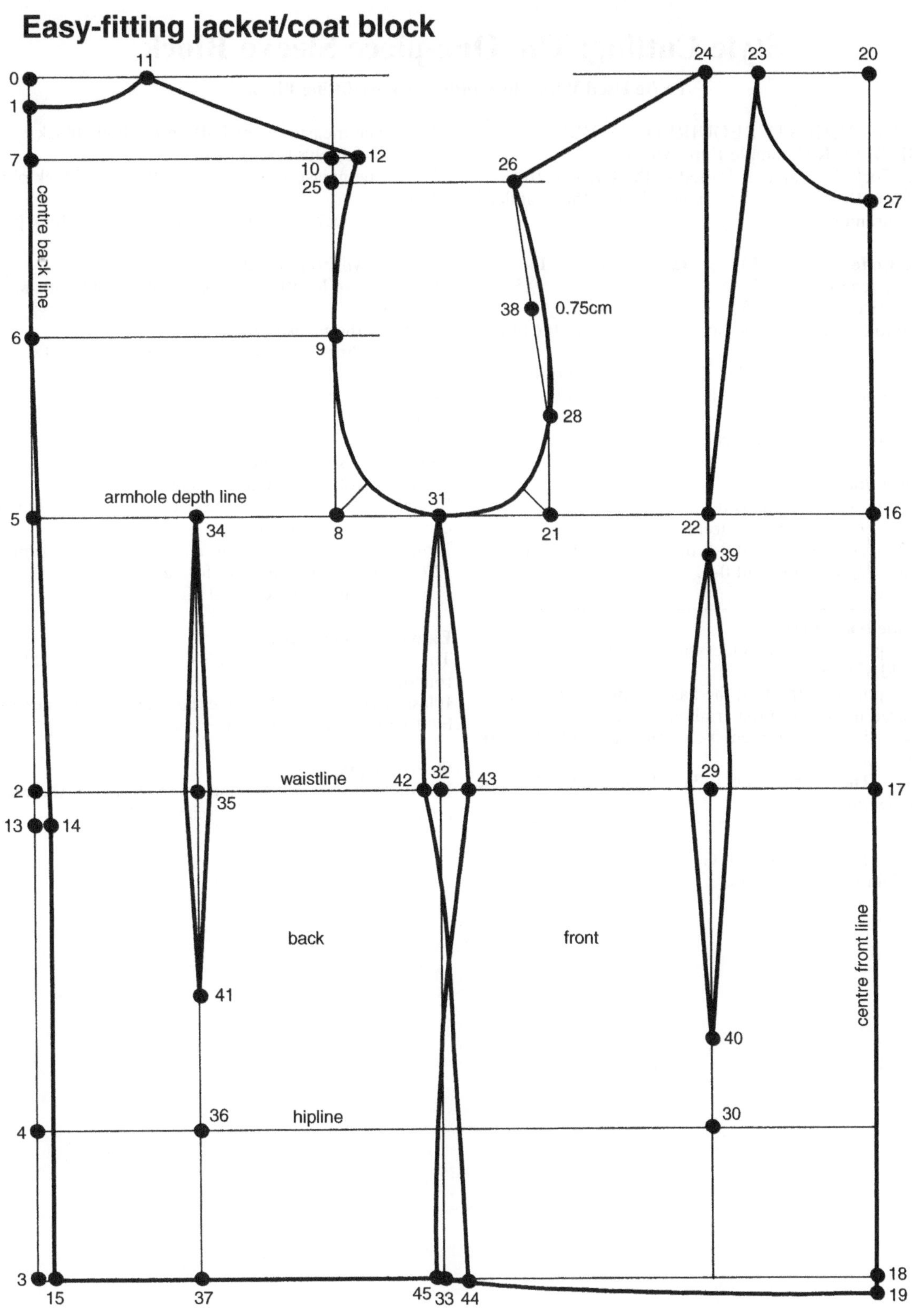

# Style Cutting: The One-piece Sleeve Block

**To Be Used With Close-fitting or Easy-fitting Blocks**

MEASUREMENTS REQUIRED TO DRAFT THE BLOCK (Example Euro size 36)
The block illustrated is drafted to the UK size 10. Refer to the 4cm size chart (page 31) for other standard measurements.

| **Size Code** | **10** | **12** | **14** | **16** |
|---|---|---|---|---|
| Sleeve length | 58 | 58.5 | 59 | 59.5 |
| Wrist size | 15.5 | 16 | 16.5 | 17 |
| Armhole (scye) | measure the armhole of the block. | | | |

**Note** It is important that the curve of the armhole is measured accurately; see the diagram opposite.

No seam allowances included.

**Sleeve draft**
Square down and across from 0.
**0–1** $^1/_3$ armhole measurement.
**1–2** $^1/_2$ measurement 0–1 minus 1cm; square across.
**0–3** $^1/_4$ measurement 0–1.

---

**On the body block**
Mark points A at the underarm point, B and C at the shoulder points.
Mark points D and E at the base of lines which are squared up to touch the armhole lines.
**D–F** The measurement 0–2 on the sleeve block; mark F *pitch point.*
**E–G** The measurement 0–3 on the sleeve block; mark G *pitch point.*

---

**3–4** The measurement G–C on the body block (straight line) plus 1.2cm.
**4–5** The measurement F–B on the body block (straight line) plus 0.8cm.
**5–6** The measurement A–F on the body block plus 0.8cm.
**3–7** The measurement A–G on the body block plus 0.5cm.
Square down from 6 and 7.
**1–8** Sleeve length plus 2.5cm; square out both ways to 9 and 10.
**7–11** $^1/_2$ the measurement 3–7.
Divide the line 3-4 into 3 sections; mark points 12 and 13.
**4–14** $^1/_2$ measurement 4–5.
**5–15** $^1/_2$ measurement 5–6.

**Draw in the sleeve head:**
From 6–5 hollow the curve 0.6cm at 15.
From 5–4 raise the back curve 1.5cm at 14; (add 0.1cm to each point for each size up).
From 4–3 raise the front curve 2cm at 13, and 1.5cm at 12 (add 0.1cm to each point for each size up).
From 3–7 hollow the curve 0.75cm at 11.

**Ease at the sleeve head**
The ease in the sleeve head is drafted to give a full rounded sleeve head.
If less ease is required reduce the length of the lines 3–4 by 0.3cm and 4–5 by 0.2cm.

**Sleeve shaping**
For slight sleeve shaping narrow the sleeve at the wrist approx. 3–5cm on each side seam.

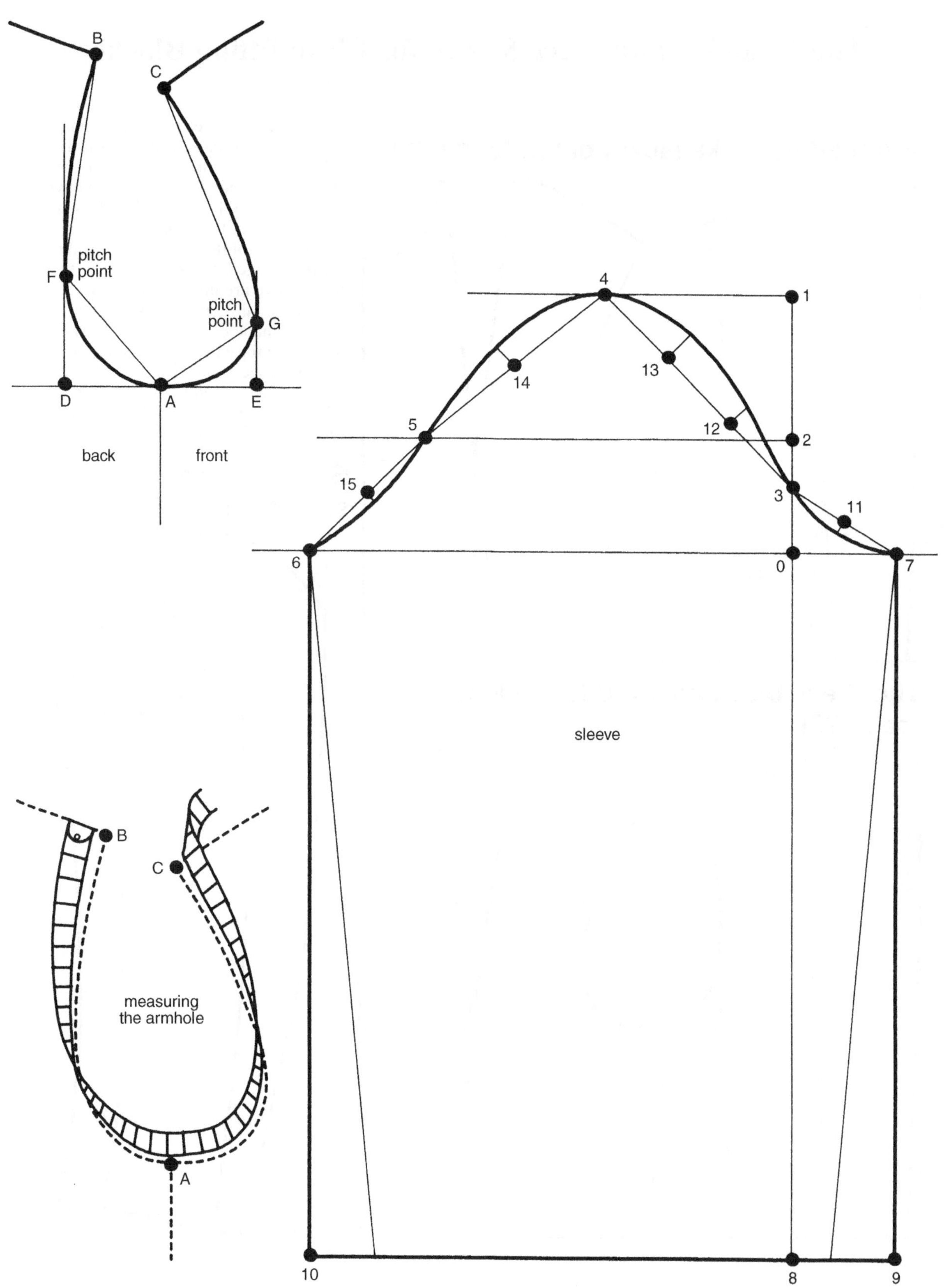
B
C
pitch
point
F
pitch
point
G
D
A
E
back
front
measuring
the armhole
B
C
A
4
1
13
14
5
12
2
15
3
11
6
0
7
sleeve
10
8
9

# The Bespoke Two-piece Sleeve for Close-fitting Blocks

If a classic two-piece sleeve is required for either of the close-fitting blocks with full bust darting, the preferred choice should be a shaped sleeve. Use the two-piece sleeve draft for the close-fitting bespoke jacket block on page 38.

The shape of the close-fitting armhole drafts on page 79 and the bespoke two-piece sleeve are illustrated below.

Note the difference between the armhole shape of close-fitting blocks and that of the easier fitting block on the opposite page. Note also the difference between the shaped sleeve illustrated below and the straighter sleeve that is often used with easier fitting styles.

## Adapted bespoke jacket block (page 78)

centre back line
back
front
centre front line

## The dress block adapted for jackets (page 78)

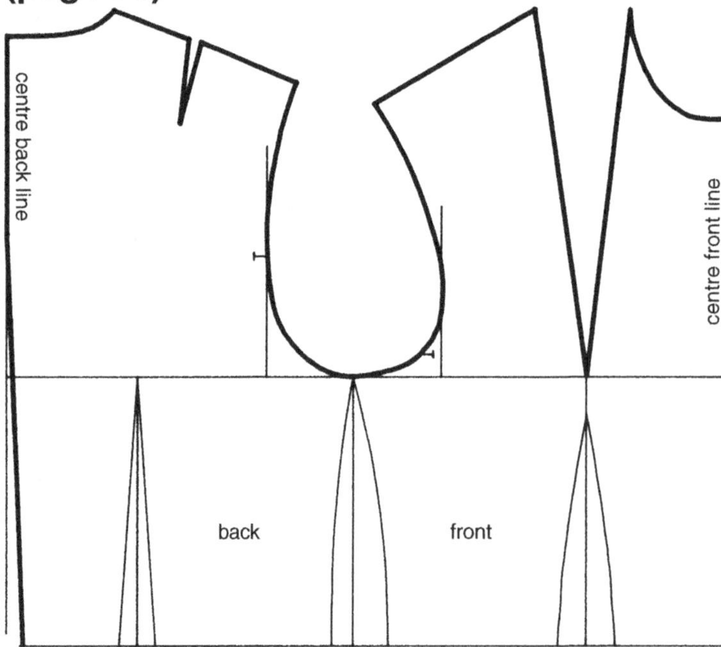


## Bespoke two-piece sleeve block (page 38)

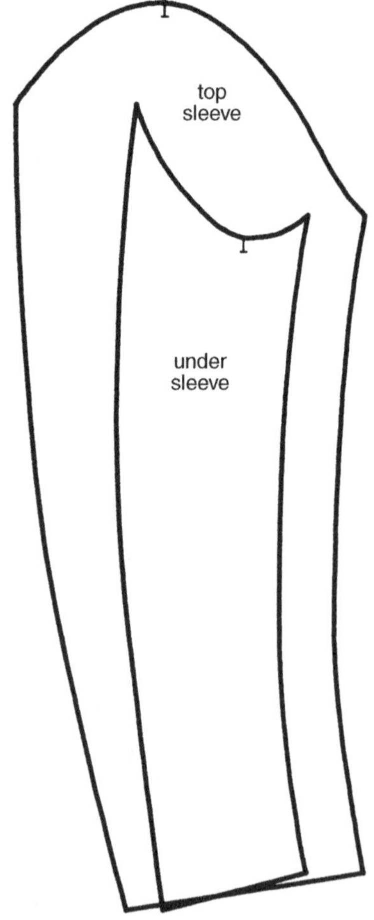

# The Classic Two-piece Sleeve for Easy-fitting Blocks

If a classic two-piece sleeve is required for an easy-fitting block with reduced bust darting, the preferred choice should be a straighter sleeve. Select the sleeve draft for the engineered jacket block on page 54.

The shape of the easy-fitting armhole draft on page 80 and the engineered two-piece sleeve are illustrated below.

Compare them with the type of shaped two-piece sleeve and the shape of the armholes of the close-fitting blocks on the opposite page.

## Easy-fitting jacket/coat block (page 80)

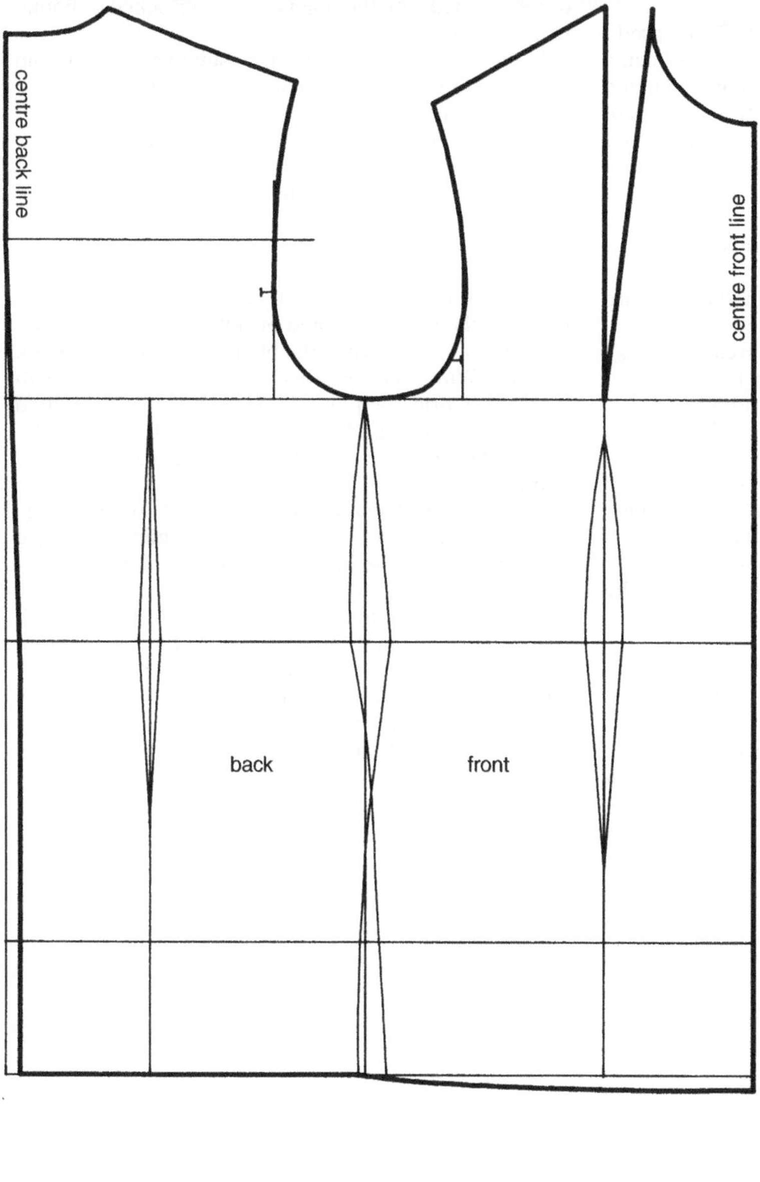

## Two-piece sleeve engineered semi-fitting classic jacket block (page 54)

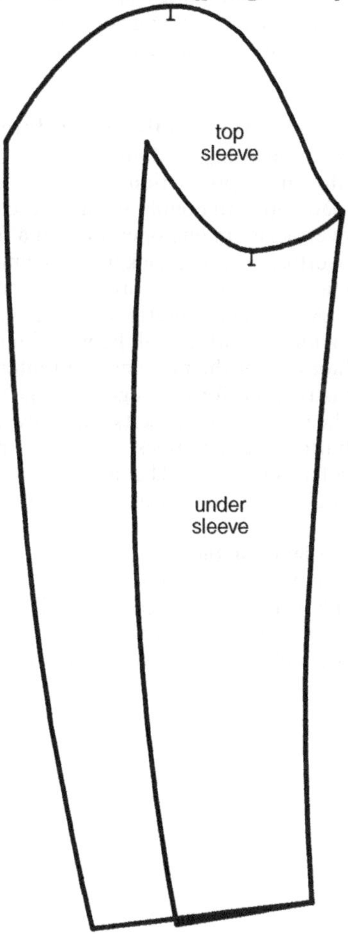

# Fabrics, Interlinings and Linings for Style Cutting

## Fabrics

Jackets cut in a *tailored style* instead of conventional tailoring make the possibilities of fabric choice and construction almost infinite. Whilst conventional tailors using bespoke methods usually select from a range of fabrics which have the quality of tailorability, designers have taken fabrics from the most delicate dress fabrics to unyielding plastics and have fashioned them into a *style tailleur.*

The use of Lycra in fabric for jackets has increased enormously. Close-fitting garments have always been a problem to market because of the fit. The introduction of Lycra into fabrics has allowed close-fitting jackets to mould to a wider range of body shapes. It also increases the crease resistance and shape retention of the garment.

## Construction Methods and Interlinings

### Manufacturing methods

Most mass-production unlined or half-lined jackets are made up with double seams; these are seamed and overlocked in one operation on a four thread overlocker. Lined jackets are seamed by lockstitch machines; the seams are pressed open and left raw.

All the main interlinings used will be fusibles, the majority of which will be warp knitted or bonded fabrics. For the placements of interlinings, see the instructions for the engineered jacket on page 59. The cheaper unlined jackets may only have the front buttonholes and pocket placings, the facings and the collar, interlined. The jacket fabric will be used for the pocket bags and to cover the shoulder pads.

### Designer methods

The historical method of mounting fabric onto muslin, silk or light-weight cotton is still used. It supports delicate fabrics and gives a luxurious appearance, particularly to soft wools. The fabric pieces are laid on top of the mounting fabric; the pieces are then tacked together and stay together throughout the whole making-up process. It is very important that the mounting is in sympathy with the main fabric and both fabrics are fully shrunk. The technique works best in designs with many seams so that fabrics do not become disconnected. Only sections of a garment may be mounted. Mounted jackets can be lined conventionally or left unlined with the seam edges overlocked or bound with fine silk.

Designers appropriate the most suitable method from historical or current dressmaking, tailoring or manufacturing techniques to effect their design.

The main features that distinguish the designer ranges from the high street ranges of jackets is the originality of cut and construction and the quality of the fabrics and the finish.

## Linings

Linings for jackets are usually light-weight with a silky finish. Jackets are half-lined or fully lined. This allows the garment to slide over the blouses and sweaters worn beneath. Whilst most jackets have linings that tone with the outer fabric, the potential for contrasts and printed fabrics is unlimited. Many jackets are half-lined or are designed to be worn directly over underwear and are unlined.

A quality finish can be given to jackets by inserting the lining underneath the facing and hemline. The edge of the facing and the hems are then bound in the lining fabric.

It would seem common sense that jackets made from fabrics which contain the stretch fibre Lycra should be lined with similar stretch linings. However, these are difficult to obtain and are expensive. The other solution is to use fabrics which have a natural stretch from either their fibre or the weaving process.

# Part Three:

# 7 BODY SHAPE VARIATIONS



All types of shapes can emerge in tailored jackets. These can be created by the proportions of length and width. It is essential that the correct fabric is used to achieve the shape of the design. Stretch fabrics allow a closer fit. Bias cutting can add ease and can give subtle qualities of drape to easy-fitting and flared designs.

Seams and darts are the principal means of creating changes of shape in jackets. This chapter gives examples of how they may be used. Examples of basic panel seaming on classic jackets are shown on pages 36, 46 and 52; however, the illustrations in this chapter demonstrate the integration of 'dressmaker' shaping into tailors' drafts and show some substantial differences of garment shape.

The design adaptation usually follows the following stages:

1. the selection of the appropriate block;
2. the modification of the block for the length and any overall ease;
3. the transfer of the dart away from the neck if required, see method below. This can be temporary to allow clear areas for seam or collar drafts.
4. the draft marked with seam lines, pocket markings and design features;
5. the collar drafts completed;
6. the pattern pieces traced from the draft, further adaptations made.

This chapter only demonstrates methods of adapting body sections; for other adaptations, such as collar drafting, it refers to the relevant pages.

BUST DART TRANSFER
Draw a line A–B from the centre of the shoulder to the bust point. Cut along the line A–B. Close the neck dart. This will transfer the dart to the shoulder line.
Using the same method, the dart can be transferred to any part of the pattern perimeter, as shown below. If the dart is then in its final position, the dart point must be shortened 2.5cm.

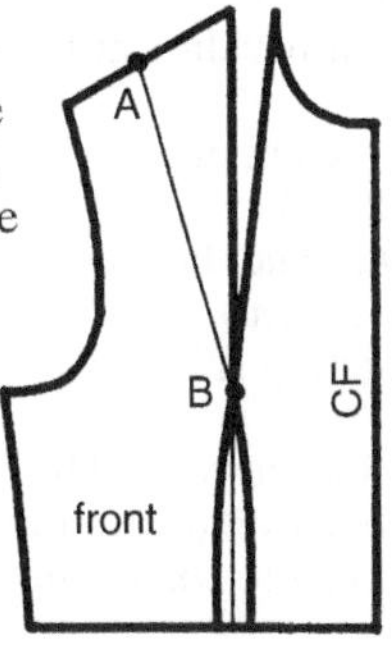


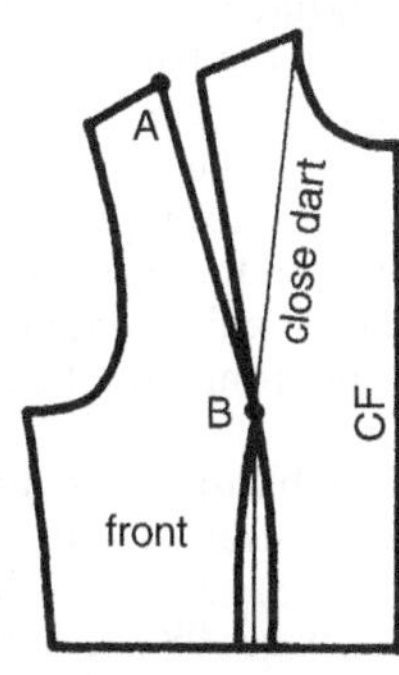


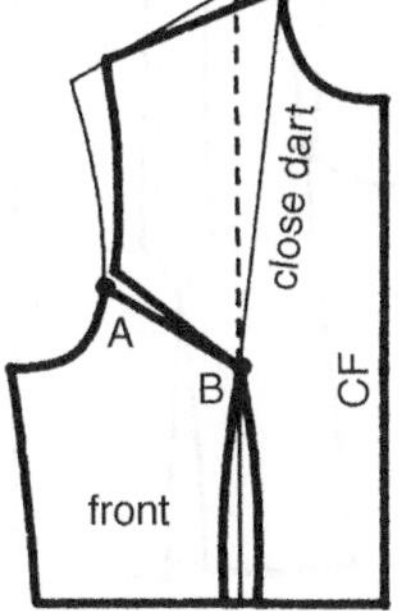


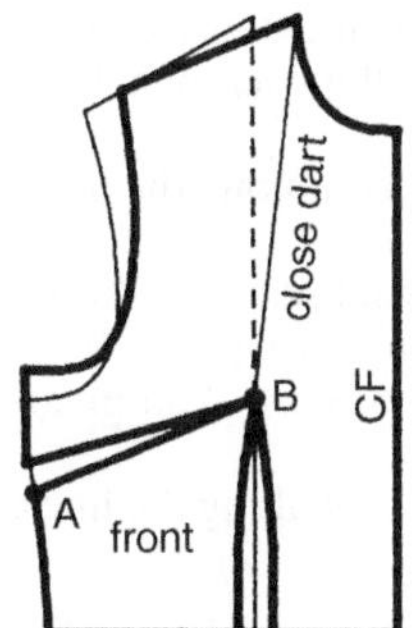


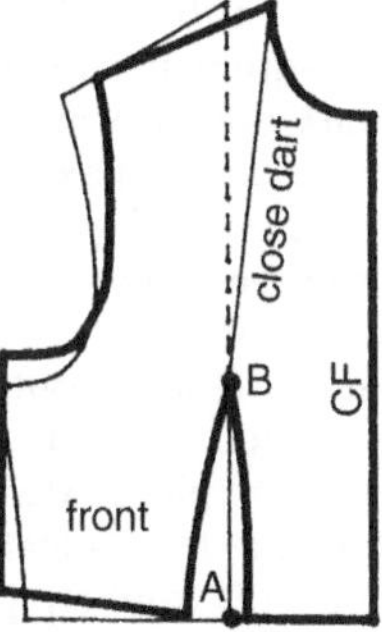

# Vertical Seams

1. CLOSE-FITTING STYLE

**Basic Draft** Trace the close-fitting block (ref. page 78). Reduce to correct length with a straight hem. Rub out waist darts and side seam shaping (11.75cm).
Draw in the main style lines on the back and front.
Draw in the vertical lines of the side panel.
Cut down the main front panel seam to bust point.
Close dart at neckline to transfer dart to the seam line.
Draw in new waist shaping back from the main seam style lines. Shape in the back and front seams 1cm.
The total shaping should not exceed 12.75cm.
Extra flare is added to the side and back panel seams.
Mark buttonholes, add buttonstand. The design demonstrates the draft of a Basic Rever Collar (ref. 1 page 100). To complete collars and facing (see pages 98 and 100).

**Back, Front and Side Panels** Trace off the individual pattern shapes.

2. EASY-FITTING STYLE

**Basic Draft** Trace the easy-fitting block (ref. page 80). Alter length if required.
Rub out any waist darting. Remove centre back waist shaping.
Redraw the side seam to give a high waist shaping.
Transfer bust dart to the side seam (ref. page 87).
The style demonstrates a low rever; therefore overlap the front neck of the draft see **Very Low Neckline** (ref. page 98).
Widen the back and front neckline at the shoulder approx. 1.5cm.
Draw in the back panel seam; draw in slight waist shaping (example is 1.25cm).
Draw in the front centre panel line; draw in slight waist shaping (example is 2cm).
Draw front strap lines; (strap is laid over front seam).
Mark buttonholes, add buttonstand. The design demonstrates the draft of a Collar with Low Revers, (ref. 4 page 100). To complete collars and facing (see pages 98 and 100).

**Back Sections** Trace off centre back panel.
Trace off back. Add back pleat extension, width = measurement of the base of the back panel.
Mark points A and B.
Trace off pleat extension. Mirror along the line A–B to create back pleat facing.

**Front Sections** Trace off front sections. Add pleat extension, width approx. 6cm. Mark points C and D.
Trace off side front; close bust dart. Add pleat extension as front.
Trace off pleat extension. Mirror along the line C–D to create front pleat facing.
Trace off front strap.

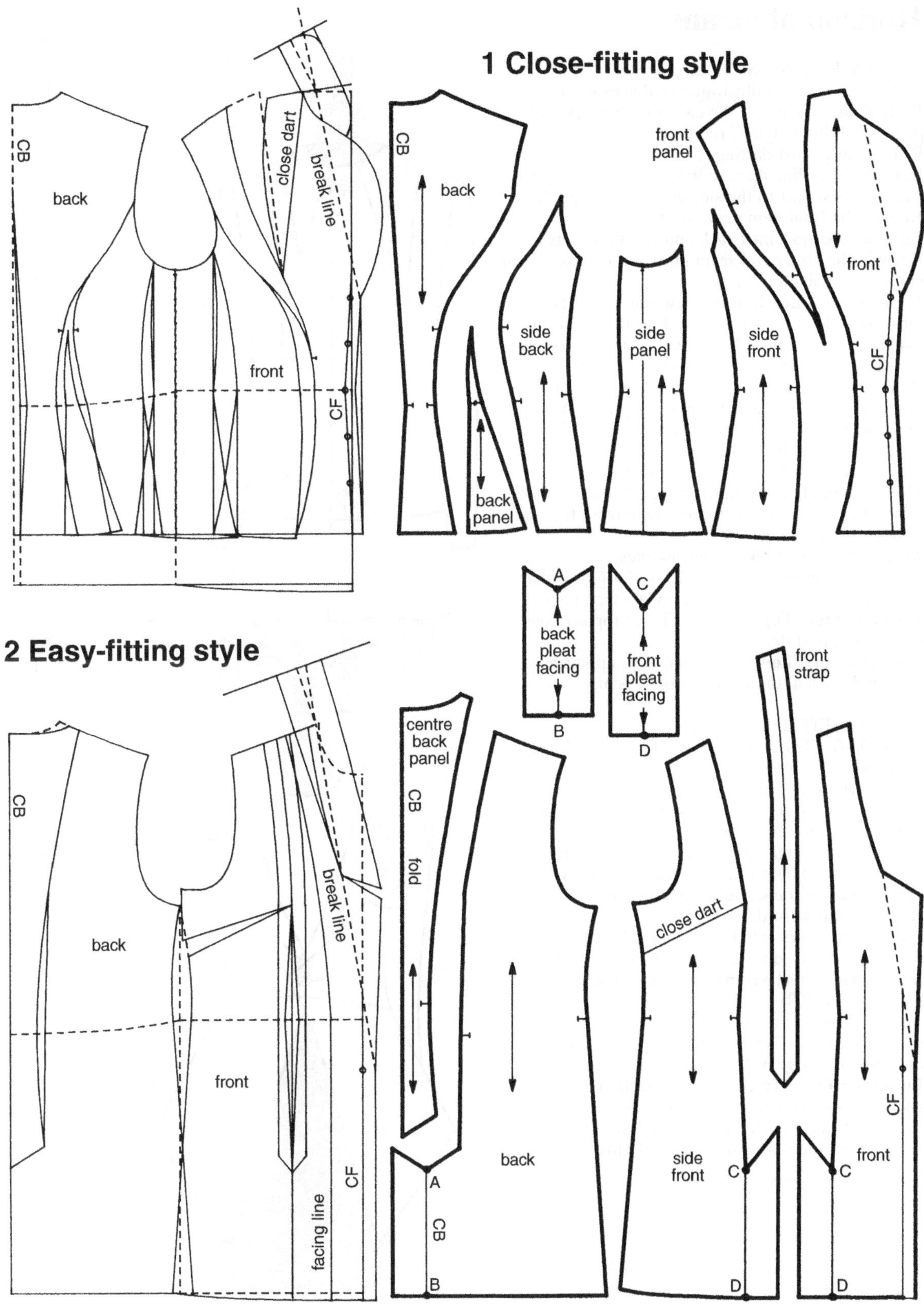
1 Close-fitting style
CB
back
close dart
break line
front
CF
CB
back
front panel
side back
side panel
side front
front
CF
back panel
2 Easy-fitting style
A
back pleat facing
B
C
front pleat facing
D
front strap
centre back panel
CB
fold
CB
back
break line
front
facing line
CF
back
A
CB
B
close dart
side front
C
D
front
C
D
CF

# Horizontal Seams

1. EASY-FITTING STYLE
A fly front facing is illustrated in this example.
**Basic Draft** Trace off the easy-fitting block (ref. page 80). Alter length if required.
Rub out any waist darting.
Raise the waistline 4cm; redraw side seam shaping.
Transfer bust dart to the side seam (ref. page 87).
Reduce the front hem curve to 0.5cm.
Separate the draft into back and front sections.
Draw in the horizontal seam line on the back; 0.5cm curved seam line on the front.
Mark points A and B at the new side waistline.
Draw in style lines C–D and E–F to the waist on the back and front bodice. Cut down the lines and across the side waist. Open the top bodices 1.5cm.
Redraw top bodice side seams from new armhole points G and H to the original waist points A and B.
Draw in 3cm back and front darts on the style lines.
Shape the 0.5cm back shoulder ease into the style line. Divide lower panels into four sections.
Mark top and bottom buttonhole, add buttonstand.
Add a further stand for fly front 6cm from top and bottom of front edge.
Trace off facing: mark fly buttonholes.
The design demonstrates the draft of a Flat Collar (ref. 1 page 106). To complete collars (see page 98).
**Back and Front Top Sections** Trace top sections.
Close front bust dart.
**Back and Front Lower Sections** Cut up vertical lines and open at the hem approx. 1.5cm.

2. CLOSE-FITTING STYLE
**Basic Draft** Trace off the close-fitting block (ref. page 78). Alter length if required.
Redraw the side seam to give a high waist shaping.
Widen the back and front neckline approx. 1.5cm at the shoulder; lower the back neckline 1cm.
Draw in horizontal curved lines across the draft.
Cut along front bodice seam to dart point. Close bust dart at neck to transfer dart to seam line.
Reduce front waist dart by 1cm.
Mark buttonholes, add buttonstand. The design demonstrates the draft of a Wide Collar with Revers, (ref. 5 page 100). To complete collars and facing (see pages 98 and 100).
**Top Sections** Trace off top sections.
**Centre sections** Trace off centre panels; close back and front darts from A–B and C–D.
**Lower Sections** Trace off lower sections. Divide each dart into two darts; draw lines to the hemline from the base of each dart. Cut up lines, close the darts, insert the required amount of flare.

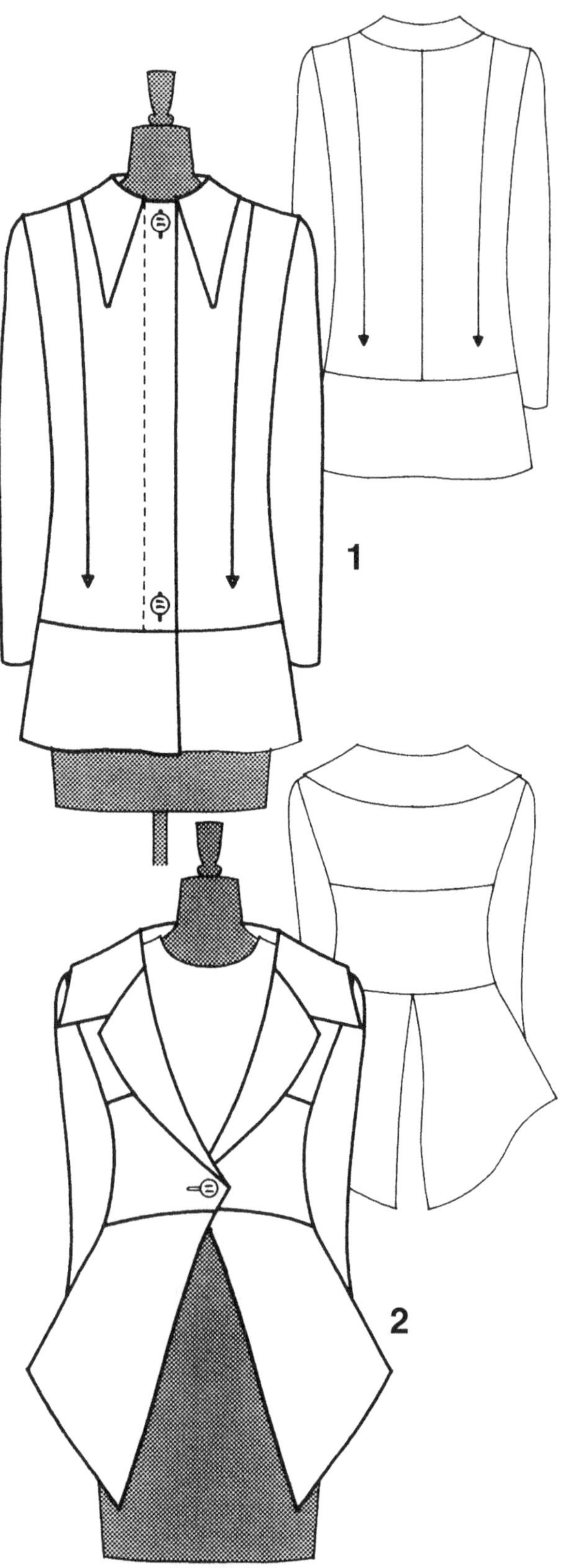

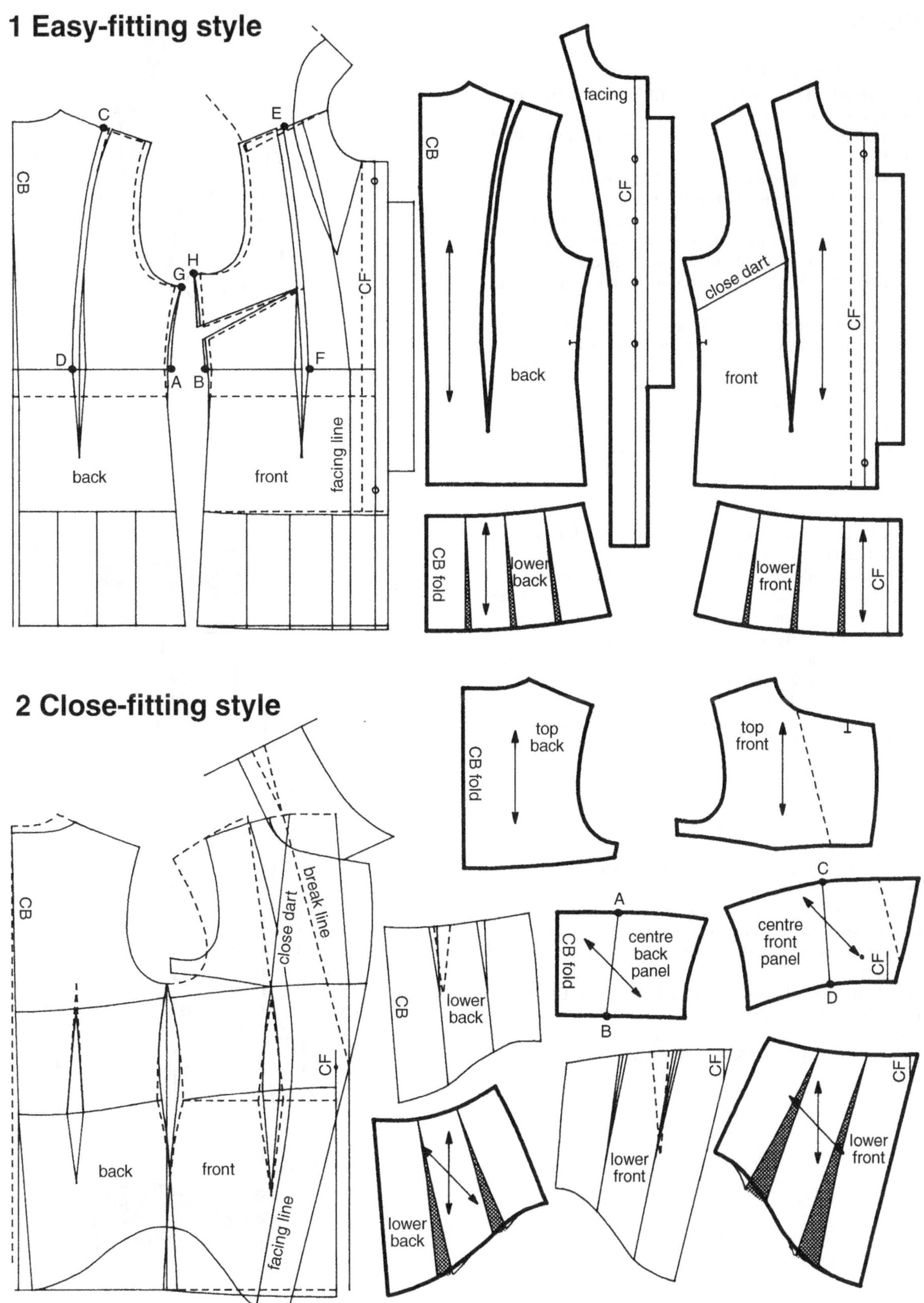
1 Easy-fitting style
C
E
CB
H
G
D
A
B
F
CF
back
front
facing line
facing
CB
CF
back
close dart
front
CF
CB fold
lower back
lower front
CF
2 Close-fitting style
top back
CB fold
top front
CB
close dart
break line
CF
back
front
facing line
A
centre back panel
CB fold
B
C
centre front panel
CF
D
CB
lower back
CF
CF
lower back
lower front
lower front

# Darts

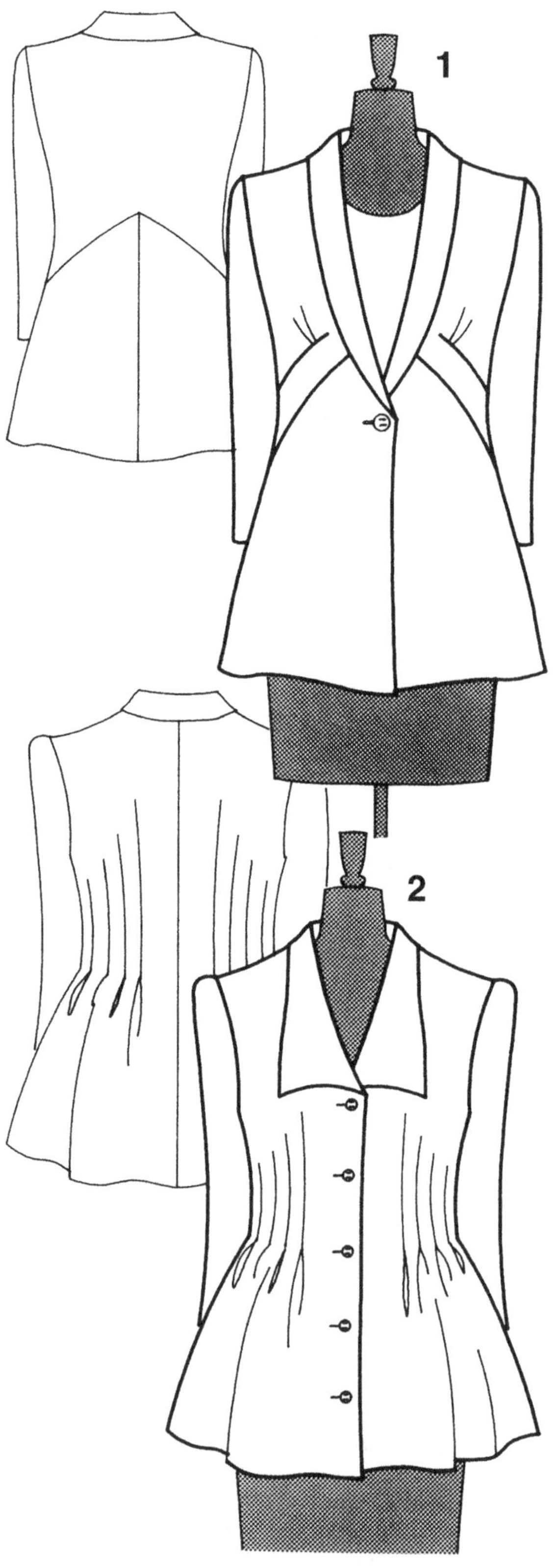


1. DARTS AND SEAMS

**Basic Draft** Trace off the easy-fitting block (ref. page 80). Alter length if required.
Draw in the asymmetrical curved seam lines across back and front.
Draw a parallel line for new bust dart position, 3cm past waist dart. Close bust dart at the neck.
Divide the lower sections in three parts as shown.
Redraw lower section dart lines with straight lines.
Mark buttonholes add buttonstand. The design demonstrates the draft of a Classic Roll Collar (ref. 1a page 102).

**Back and Front Sections** Trace off top sections.
On the front, draw a line from the centre shoulder at A to top of waist dart at B. Cut and open approx. 4.5cm.
Mark two tucks each 2.25cm on the dart line as shown.
Close the bottom section of the waist dart at C–D.

**Lower Sections** Trace off the lower sections. Cut up the vertical lines. Close the darts and open the lines at the hem to the amount of flare required.

2. DARTS AND TUCKS

**Basic Draft** Trace off the easy-fitting block (ref. page 80). Alter length if required.
Redraw the side seam to give a high waist shaping.
Add 2cm extra flare to the side seam, 1cm flare to the back seam. Rub out the waist darting.
Draw new lines 4cm below the waistline.
On the back section draw a vertical line approx. 7cm from centre back to A approx. 9 cm from the neckline.
Draw in 0.5cm shoulder ease as a dart to point A.
A–B approx. 9cm; B–C approx. 11cm; C–D approx. 15cm. Join A–D.
On the front section draw a vertical line from the bust point. Mark point E at the waist; E–F = 2cm. Square up to the armhole line at G.
F–H is approx. 13cm; H–I is approx. 14cm. Join I–G.
Mark buttonholes, add buttonstand. The design demonstrates the draft of a High Roll Collar (ref. 1c page 102).
Separate the front and back sections.

**Front and Back Sections** Close back shoulder dart and front bust dart to add flare to hemline. Add extra flare if required.
Divide the two changed constructed areas ABCD and FGHI into three even sections.
On each line construct 0.75cm darts at the waistline.
Narrow the darts to 0.5cm on the lower line.

## 1 Darts and seams

## 2 Darts and tucks

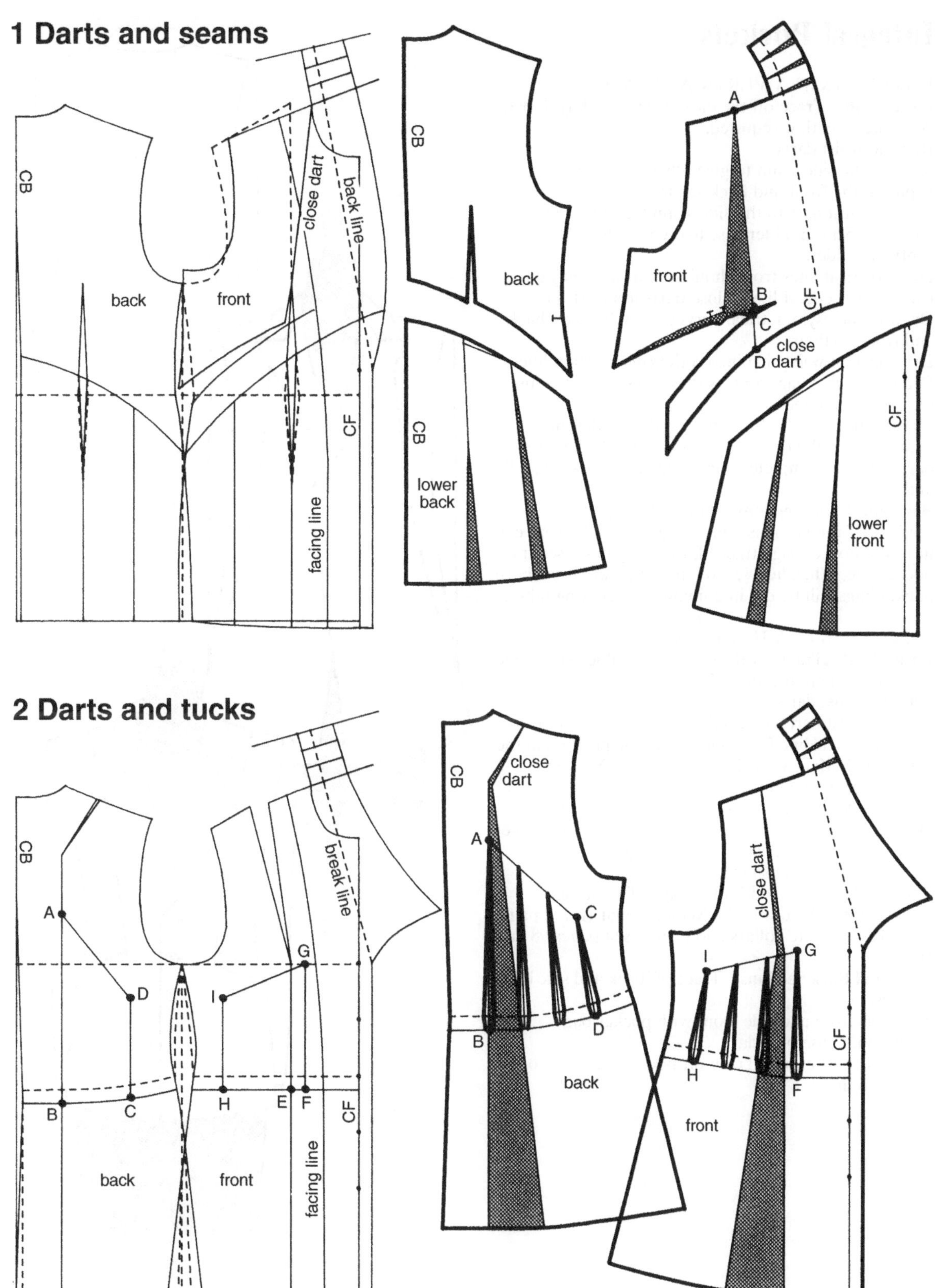

# Integral Pockets

1. POCKETS IN A VERTICAL SEAM

**Basic Draft** Trace off the easy-fitting block (ref. page 80). Alter length if required.

Rub out waist darts.

Redraw the side seam to give a high waist shaping.

Separate the front and back sections.

Transfer bust dart to the side seam (ref. page 87).

Use the 0.5cm shoulder ease to create a 7cm dart at the centre shoulder.

Draw vertical lines from shoulder dart and bust dart.

Cut up the vertical lines, close darts to insert flare.

Draw in the asymmetrical curved seam lines on back and front sections.

Draw in 1cm waist shaping on the curved seam lines.

Draw in pocket bag from A–B as shown. Mark point C on front panel line.

Mark buttonholes, add buttonstand. The design demonstrates the draft of a Basic Rever Collar (ref. 1 page 100). To complete collars and facing (see pages 98 and 100).

**Back and Front Sections** Trace off all pattern sections. If the fabric is light-weight, the side front can have the pocket bag attached; the front has a separate pocket bag. When heavier weight fabrics are used, both pocket bags will be cut in a lining or pocketing fabric.

2. POCKETS IN A HORIZONTAL SEAM

**Basic Draft** Trace off the easy-fitting block (ref. page 80). Alter length if required.

Rub out waist darts.

Transfer bust dart to the side seam (ref. page 87).

Draw a vertical line from point A–B, the position of the back panel. Mark C at the waistline. C–D 2.5cm.

Draw in back seam curve A, D, B.

B–E = 1.25cm; draw in side panel line, A, G, E.

Draw in front panel line F, G, H. Draw in welt pocket line I–J. Draw in 1.25cm waist shaping.

Draw in pocket bag shape.

Mark buttonholes, add buttonstand. The design demonstrates the draft of a Reefer Collar (ref. 2 page 100). To complete collars and facing (see pages 98 and 100).

**Front and Back Sections** Trace off back and side back sections.

Trace off front and side front with pocket bag extension. Close bust dart.

Trace off pocket bag. Trace off pocket welt, mirror along the line I–J.

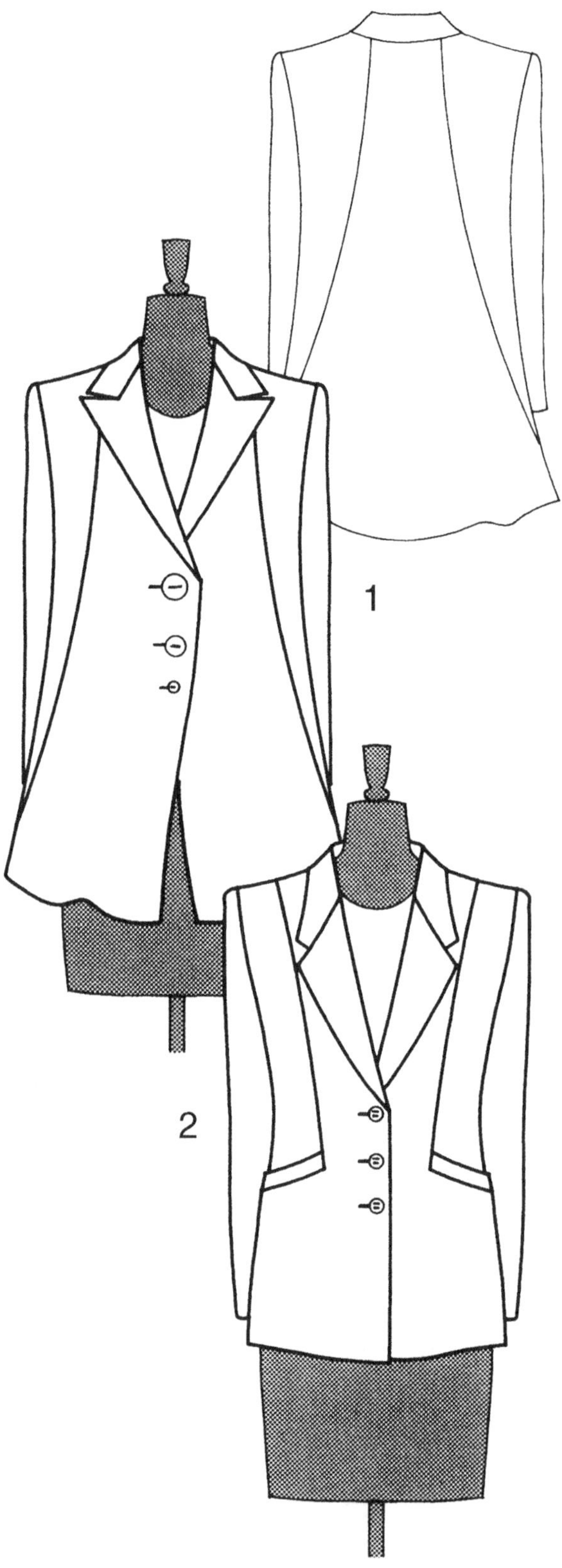

## 1 Pockets in a vertical seam

## 2 Pockets in a horizontal seam

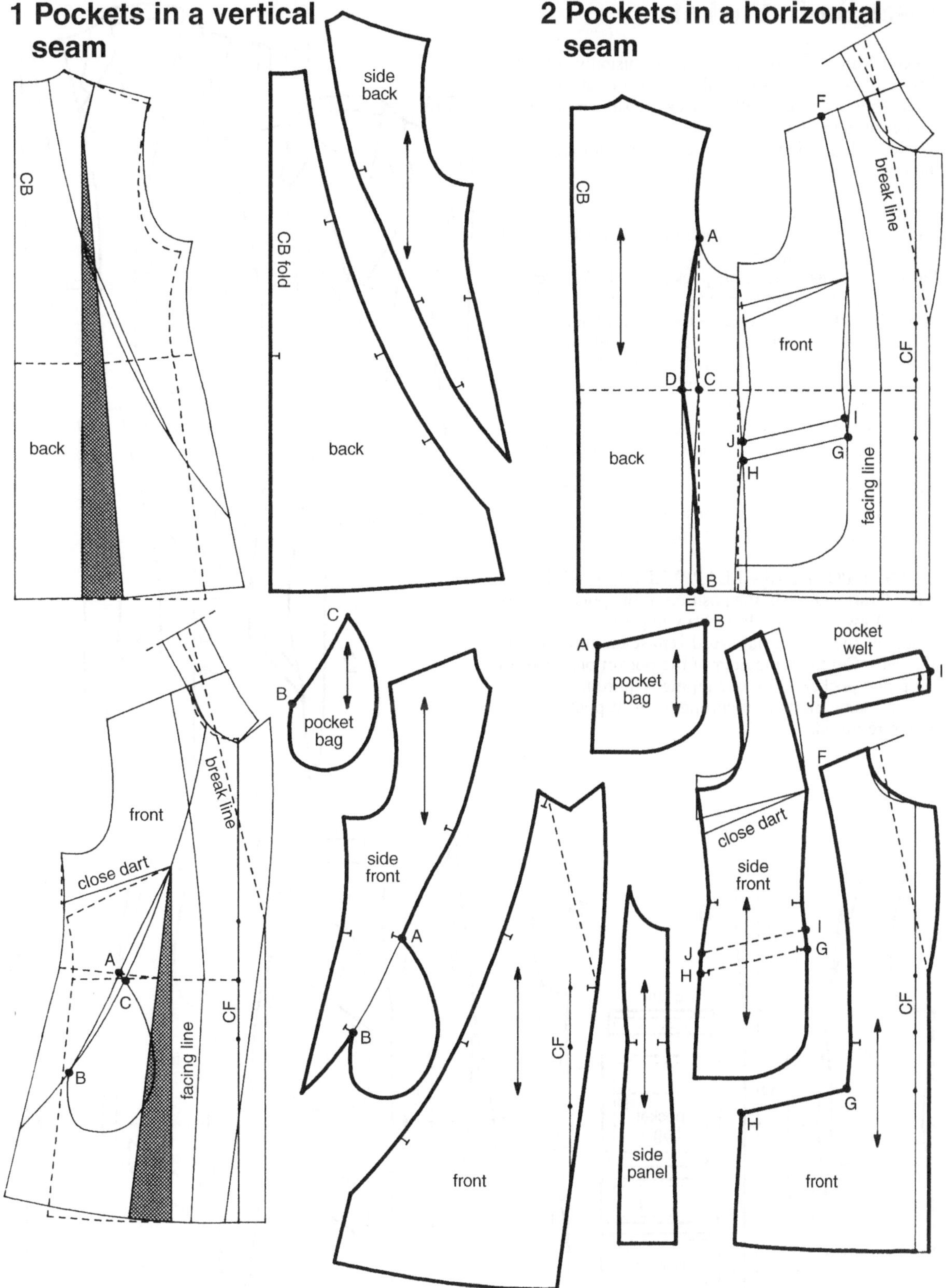

# Inset Basic Pockets

**Special Note** The pocket pieces are usually cut with different amounts of seam allowances on particular lines. Therefore, **seam allowances are shown on the pocket pattern pieces**.

The pocket facing is usually cut in the suit fabric and the pocket bags in lining.

1a. PIPED POCKET
**Basic Draft** Draw in the position of the pocket mouth A–B. Draw in pocket bag.
**Pocket Patterns** Trace off pocket bag 1. Add 1cm seam allowance on the top edge; 2cm on remainder. Mark in pocket facing line on the pocket bag.
Trace off pocket facing; Add 1cm seam allowance to top and bottom edges; 2cm to side lines.
Trace off pocket bag 2. Add 1cm seam allowance on the top edge; 2cm on remainder.
Pipings – construct two rectangles twice the depth of the piping. Add 1cm seam allowance to all edges.

1b. PIPED POCKET – DART TRANSFERRED
The draft demonstrates the bust dart transferred into the waist dart and the pocket line.

2. INSET POCKETS – FLAP/WELT POCKETS
**Basic Draft** Draw in the position of the pocket mouth A–B. Draw in pocket flap. Draw in pocket bag.
Trace off the pocket flap. Add 1cm seam allowance to all edges. Cut the remainder of the pocket pieces as for the piped pocket. Only one piping required.
Use the same method of cutting for welt pockets. No piping required.

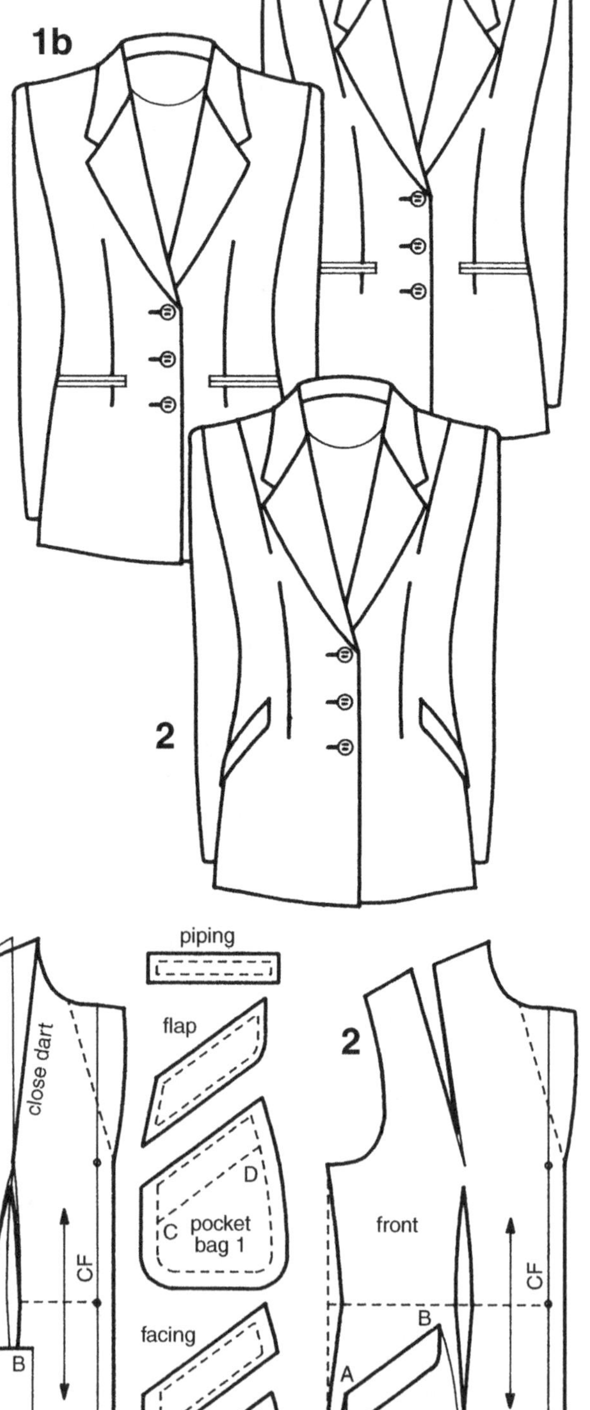

# Part Three:

# 8 COLLAR VARIATIONS



The collars illustrated and constructed in this chapter are related specifically to jacket cutting. It includes basic collar shapes and some added variations.

# General Principles

### Basic Terms
TERMS used when constructing collars.
*Neckline* the line where collar is joined to neck.
*Style Line* outer edge of collar or rever.
*Roll Line* the line where the collar rolls over.
*Stand* rise of the collar from neckline to roll line.
*Fall* depth of collar from roll line to style line.
*Break Point* where the rever turns back to form lapel.
*Break line* line along which lapel rolls back.
A description and illustration of collar terms can be found on page 40.
**Collar Types** collars fall into four basic groups.
1. *Collars with revers,* separate collar and rever.
2. *Collars cut in one with the garment* (roll).
3. *Standing collars* stand up around the neck or stand, fold over then fall.
4. *Flat collars* sit flat (or almost) around shoulders.

### Before Drafting a Collar
If the style adaptation has not transferred the bust dart from the neck point it can be transferred temporarily to another area, usually the underarm, see page 87.
FRONTS
**Single Breasted Front**
Mark buttonline, buttonhole positions.
Add button stand approx. 2cm.
**Double Breasted Front**
Mark two buttonlines an equal distance each side of the centre front. Mark buttonholes.
Add button stand approx. 2cm.

NECKLINES
Lower neckline if required. Example shown opposite 1cm at the centre back, 2cm at the shoulders, 1.5cm at the centre front. This will vary according to the style.
**Very Low Neckline**
Draw a line from the centre of neck line to bust point. Cut up the line and overlap 0.6cm–0.8cm at the neckline. This widens the bust dart.
(Collar illustration ref. 4 page 100).
**Draped Neckline**
Draw a line from the centre of the neckline to the armhole and open the neckline the required amount.
(Collar illustration ref. page 108).

### Drafting a Collar
UNDERCOLLAR
The drafts on the following pages are for the construction of undercollars.
The *undercollar* provides the basic draft for the collar.
**General Points**
When drawing the style line, allow for the depth of the collar stand.

Widening the style line of a rever, roll or stand collar reduces the stand and also allows the collar to sit lower on the shoulders (see pages 101, 103 and 105).

Reducing the style line of a flat collar draft makes the collar stand rise and also makes the collar rise up the shoulders (see page 107).

Measuring the length of the style line in its position on the shoulders gives a good guide.
Experiment on a dress stand or figure for final effects.

### After Drafting a Collar
TOP COLLARS
Add 0.25cm to outer edge of the top collar from point A to B and C–D as shown.
This ensures the seam line of outer edge of collar will not show when made up, and the back neck of collar will sit properly. Add 0.5cm for thick fabrics.

FACINGS
Draw in the facing line. Trace off the facing.
**Facings for Collars with Revers**
Add 0.5cm to the style line of the rever from collar point A to break point B.

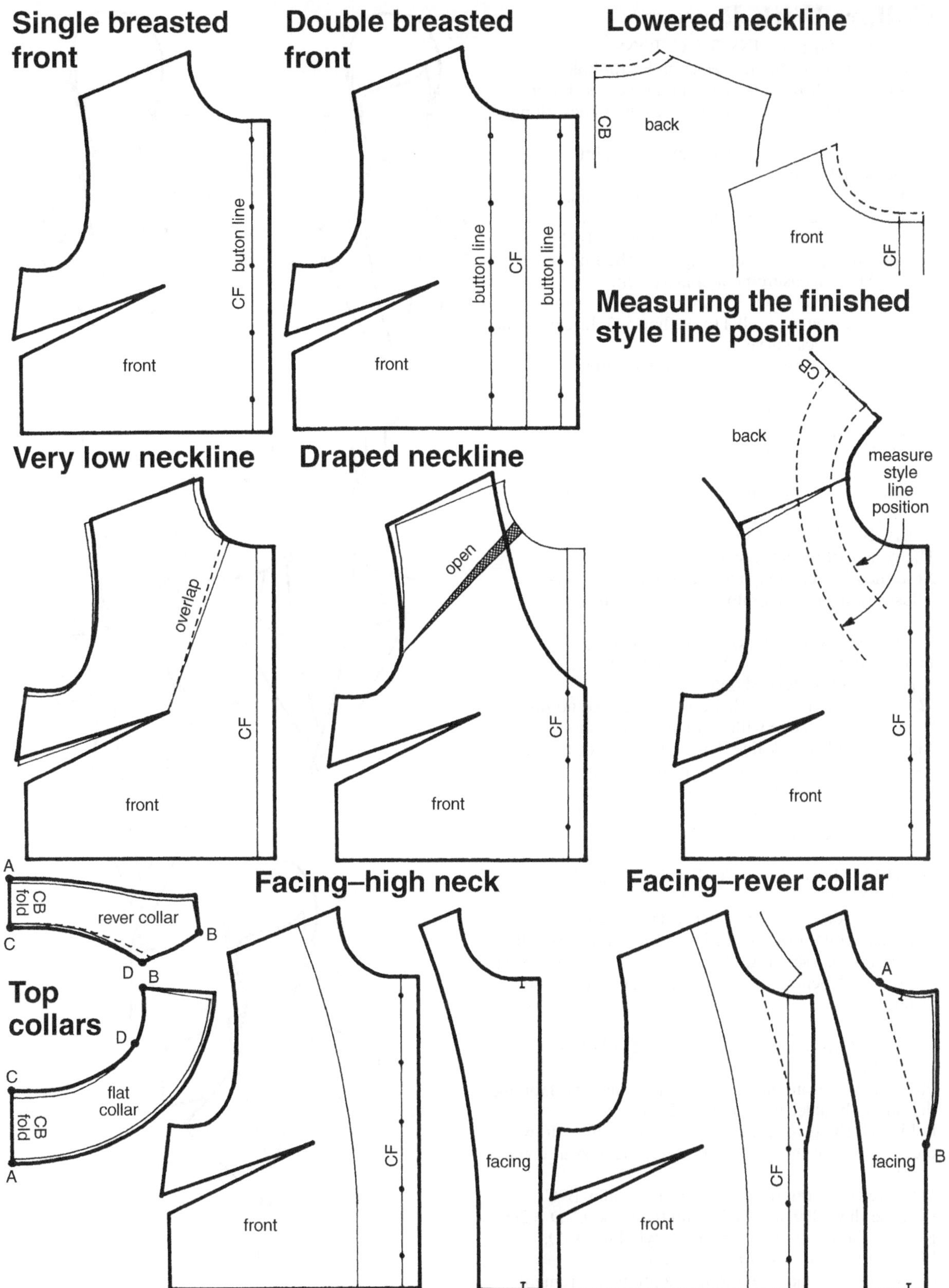
Single breasted front
CF
buton line
front
Double breasted front
button line
CF
button line
front
Lowered neckline
CB
back
front
CF
Measuring the finished style line position
CB
back
measure style line position
CF
front
Very low neckline
overlap
CF
front
Draped neckline
open
CF
front
A
CB fold
rever collar
C
B
D
B
Top collars
D
C
flat collar
CB fold
A
Facing–high neck
CF
front
facing
Facing–rever collar
CF
front
A
facing
B

# Collars With Revers

1. BASIC COLLAR INSTRUCTIONS
Trace round front bodice. Mark in buttonholes, buttonstand. Draw in neckline and rever. Rub out existing neckline (check shape by folding back along break line).
Mark point 1 at break point, 2 at neck point.
Extend shoulder line.
**2–3** 2cm; join 1–3 with a dotted line; extend line.
**3–4** Back neck measurement plus 0.5cm.
**4–5** 2cm (5–3 is same measurement as 4–3); square a line across at right angles to the line 5–3.
**5–6** Stand measurement approx. 2cm.
**5–7** Fall meas. 2cm–3cm more than the stand.
Draw a line from 6 parallel to the line 5–3. Integrate the line into the neck curve.
Mark point 8 at break line, 9 at collar point.
Draw in collar 7, 6, 8, 9 and style line. Trace off collar.
**8–10** 1 cm; draw in the stand line from 5–10.
Trace off separate collar and stand.
Divide the distance 3–5 into 3 sections. Cut and open the style line 0.2cm–0.3cm.
Mark balance points on neck, stand and collar.

2. BASIC REEFER COLLAR
The construction is the same as for a 'gents' collar. Note the different shape at the top of the revers. (Illustration shows a double-breasted front).

3. CHANGING THE REVER ANGLE
Trace round front bodice. Mark point 1 at break point, 2 at neck point. Extend shoulder line.
**2–3** 2cm; join 1–3 with a dotted line; extend line.
Draw in the neckline with straight lines as shown, point 4 is 2cm inside break line. Draw style line of the rever.
**3–5** Back neck measurement plus 0.2cm.
**5–6** Stand measurement; 5–7 fall measurement.
Trace off collar draft. Complete collar and stand, but open the style line of collar a minimum of 0.3cm.

4. CHANGING THE STYLE LINES – LOW REVERS
For low revers make 0.6cm neck dart (page 98). Complete collar draft as for basic collar but this collar does not have a separate stand. The meas. 4–5 and 5–11 is reduced depending on the rever angle. Trace off collar.

5. CHANGING THE STYLE LINES – WIDE COLLARS
Place back to front along the shoulder line overlapping the outer shoulder lines approx. 2cm.
Fold back the rever area along the break line; draw in the style line of the collar and rever. Mark A at collar point.
Measure the depth of the back of the collar B–C.
Because the collar will sit 2cm up the neck, C–D = 2cm
Redraw the *position* of the collar style line A–D.
Measure the *collar position line* A–D.
Construct a standard collar, the depth measurement B–C.
Cut and open collar style line A–C to measuremnt A–D.

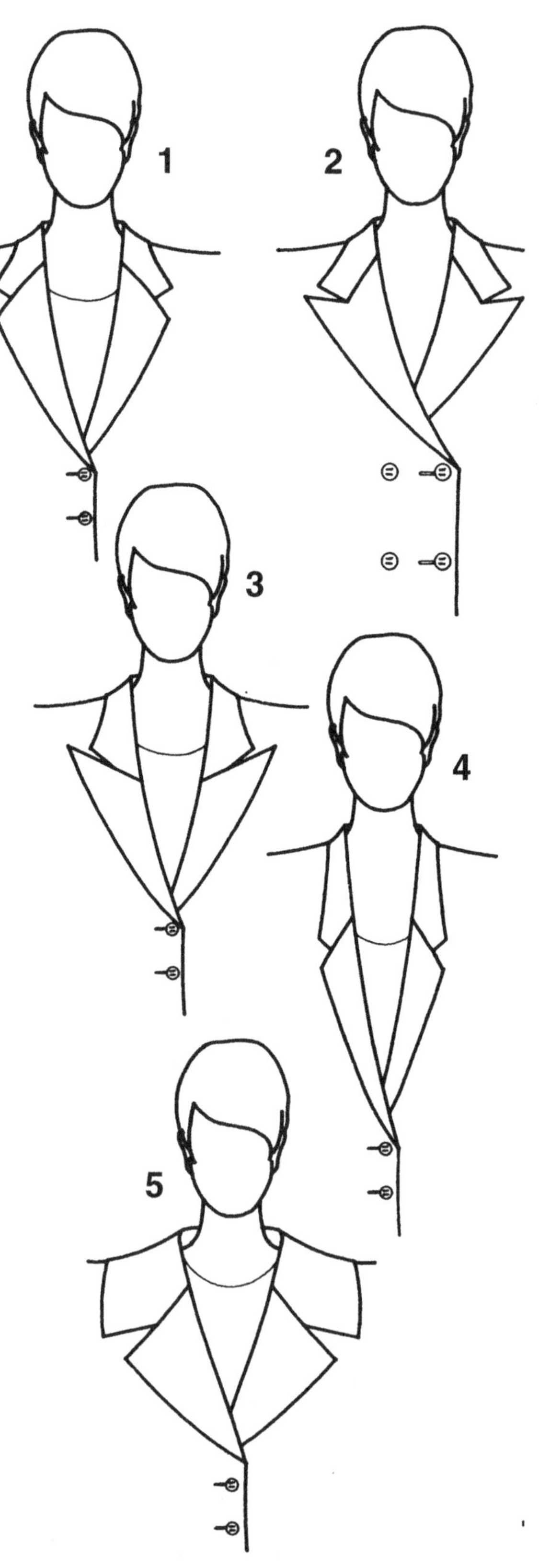

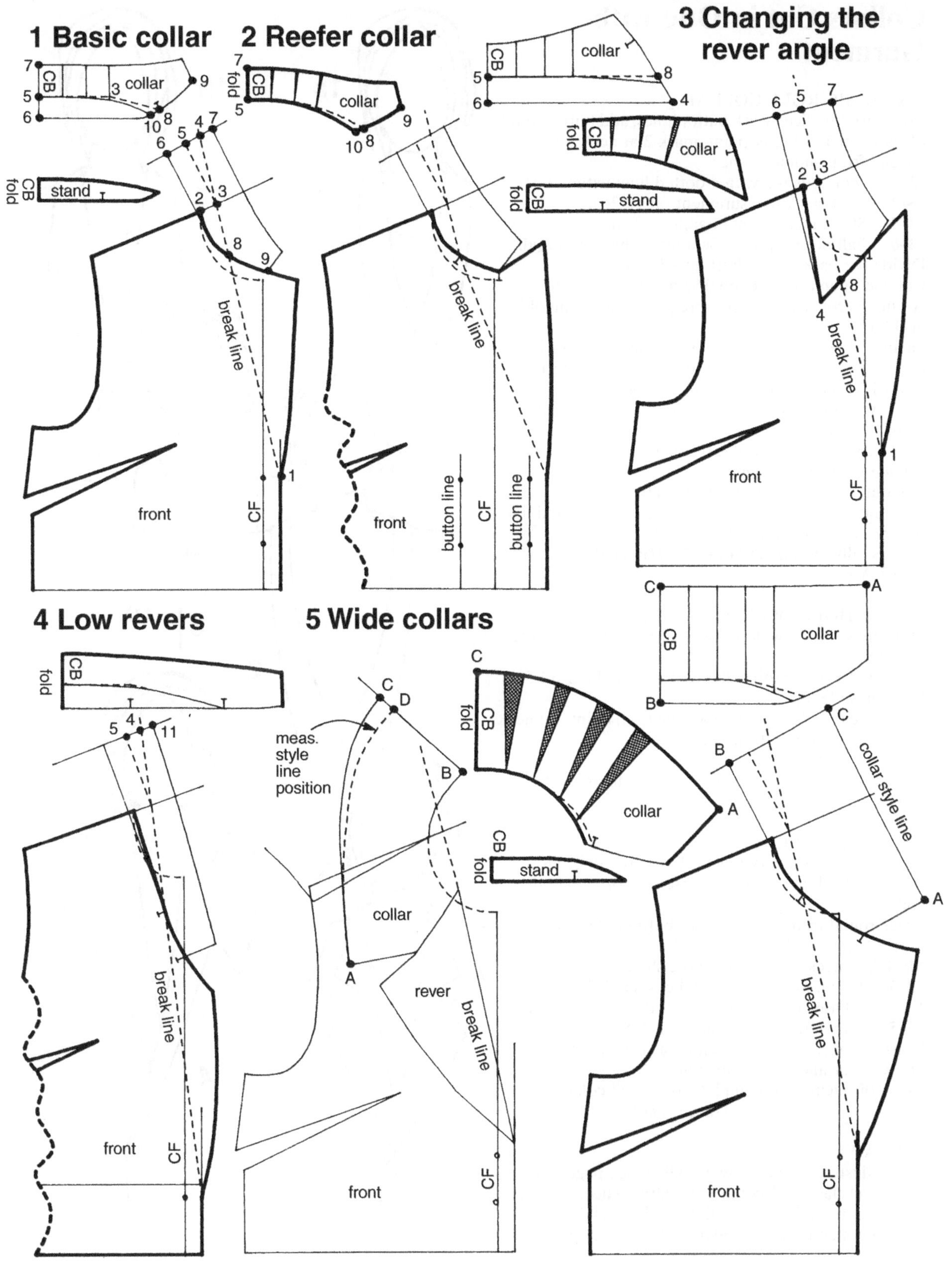
1 Basic collar
2 Reefer collar
3 Changing the rever angle
4 Low revers
5 Wide collars
CB
collar
stand
fold
front
break line
CF
button line
meas. style line position
rever
collar style line

# Collars Cut in One with Garment

1. CLASSIC ROLL COLLAR
Trace front bodice. Mark buttonholes, add buttonstand. Mark point 1 at break point, mark 2 at neck point. Extend front shoulder line.

**2–3** 2cm; join 1–3 with a dotted line; extend line.
**3–4** Back neck measurement plus 0.2cm.
**4–5** Stand measurement approx. 2cm.
**4–6** Fall meas. approx. 3cm more than the stand.

Divide the back collar draft into 3 sections.
Cut and open each section 0.8cm at the style line.
An under collar can be cut if required along the old neckline.

**Facing** Trace off facing. Draw line across facing below rever. This allows the facing to be cut in two parts, lower half on the straight grain of fabric. The top half can have centre back line placed to a fold of the fabric to avoid a back seam.
Add 0.25-0.5cm round edge of collar and rever from 1-6.

**Changing the Style Line**
The outer line of the roll collar can be changed in many different ways to produce new designs, see dotted line on draft and illustration 1b.
See also illustration and draft 1c, HIGH ROLL COLLAR.

2. LOW HOLLOWED NECKLINE
Draft illustrates a widened and very low neckline (see page 98).
Construct a classic roll collar draft, but make 2–3 1.5cm.
Draw in style line.
Draw line parallel to the break line from point 2 at neck to 5cm above top buttonhole.
Draw in 1.5cm dart on this line.
Trace off facing including dart, complete as for roll collar.

3. DARTED NECKLINE
Draft illustrates a very low neckline (see page 98).
A darted neckline allows the insertion of a second collar.
Trace round front bodice, mark buttonholes and buttonstand. Mark break point 1.
Mark 2 at neck point, extend the shoulder line.

**2–3** 1.5cm. Mark 4 midway between 2–3.

Join 4–1. Draw neck dart $^1/_2$ to $^3/_4$ distance down line.

**3–5** 2cm. Draw break line from 1–5.

Construct roll collar, use point 3 as neck point.
Draw collar and shaped style line.
Trace off facing and complete as for roll collar.
Draw in separate collar. Trace off collar.

4. SHAWL COLLAR
Draft illustrates a very low neckline (see page 98).
Construct classic roll collar draft. Draw a deep style line.
Measure the style line position on the back bodice.
Cut and open the back collar to this measurement.

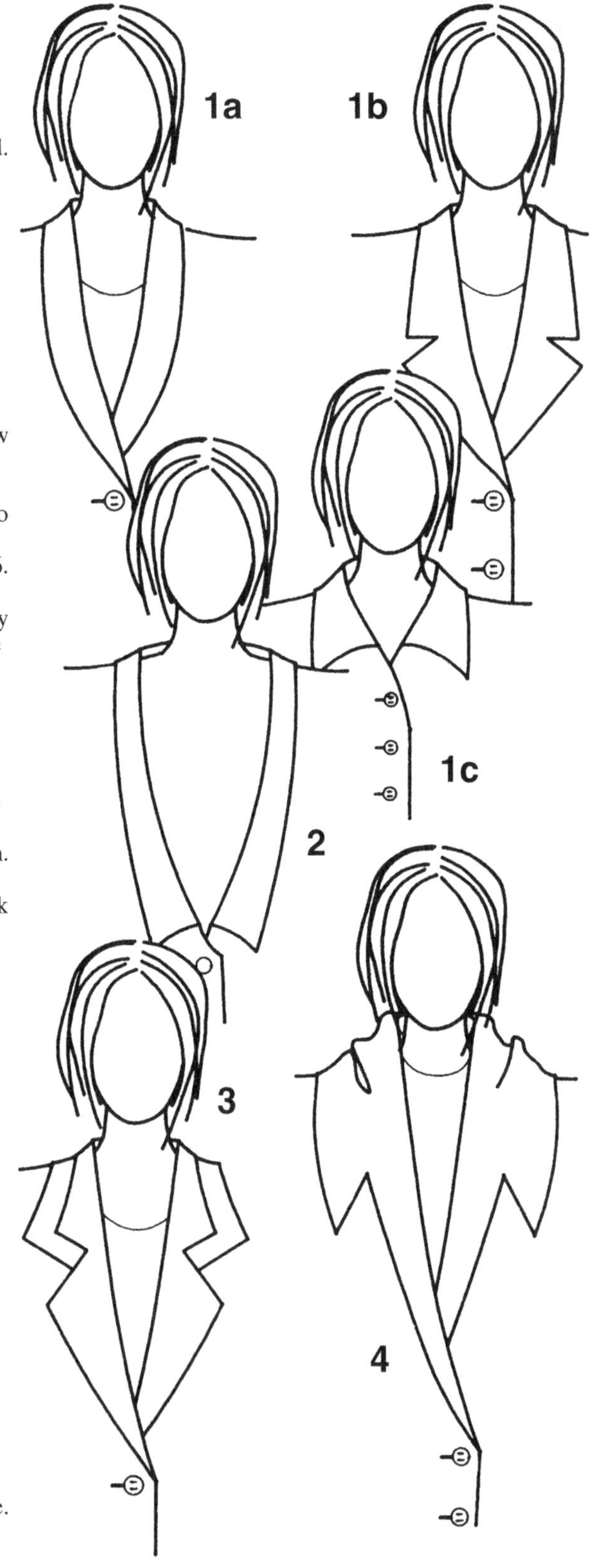

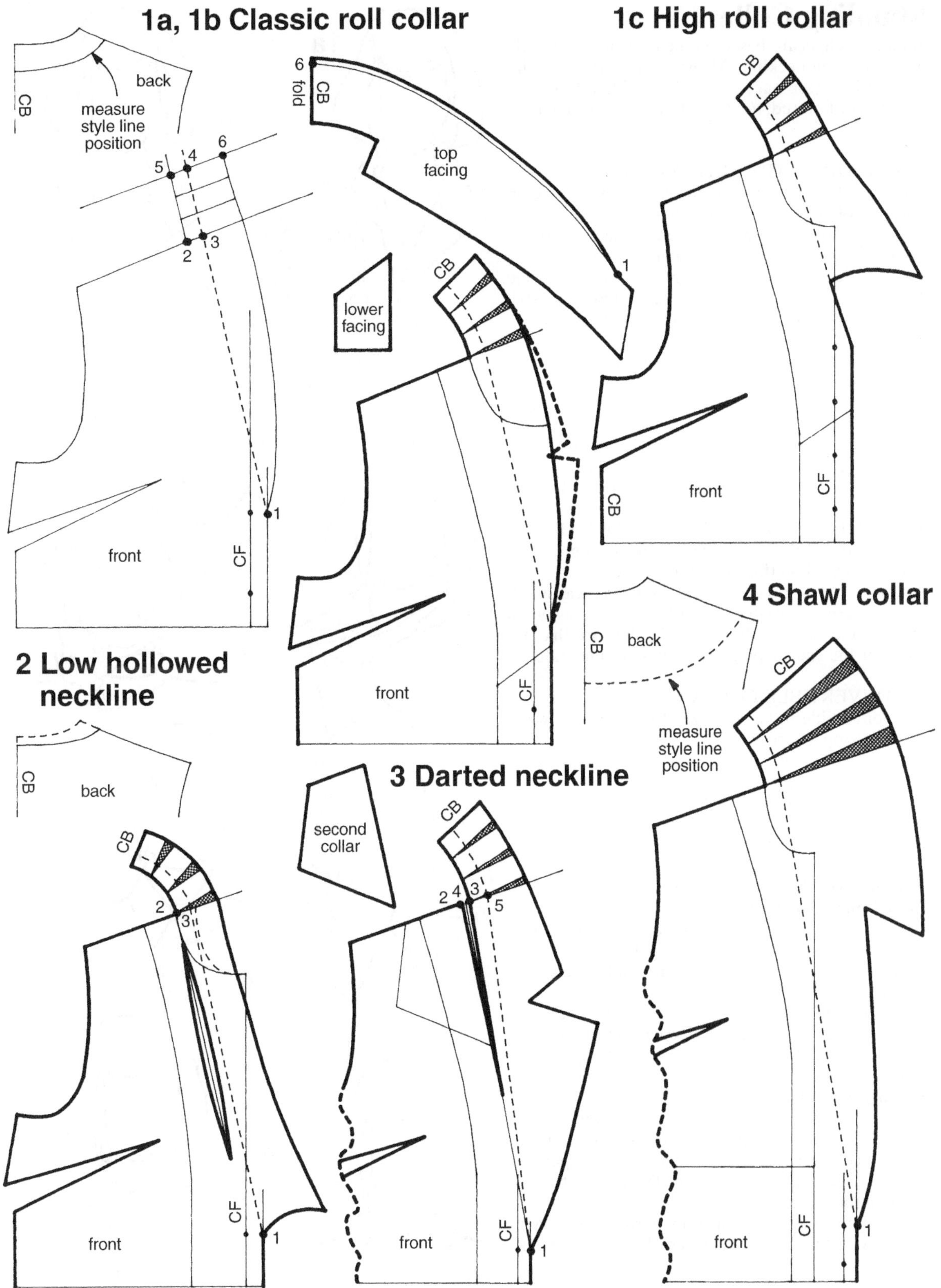
1a, 1b Classic roll collar
1c High roll collar
CB
back
measure
style line
position
6
5
4
2
3
1
front
CF
6
fold
CB
top
facing
1
lower
facing
CB
front
CF
CB
front
CF
CB
2 Low hollowed
neckline
CB
back
CB
2
3
1
front
CF
second
collar
3 Darted neckline
CB
2
4
3
5
front
CF
1
4 Shawl collar
CB
back
measure
style line
position
CB
front
CF
1

# Standing Collars

Standing collars are based on the measurement of the back and front neckline. Measure the curve with the tape upright, (see page 39). If the neckline is to be widened or lowered, *do this before the measurement is taken.*

1. STANDING STRAIGHT COLLARS

**1–2** $^1/_2$ the new neckline measurement; square up.
**1–3** Collar depth; square across.
**2–4** Button stand measurement; square up to 5.
**1–6** $^2/_3$ measurement 1–2; square up to 7.
**4–8** 0.5cm; join 6–8 wth a curve. Draw in style line.

The basic rectangle provides a base for unlimited style changes. See illustrations and diagrams 1b and 1c.

2. STANDING STRAIGHT COLLARS (BUTTONED)

Lower the back neckline 1cm, centre front 2cm; widen neckline approx. 1.5cm at the shoulders.
This can be increased depending on the style.
Construct rectangle as above; shape the front edge line and buttonstand line in 1.5 cm at 5. Mark buttonhole.

3. DEEP FOLDED OR DRAPED COLLARS

Lower and widen the neckline; the measurements are often increased on this kind of neckline.
A simple fold over rectangle cut on the bias can create many different types of drape or fold depending on the shape of the neckline, fastening, depth or width of the collar or the end shaping. Examples are illustrated.

4. CONVERTIBLE COLLAR

The convertible collar sits high at the neck but will open to form a narrow rever.

**1–2** $^1/_2$ the new neckline measurement; square up.
**1–3** Collar depth; square across to 4.
**1–5** $^2/_3$ measurement 1–2; square up to 6.
**2–7** 0.5cm; join 5–7 with a curve.

Draw in any front style line shape from 6.

5. COLLARS WITH STANDS

**Basic Collar and Stand** Construct stand rectangle; length = $^1/_2$ neck measurement; depth = stand depth. Add shaped buttonstand and buttonhole.

**1–2** 0.5cm. Draw a curve to the front edge as shown.

Construct collar rectangle; length = $^1/_2$ the neck measurement; depth =1.5cm deeper than the stand.

**3–4** 0.5cm. Draw a curve to the front edge as shown.

**Shaping the Collar**

Divide the collar and stand into four sections.
Cut and overlap the top edge of the stand 0.1cm.
Reduce collar at back edge 0.3cm. Cut and open the outside edge of the collar 0.3cm. Trace new shapes.

**Darting the Collar**

The collar can also be shaped by darting. Lengthen collar by 3.2cm. Create four 0.8cm darts at collar edge.

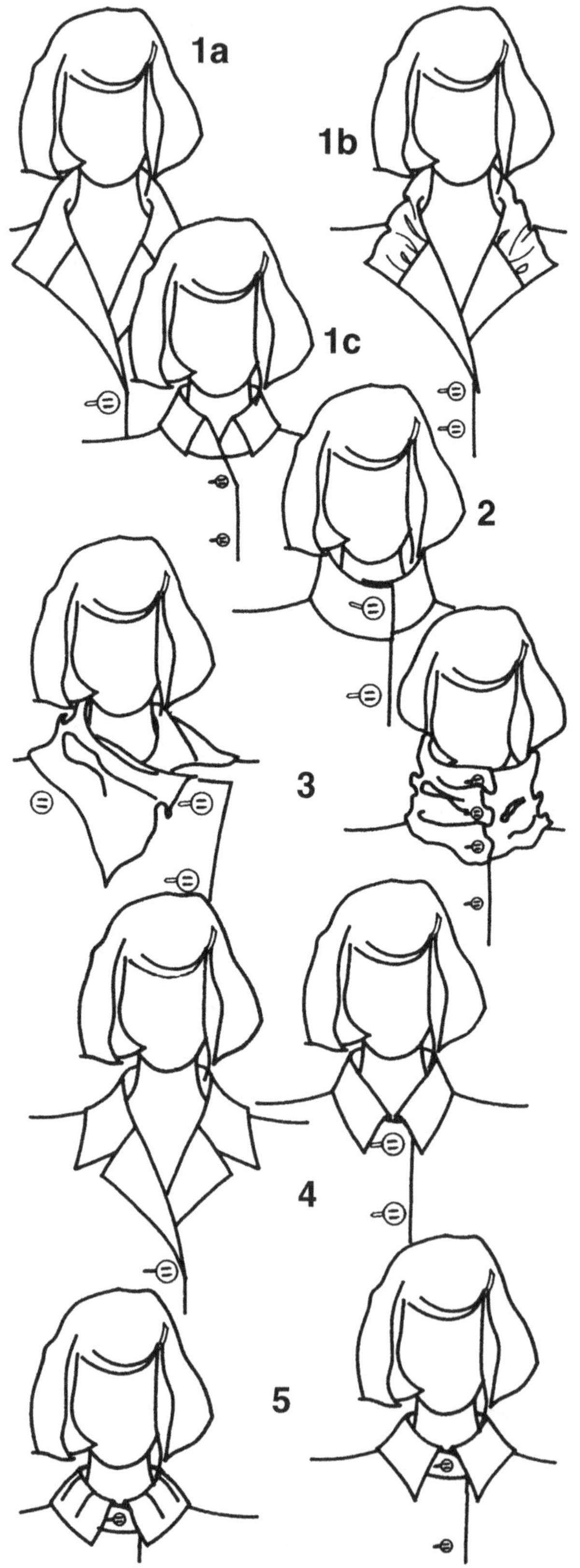

## 1 Standing straight collars

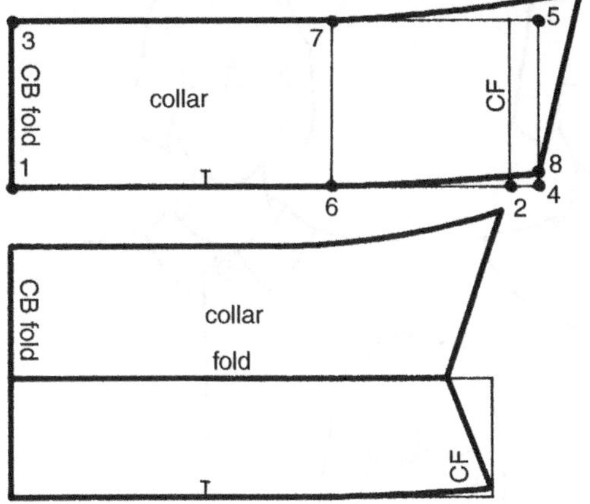


## 2 Standing straight collars/ buttoned

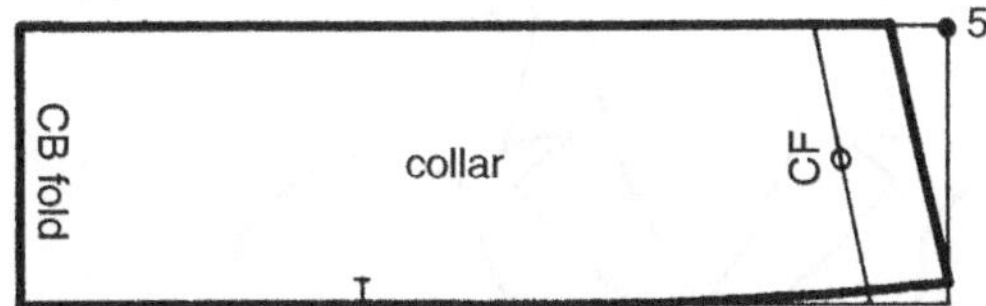


## 3 Deep folded or draped collars

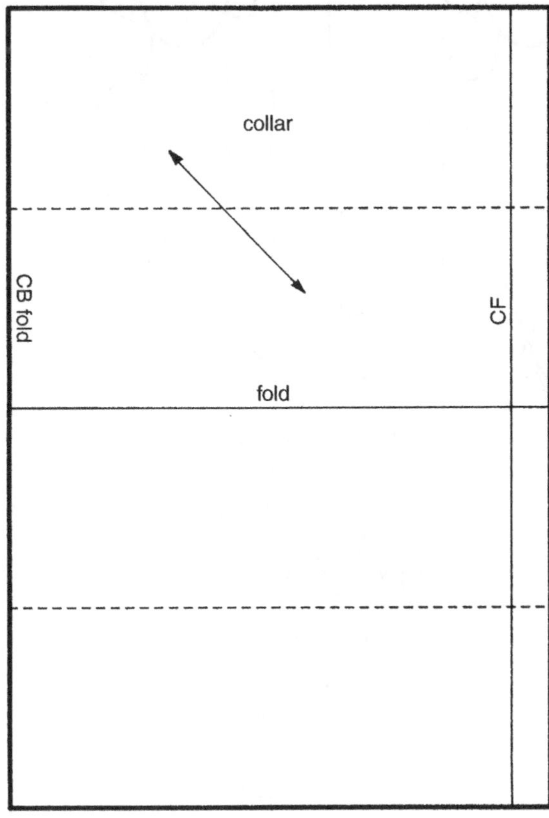


## 4 Convertible collar

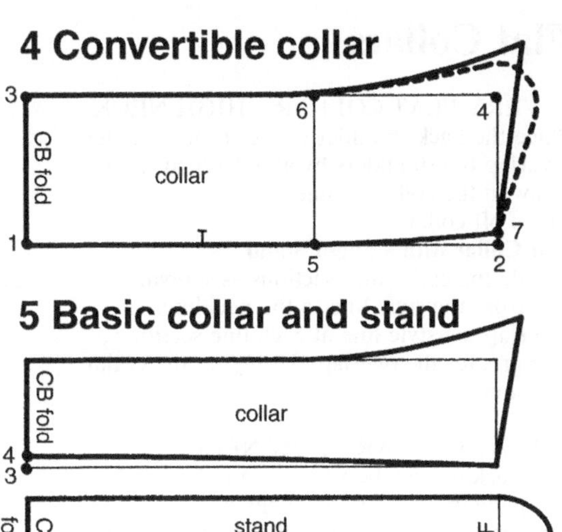


## 5 Shaping the collar

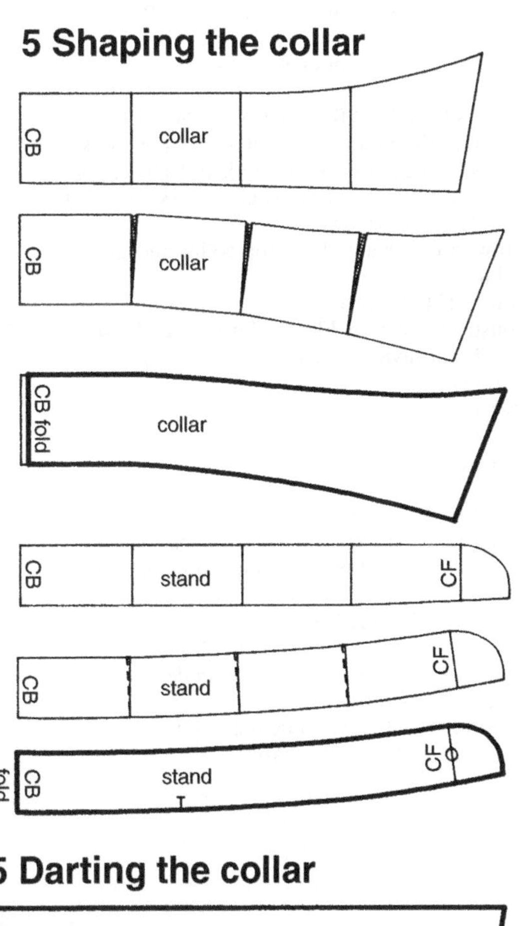


## 5 Darting the collar

CB fold

collar

# Flat Collars

1. VERY FLAT COLLAR – HIGH NECK
Place the back shoulder to the front shoulder.
Overlap the shoulders by about 1.5cm–2cm.
Draw in the collar outline.
Trace off collar.
**Flat Collar with a Slight Stand**
Divide the collar into sections as shown.
Cut from the style line to the neckline.
Overlap the style line at each line section.
The greater the overlap, the higher the collar will stand.

2. FLAT COLLAR – LOW NECK
The neckline can be widened and lowered.
See page 98 – lowering necklines.
Construct collar as **Flat Collar with a Slight Stand,** but divide only the back collar part into sections.
Overlap the style line at each line section.
Trace round the new collar shape.
Example shows a mock rever collar.

3. FLAT COLLAR – VERY LOW NECK
Example shows a collar with a very low neck.
The neckline has been lowered, and a 0.6cm dart has been taken from the neck to make a wider bust dart, see page 98.
Draw in the shape of the top collar and under collar.
Trace off the top collar.
Construct collar as **Flat Collar with a Slight Stand,** but divide only the back collar part into sections.
Overlap the style line at each line section.
Trace round the new collar shape.
Trace off the second collar.

4. VARIATIONS
Using the basic flat collar draft construction, almost any variation of shape can be adapted.

5. FLARED COLLAR
Any drawn collar shape can be flared.
Draw in collar shape. Trace off collar.
Divide into sections.
Cut and open the style line the required amount.
Trace around the new shape.

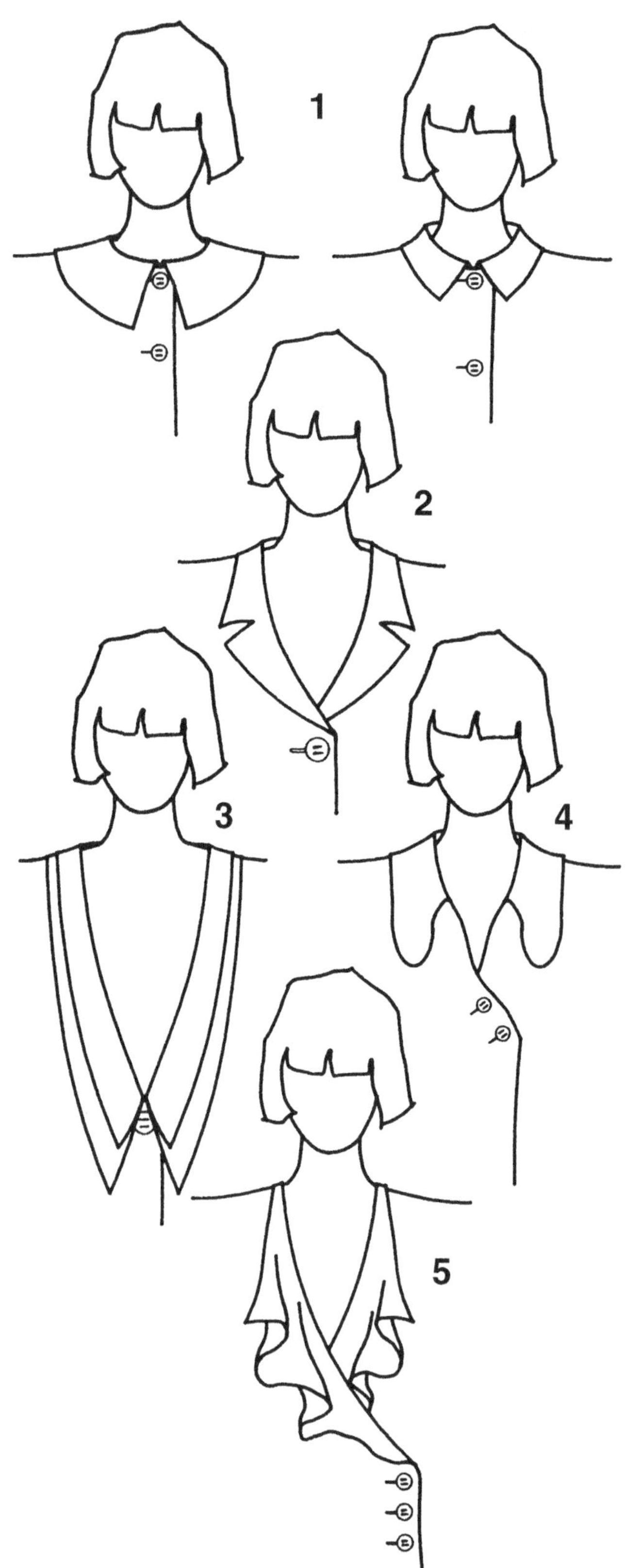

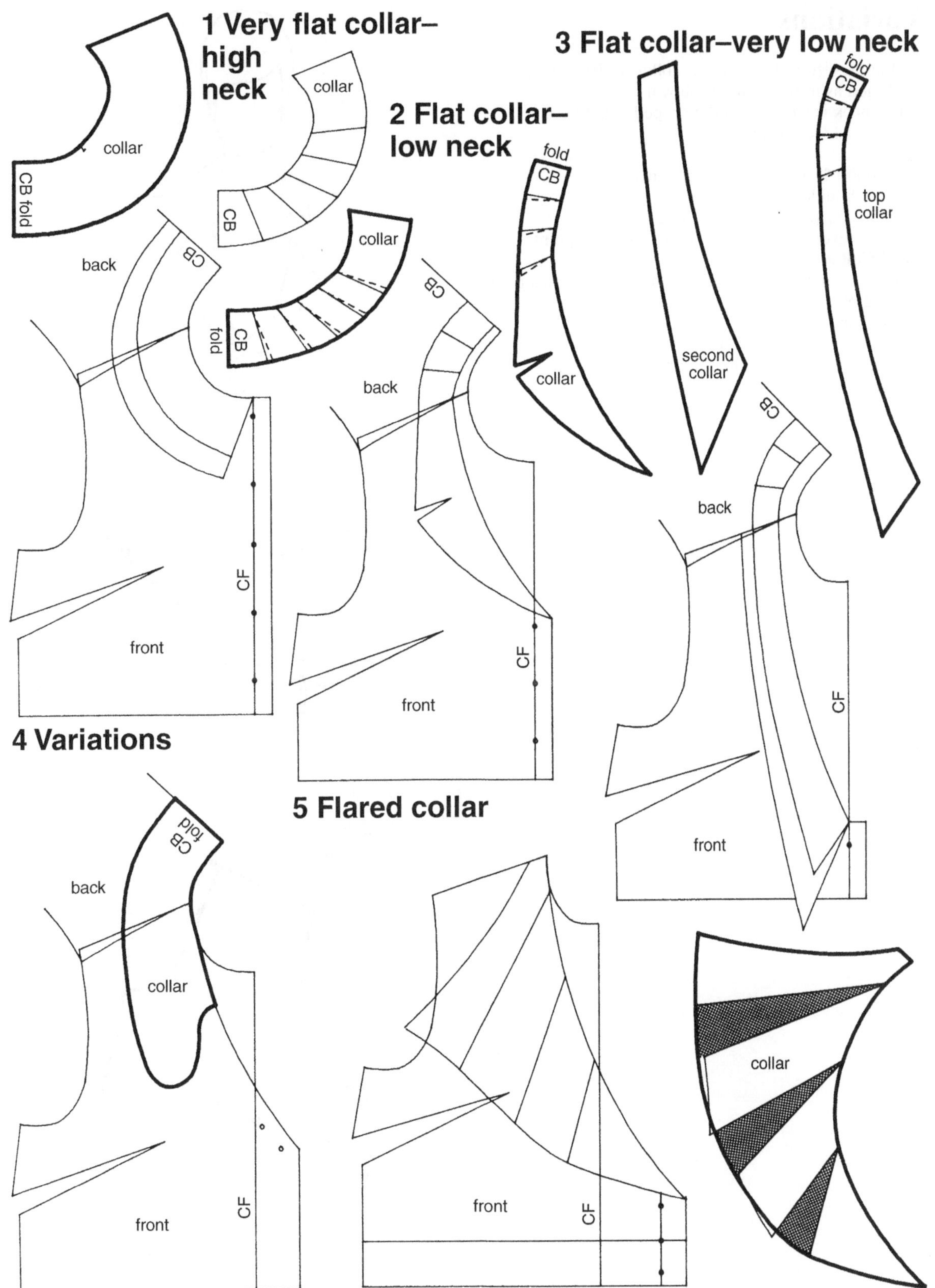
1 Very flat collar–high neck
collar
collar
CB fold
CB
back
CB
fold
CB
collar
front
CF
2 Flat collar–low neck
fold
CB
collar
CB
back
front
CF
3 Flat collar–very low neck
fold
CB
second collar
top collar
CB
back
front
CF
4 Variations
CB fold
back
collar
front
CF
5 Flared collar
front
CF
collar

# Variations

Techniques from the different collar drafts can be combined as in the example shown.

The neck is widened and a draped neckline is constructed (see page 98).

**Rever**

Mark point 1 at break point, 2 at neck point.
Extend shoulder line.
**2–3** 1cm. Join 1–3 with a dotted line.
Draw in rever shape. Mark point 4 at rever point.

**Stand Collar**

Draft a rectangle 5–6 the measurement of the back neck plus the measurement 2–4.
Shape front edge.
Divide the collar into sections as shown.
Cut and open the style line the required amount (example shows 0.3cm).

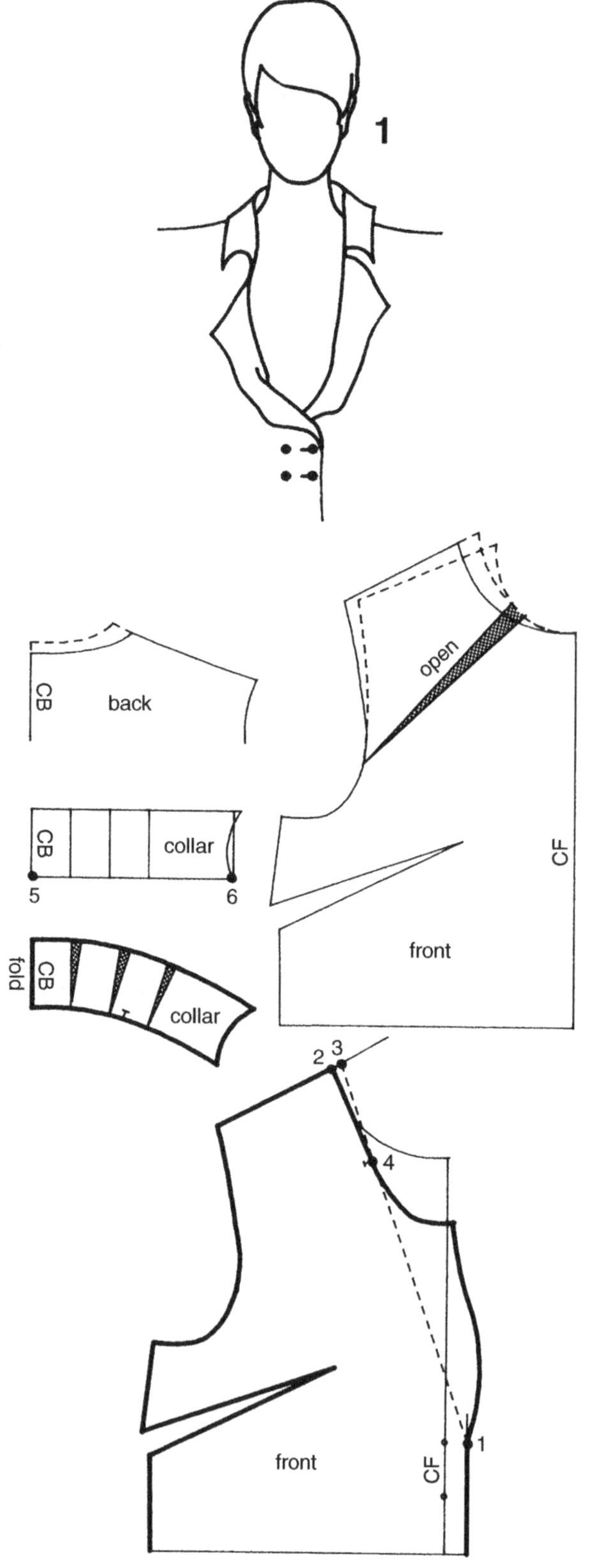

# Part Three:

# 9 SLEEVE VARIATIONS



The tailored jacket is usually associated with classic two-piece sleeves. However, not only can the two-piece sleeve be varied, but completely different shapes in a 'tailoring style' can be achieved by using the softer one-piece sleeve block and cutting sleeves from the kimono block.

There is a reluctance to use anything but the classic two-piece sleeve in tailored jackets. One of the main reasons is the mass production of pre-formed shoulder pads. Sleeves, where the adaptation includes modification to the sleeve head, often require the construction of special shoulder pads.

# Two-piece Sleeves

Two-piece sleeves are a defined shape but modifications to them can create design interest. This is particularly important at the sleeve head, where extra ease can offer a more comfortable fit.

Cutting the under sleeve or the top sleeve on the bias can also increase comfort.

EXTRA PADDED SHOULDERS
Draw a line from the armhole to the shoulder point. Cut up line and open the extra depth of the new pad. Cut across the sleeve head and up the centre line. Open the same amount that is inserted in the armhole.

1. SINGLE DARTED HEAD
Mark points A, B and C, D on shoulder, front and back pitch points on the body sections. Mark sleeve pitch points E, F, G. Square across from E to H.
C–I on the body block is the measurement G–H.
Cut across the sleeve head and up the centre line.
Open the sleeve head 1cm at F.
E–K is the meas. A–B. L–H is the meas. I–D.
Draw in dart K, J, L as shown.

2. THREE DARTED HEAD
Mark points A–I on body and sleeve as above.
Cut across the sleeve head as above but divide the sleeve head into three sections.
Cut and open raising the sleeve head approx. 4cm at J.
Create darts as shown. Ensure the finished sleeve head measurement from H–E is the same as the measurement A–B and D–I on the body block.

3. STRAPPED HEAD
Mark points A–I on body and sleeve as above.
Draw strap line approx. 3.5cm wide across the top of sleeve. Mark points J and K on strap.
Draw new sleeve head J, F, K.
Square up from E–L the measurement A–B.
Square up from H–M the measurement I–D.
Draw new strap lines 3.5cm wide.
Make the inside of the strap lines J–N and K–O equal the measurement of the new sleeve head J, F, K.

4. SEAMED TOP SLEEVE 1
Construct as for single darted head, but extend vertical line to centre of hemline. Separate the sections.
Curve the seam line outwards 0.5cm as shown.

5. SEAMED TOP SLEEVE VARIATIONS
Many alternative design lines can be inserted into the top sleeve, and the sleeve head ease incorporated into the seam as example.
Added shape can be included by tucks and darting as in the examples above.

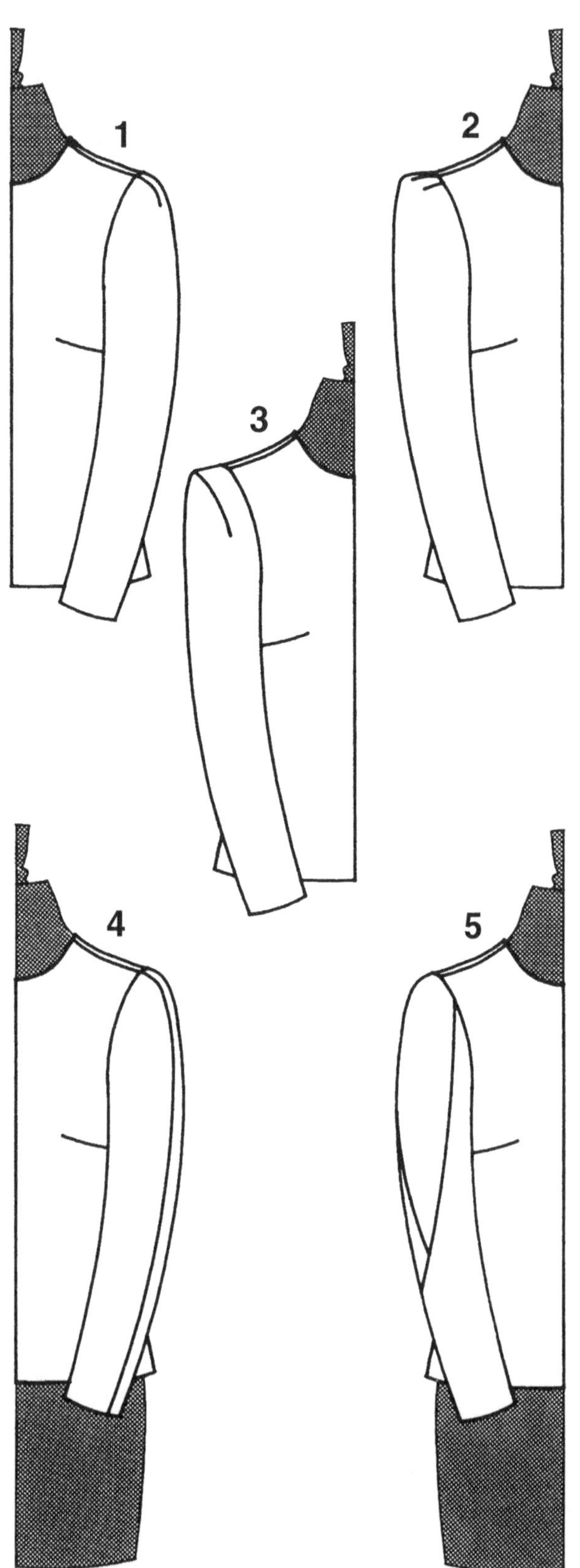

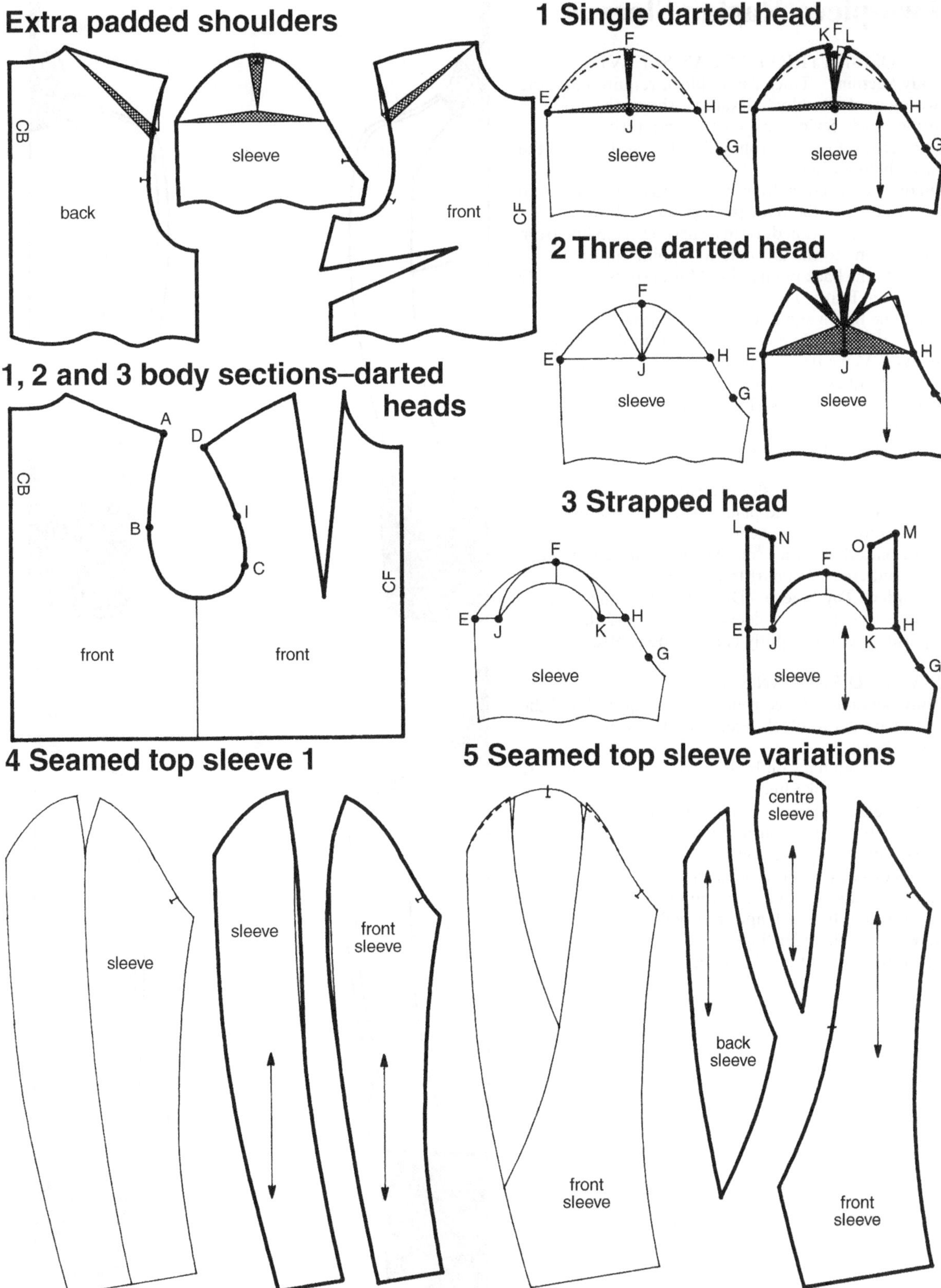
Extra padded shoulders
CB
back
sleeve
front
CF
1 Single darted head
F
E
J
H
G
sleeve
K F L
E
J
H
G
sleeve
2 Three darted head
F
E
J
H
G
sleeve
E
J
H
G
sleeve
1, 2 and 3 body sections–darted heads
CB
A
D
B
I
C
CF
front
front
3 Strapped head
F
E
J
K
H
G
sleeve
L
N
O
M
F
E
J
K
H
G
sleeve
4 Seamed top sleeve 1
sleeve
sleeve
front sleeve
5 Seamed top sleeve variations
front sleeve
centre sleeve
back sleeve
front sleeve

# Two-piece Raglan Sleeves

1. CLOSE-FITTING RAGLAN SLEEVE
**Body Sections** Trace round block required and the two-piece sleeve block. Example shows the close-fitting block. Swing bust dart to underarm.
Take 1cm off the front shoulder line; add 1cm to the back shoulder line.
On the back section draw in a curved raglan line from the neckline to the back pitch point as shown.
On the front section draw in a curved raglan line from the neckline to the armhole to a point approx. opposite the back pitch point. Mark points A, B, C, D on raglan, E at front pitch point.
Place the 0.5cm shoulder ease into a dart.
Trace off the body pieces. Trace off raglan pieces.
**Sleeve** Move balance point at the sleeve head 1cm forward; square down 4cm to point F.
Mark point G at back sleeve pitch point; H on front pitch point.
Measure the distance D–E on body sections; H–I = D–E.
Place raglan pieces to sleeve head as shown, matching B to G and D to I and placing shoulder points 1.5cm away from the sleeve head.
Close back dart. Trace round making curved shoulder lines and creating a dart to point F.
**Two-piece Top Sleeve** Draw a curved line from point F to hemline of sleeve. Trace round the separate sections slightly curving the centre line.

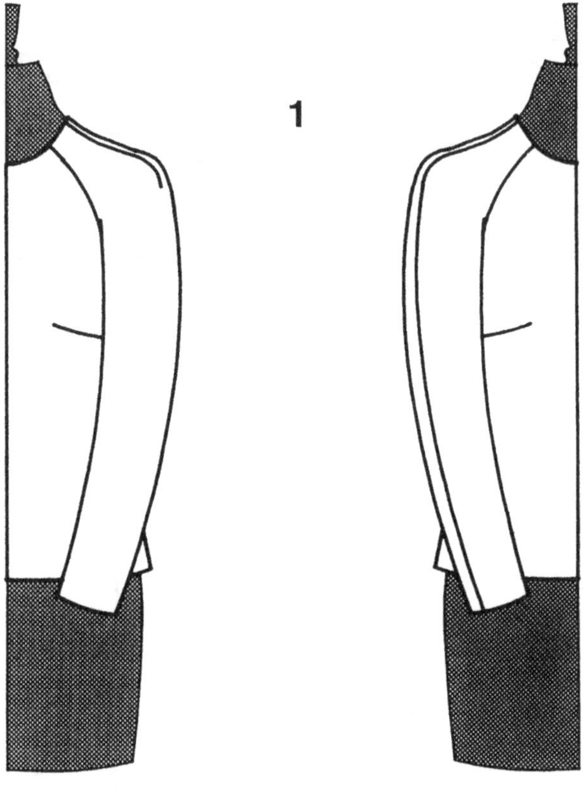


2. YOKED RAGLAN SLEEVE
**Body Sections** Trace round block required and the two-piece sleeve block. Example shows the easy-fitting block.
Draw in yoke lines on body sections; mark points A and B on the yoke line.
**Yoke/sleeves** Draw a curved line down the centre of the top sleeve; separate the sections.
Place sleeves to yoke points A and B with the pitch points of body sections adjacent.
Raise shoulders 1cm at the armhole edges.
Trace round the back and front yoke/sleeves with new curved shoulder lines.
Trace round front and back sections.

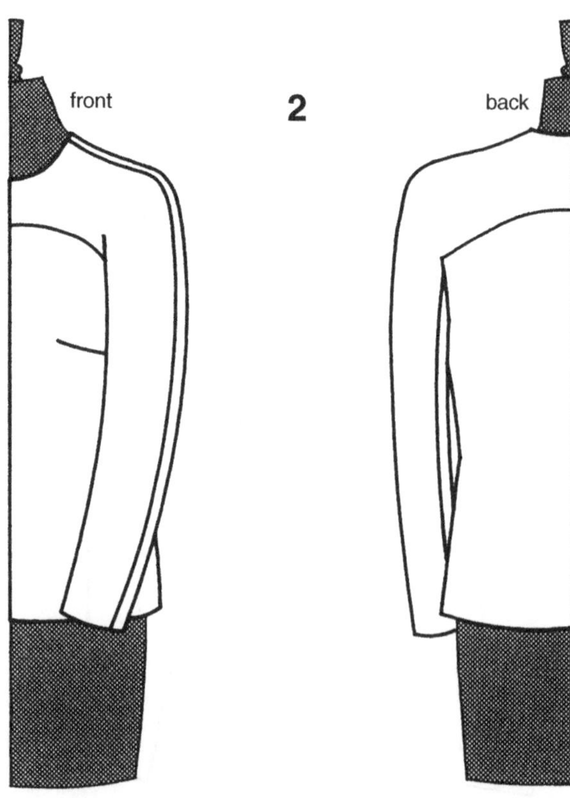

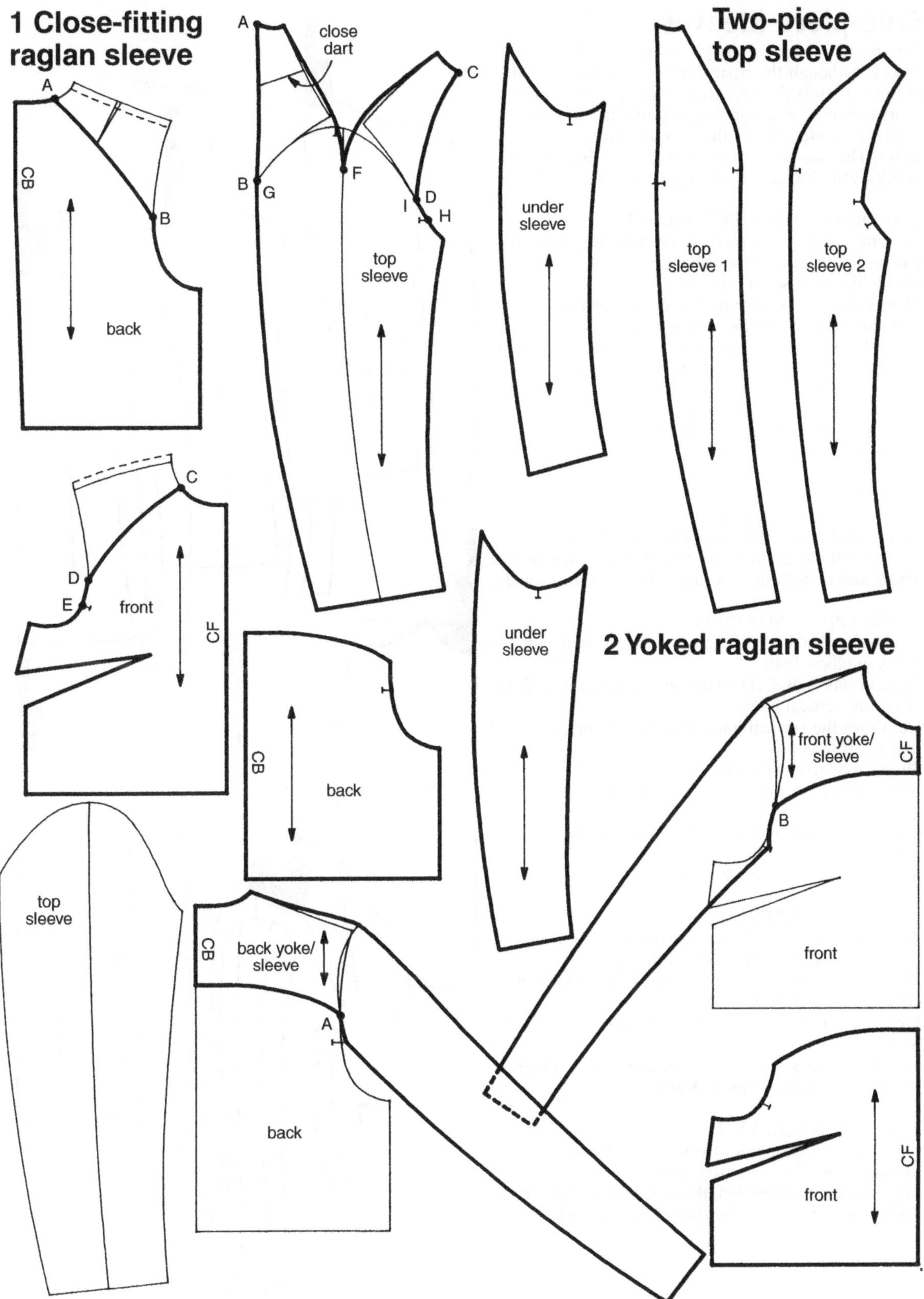
1 Close-fitting raglan sleeve
A
B
CB
back
C
D
E
front
CF
top sleeve
A
close dart
B
G
F
C
I
D
H
top sleeve
under sleeve
Two-piece top sleeve
top sleeve 1
top sleeve 2
under sleeve
CB
back
2 Yoked raglan sleeve
front yoke/ sleeve
CF
B
front
CB
back yoke/ sleeve
A
back
front
CF

# One-piece Sleeves

One-piece sleeves usually give a softer outline to a jacket. Although the basic draft creates a straighter outline, it offers the opportunity to create many of the simple or more extreme shapes found in 'dressmaker' drafts. It is often cut on the bias for softly draped styles. The one-piece sleeve can also be shaped and divided into the curved shaping of a two-piece sleeve.

1. DARTED ONE-PIECE SLEEVES
1a. Trace off the one-piece sleeve with slight shaping.
Curve the underarm seam slightly.
Divide the back seam; square across.
Mark point A at centre point; square down to B.
Cut along the elbow line to point A.
Pivot the back section forward 4cm to create a dart at the elbow line. Halve the length of the dart.
Mark point C at centre of wristline.
1b. Draw a vertical line from the sleeve head at D to touch the point of the new dart. Close the dart to create a dart from the wristline.

2. SLEEVE WITH BACK SEAM
Create the sleeve 1b with wrist dart.
Trace off the back and front sleeve from D.
Draw slight curves along the back lines of each sleeve.
The seams of both sleeves should have smooth curves.

3. TWO-PIECE SHAPING
Draw a vertical line from pitch points to wrist line.
Mark in elbow line.
Mark points A, B, C, D on the underarm seam; E, F, G, H on the vertical lines.
Cut down the vertical lines; join the side pieces at the underarm seam.
Shape in hem of under sleeve, 1.25cm at F, 2.5cm at H.
Shape in hem of top sleeve, 3.75cm at F and 2.5cm at H.
Cut along elbow line. Pivot both sections to touch point H.
Shape all seam lines with curves.

4. SEAMED SLEEVE 1
Trace off the elbow darted one-piece sleeve with centre line. Mark centre of wrist line point A.
Draw a curved line. Extend elbow dart to touch the curved line at B. Join A–B.
Divide the front section of the sleeve into two sections; mark point C.
Cut off the back piece. Close the elbow dart, Overlap the front sections 0.5cm at A and C.

5. SEAMED SLEEVE 2
Draw vertical seam lines through the sleeve.
Lengthen the sleeve approx. 4cm.
Separate the sections; lengthen and shape the seams and the lower edge of the sleeves as required.

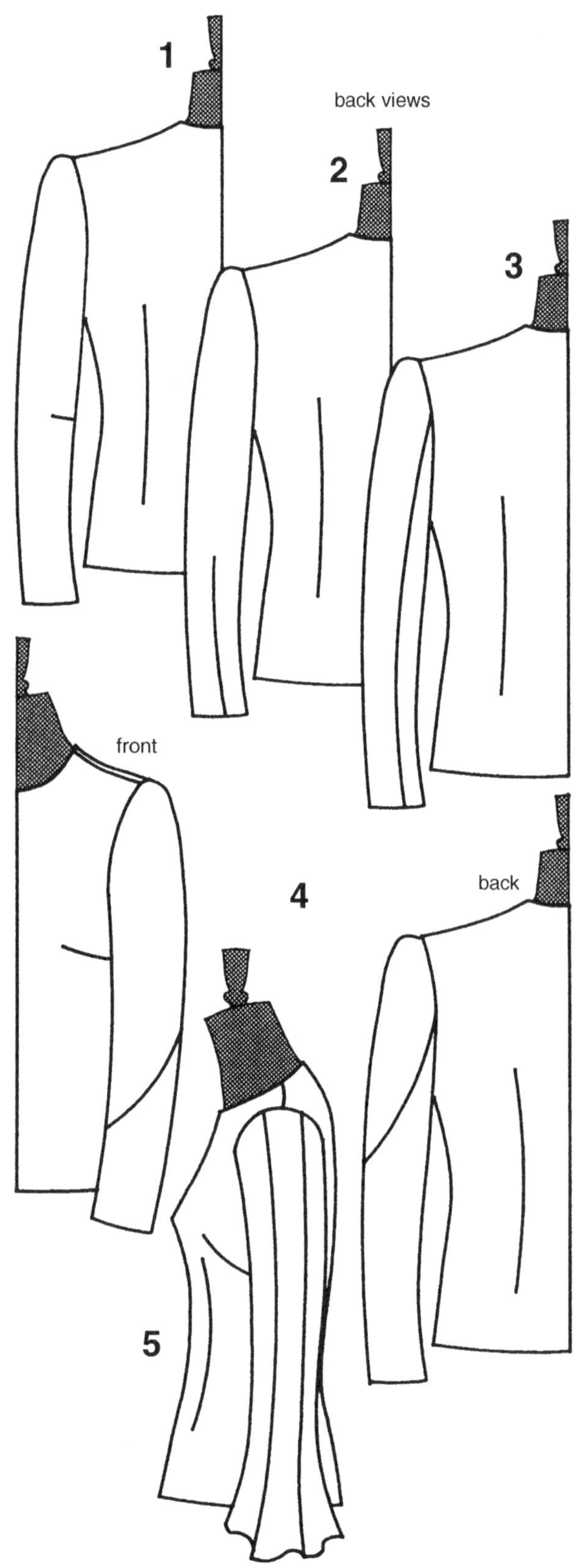

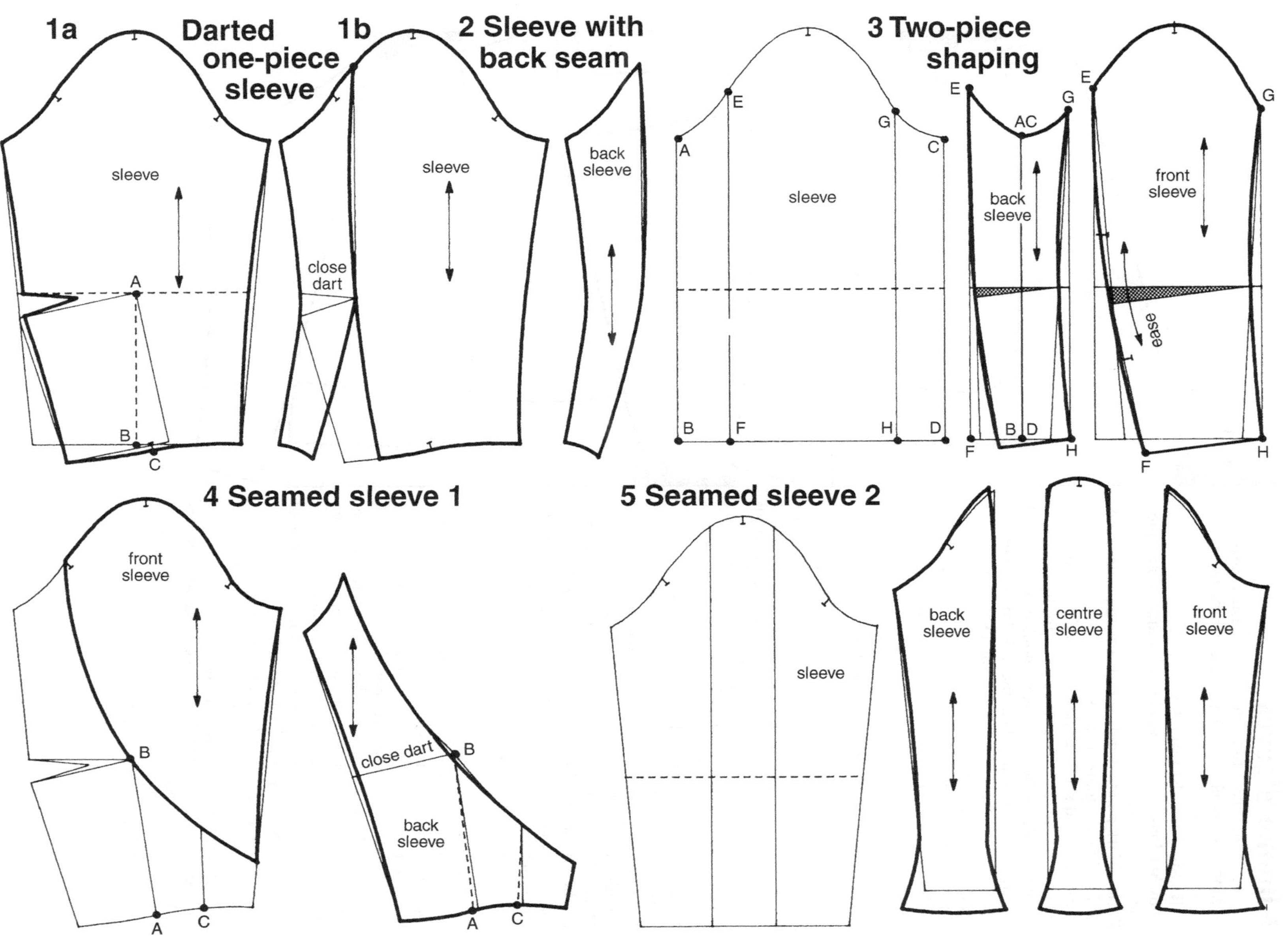
1a
Darted one-piece sleeve
1b
sleeve
A
B
C
close dart
sleeve
2 Sleeve with back seam
back sleeve
3 Two-piece shaping
sleeve
A
E
G
C
B
F
H
D
E
AC
G
back sleeve
F
B D
H
E
G
front sleeve
ease
F
H
4 Seamed sleeve 1
front sleeve
B
A
C
close dart
B
back sleeve
A
C
5 Seamed sleeve 2
sleeve
back sleeve
centre sleeve
front sleeve

# Kimono Sleeves

Although the easy-fitting block is the usual basis for kimono designs, close-fitting blocks can be used.

1. BASIC KIMONO BLOCK

**Body Sections** Trace round block required and the one-piece sleeve.

**Back** Mark points 0 and 1 on side seam; square out.

**1–2** 3.5cm; square up to 3.

Mark point 4 at shoulder point, 5 at neck point.

Divide the sleeve block down the centre line.

Place back sleeve head to touch shoulder point 4 and underarm of sleeve to touch line 2–3. Mark point 6.

**0–7** $^1/_3$ the measurement 0–1 minus 0.5cm.

Join 7 to wrist point 8.

**7–9** 6cm. **7–10** 6cm; join 9–10 with a curve.

**4–11** 1.5cm; join 5–11 and 11–12 at wrist point.

**Front** Transfer the bust dart to the waistline.

Mark points 13 and 14 on the side seam.

**13–15** 3.5cm. **14–16** 3.5cm; join 15–16.

Mark point 17 at shoulder point, 18 at neck point.

**16–19** the measurement 3–6 on the back section.

Place underarm of front sleeve to point 19 and sleeve head to shoulder (it will rise above shoulder point).

**14–20** the measurement 0–7; join 20 to wrist point 21.

**20–22** 6cm. **20–23** 6cm; join 22–23 with a curve.

**17–24** 1.5cm; join 18–24 and 24–25 at wrist point.

2. GUSSETING THE KIMONO BLOCK

Gusseting the block gives it a better 3D shape.

Trace round kimono block. Mark points 9, 10, 22, 23. G is midway 9–10; H is midway 22–23; square out.

Mark side and underarm panels to touch the lines (they can be any shape). Mark points A, B, C, D, E, F.

Cut off the side panels, cut along the lines G–B, H–E.

Open the lines, and place together to match points.

Trace round side panel gusset.

3. DOLMAN SLEEVE

Trace round kimono block; mark points A and B at the centre of the underarm.

Draw in the armhole shape to points A and B.

Mark points C and D at the shoulder.

The armhole shape can start above the shoulder point or lower, (it should start at the same distance from the shoulder point on back and front sections).

Remove 1.5cm shaped sections, $^2/_3$ of the front armhole and $^3/_4$ the length of the back shoulders.

Mark points E and F at the centre of each section.

A–G and B–H is approx. 4cm. Join G–E and H–F.

Cut off sleeve sections; join at the centre.

Cut up lines G–E and H–F; open 4cm. Redraw underarm curves, redraw sleeve head with smooth curves.

4. DEEP RAGLAN SLEEVE

see overpage.

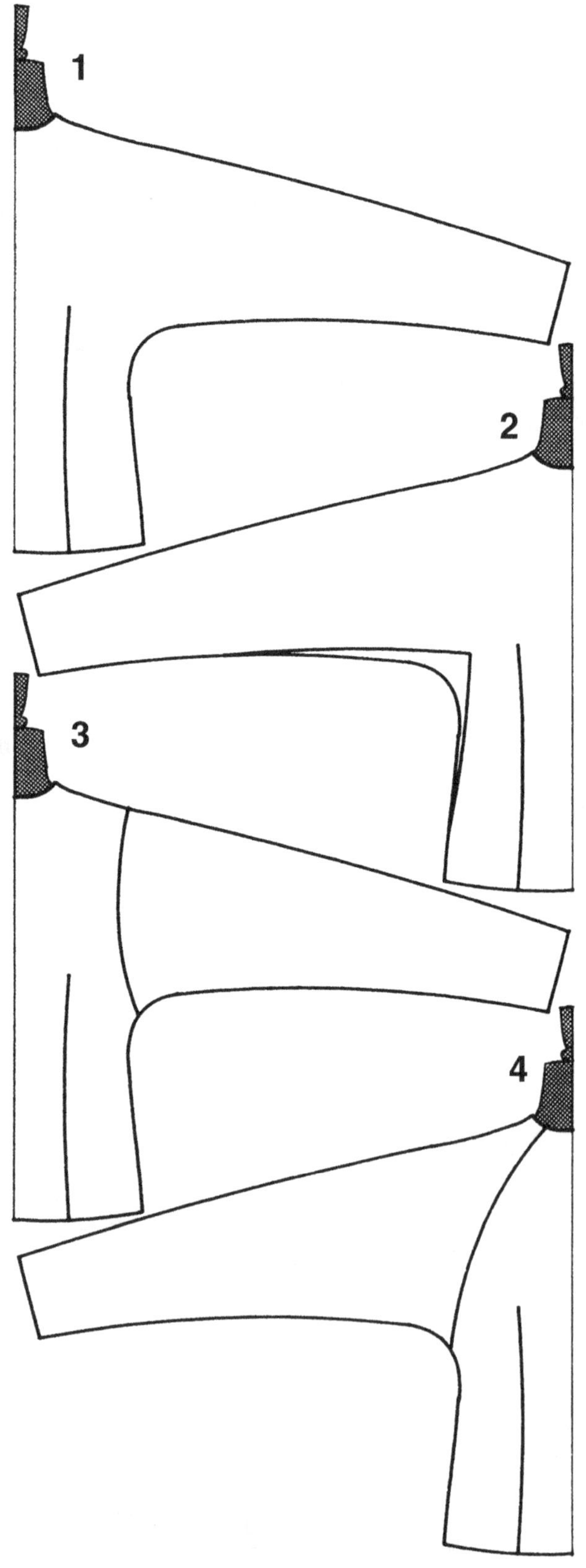

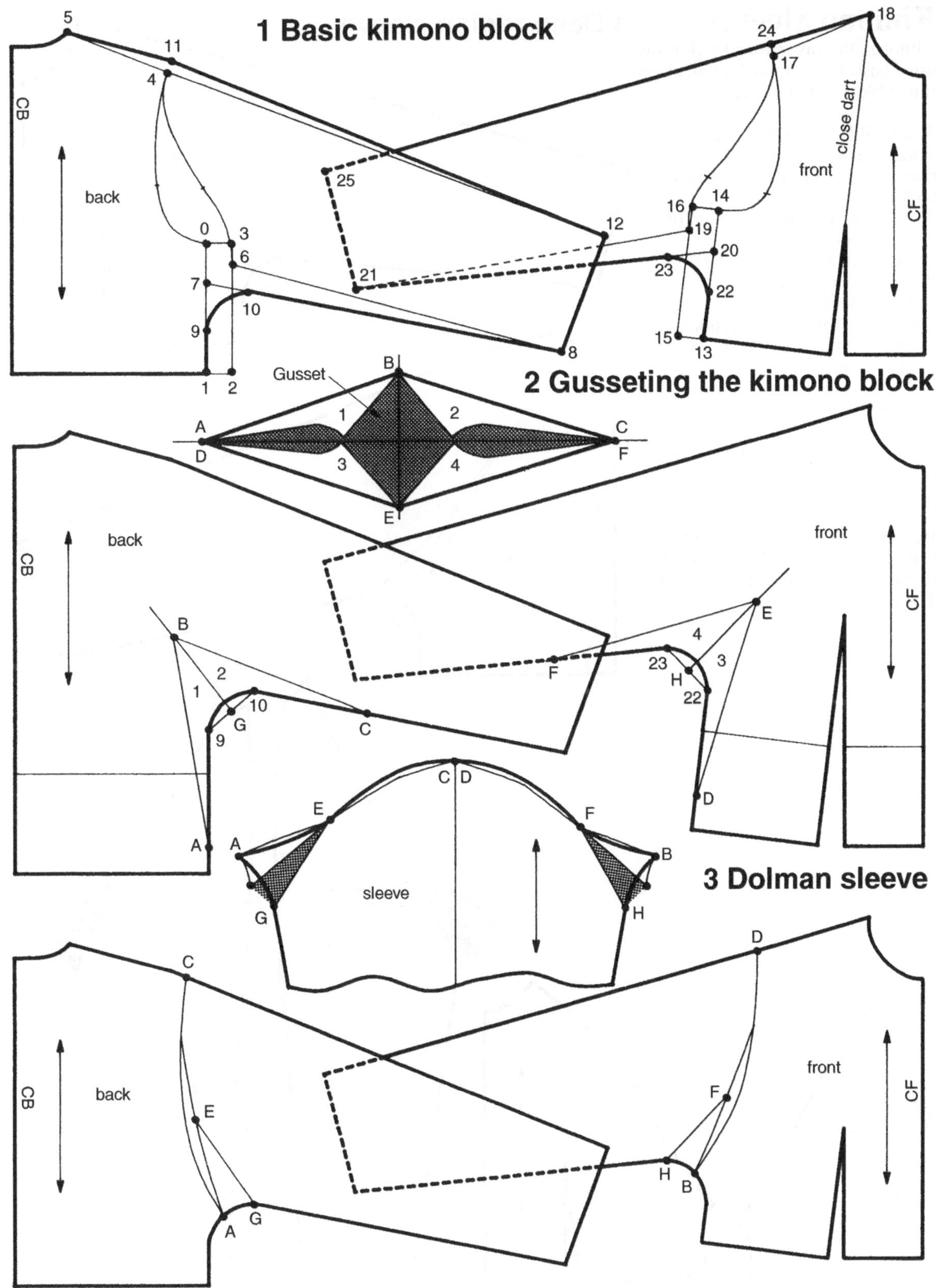
1 Basic kimono block
CB
back
front
CF
close dart
5
11
4
0
3
6
7
9
10
1
2
8
12
25
21
24
18
17
16
14
19
20
23
22
15
13
2 Gusseting the kimono block
Gusset
A
B
C
D
E
F
1
2
3
4
CB
back
front
CF
G
H
9
10
22
23
sleeve
3 Dolman sleeve
CB
back
front
CF

# Kimono Sleeves

## 4 Deep raglan sleeve

Although the easy-fitting block is the usual basis for kimono designs, close-fitting blocks can be used.

4. DEEP RAGLAN SLEEVE
Trace round kimono block; mark points A and B at the centre of the underarm.
Draw in the raglan shape from the neck to points A and B.
Mark points C and D.
A–E is $^{2}/_{3}$ length of A–C.
B–F is $^{3}/_{4}$ length of B–D.
Take out 1.5cm shaped sections.
Mark points G and H at the centre of each section.
A–I and B–J is approx. 4cm; join I–G and J–H.
Trace off sleeve sections.
Cut up the lines H–J and G–I; open 4cm.
Redraw underarm curves from A–I and B–J.
Redraw the armhole with slight curves.
Curve outer lines slightly outward, shaping in at the hem approx. 2cm.
Trace off body shapes.

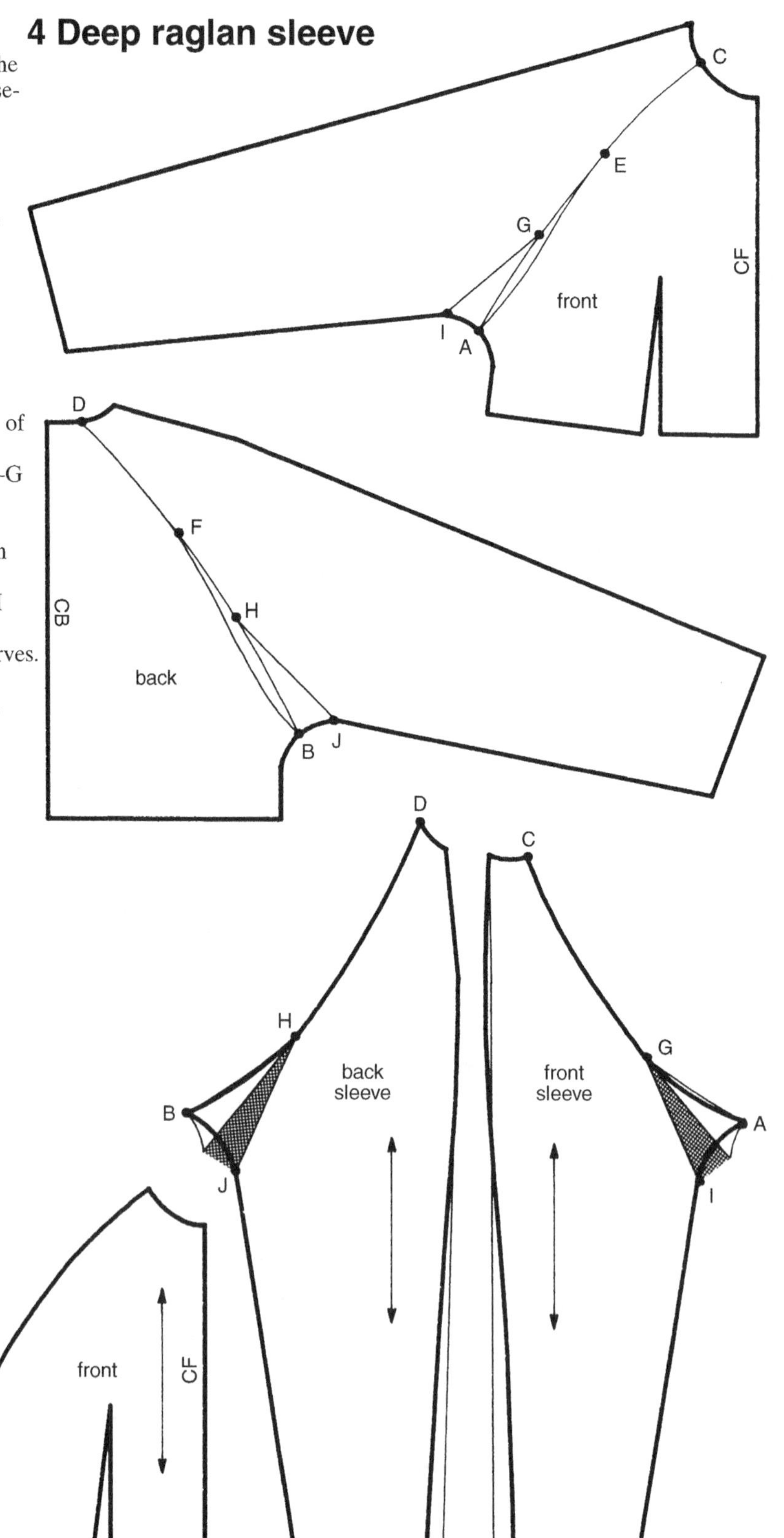

# References


## Chapter 1 The Evolution of the Woman's Tailored Jacket

[1] W. D. F. Vincent, *The Cutters' Practical Guide to the Designing, Cutting and Making of Ladies' Garments,* London: John Williamson & Co. Ltd (1914), p. 3.

[2] Xavier Chaumette, *Le Costume Tailleur,* Paris: ESMOD (1989), p. 11.

[3] Edward B. Giles, *The Art of Cutting-and-History of English Costume,* London: F. T. Prewett (1887), p. 55.

[4] Claire Walsh, 'Shop Design and the Display of Goods in Eighteenth-Century London', *Journal of Design History,* VIII (1995), p. 159.

[5] Beverly Lemire, 'In the hands of work women: English Markets, Cheap Clothing and Female Labour, 1650–1800', *Costume,* XXXIII (1999), p. 26, and 'Redressing the History of the Clothing Trade in England: Ready-made Clothing, Guilds and Women Workers, 1650–1800', *Dress,* XXI (1994), p. 69. Ivy Pinchbeck, *Women Workers and the Industrial Revolution 1750–1850,* London: Virago (1981), p. 287. Judith G. Coffin, *The Politics of Women's Work: the Paris Garment Trades 1750–1915*, New Jersey: Princeton University Press (1996).

[6] Winifred Aldrich, 'Tailors' Cutting Manuals and the Growing Provision of Popular Clothing', *Textile History,* Vol. 31 No. 2 November (2000), pp. 163–201.

[7] Winifred Aldrich, 'Tailors' Cutting Manuals and the Growing Provision of Popular Clothing', *Textile History,* Vol. 31 No. 2 November (2000), pp. 163–201.

[8] Amanda Jones, *The Tailor's Assistant Comprising Rules and Directions for Cutting Men's Clothes by the Square Rule* Second Edition, London: William Sumner (1923).

[9] John Leslie, *Measuring the Human Figure,* 1839, British Patent No. 8306. An example of many patents.

[10] Elise Mangold, *Selbft-Unterrichlim Damen-kleidermachen,* Sarburg (1861).

[11] Guillaume Compaing, *L'Art du Tailleur: Application de la Géométrie à La Coupe de L'Habillement,* Paris (1828); Charles Compaing, *Méthode de Coupe D'Habillements*, Paris (1842). His method could be used for direct measurement cutting or proportional cutting. H. F. Wampen, *Instruction, in Mathematical Proportions and Construction, of Models for Gentlemen's Dresses,* London (1837). Wampen continued to write many books on Anthropometry and Proportional Drafting, and produced in 1864 his major comprehensive work, *Anthropometry; or, Geometry of the Human Figure*, London (1864).

[12] Heinrich Klemm 'Lehrbuch der Modernen Bekleidungskunst fur Damen' in Norah Waugh, *The Cut of Women's Clothes,* London: Faber and Faber Ltd (1968), pp. 195–197. Claudia Kidwell, *Cutting a Fashionable Fit*, Washington: Smithsonian Institution Press (1979), pp. 22–26.

[13] 'Our Ladies' Academy of Cutting', an advertisement in *The Ladies' Tailor,* London, The Tailor and Cutter, No. 1 Vol. 1 (1884), p. 2.

[14] During the 1920s, most British tailors still used the 'forward swing' to create fullness over the bust; see the drafts in W. D. Vincent, *The Cutters Practical Guide to the Designing, Cutting and Making of Ladies' Garments,* London: John Williamson & Co. Ltd (1924), and B. W. Poole, *The Science of Pattern Construction for Garment Makers*, London: The New Era publishing Co. Ltd (1927).

[15] Charles Hecklinger, *The Dress and Cloak Cutter*, Burlington (1881).

[16] See extracts on slopworkers, needlewomen and tailors in Henry Mayhew's letters to The Morning Chronicle in 1849, in E. Yeo and E. P. Thomson, *The Unknown Mayhew,* New York: Pantheon Books (1971).

[17] Jessica Davies, *Ready-made Miracle*, New York: Putnam's Sons (1967), p. 29.

[18] *Manual of Grading and Proportions*, The Berkowitch Designing Academy, New York (1904).

[19] Nancy L. Green, *Ready-to-wear and Ready to Work,* Durham and London: Duke University Press (1997) pp. 189–192.

[20] Katrina Honeyman, *Well Suited: A History of the Leeds Clothing Industry 1850–1990,* Oxford: Oxford University Press (2000), p. 81.

[21] Margaret Stewart and Leslie Hunter, *The Needle is Threaded*, London: Heinemann (1964) pp. 58–62 and 121–131.

[22] Mrs Ewing, in her publication, *The Tailor System: Dress Cutting Made Perfect*, Indianapolis (1869), states that she developed her system of dress cutting by 'tape

and square' by studying the methods of her tailor husband. The quote is from an advertisement for 'S. T. Taylor's System of Dress Cutting', *Harpers Bazar*, Vol. IX, No. 15 April 8th (1876).

[23] Before 1880 books on garment cutting for women's wear were found principally in tailoring publications. My examination of the titles in the British Library showed that after 1880 there were more dressmakers than tailors publishing books containing women's garment cutting. The popularity of tailors' journals may explain this bias.

[24] Harriet A. Brown, *Scientific Dress Cutting and Making,* Published by the author (1902), p. 52.

[25] Claudia Kidwell, *Cutting a Fashionable Fit*, Washington: Smithsonian Institution Press (1979).

[26] Alexis Lavigne, *Méthode du Tailleur*, Paris (1847); *Méthode de Coupe Pour Dames à L'Usage des Tailleurs, Couturières et Apprentis de Deux Professions*, Paris (1869).

[27] ESMOD, *L'École Lavigne,* Paris (1991).

[28] Guerre-Lavigne, *Dress Cutting: Theoretical and Practical,* Leeds: E. J. Arnold & Son, Limited (1907 and 1914). In 1893 a leaflet advertised a visit by her to the Training School of Dressmaking and Needlework in Leeds to demonstrate her methods, L'Archives de Lavigne, Paris: ESMOD.

[29] Mrs Willett Cornwell, *Columbian Sewing Book*, Chicago (1892). Mrs Cornwell exported her system to Europe, Australia and England and set up a cutting and sewing school in Nottingham.

[30] Doris Langley-Moore, *Fashion Through Fashion Plates,* London: Ward Lock (1971).

[31] *Journal des Demoiselles*, 16th Fevrier 1899, included cut paper patterns with the magazine. The journal also included an instruction sheet with an illustration of the design and the pattern pieces, and instructions for making up.

[32] Carol Anne Dickson, *Patterns for Garments: A History of the Paper Pattern Industry in America to 1976,* A PhD Thesis, The Ohio State University (1979).

[33] *The Delineator*, New York: The Butterick Publishing Company, January (1911).

[34] *The Delineator*, New York: The Butterick Publishing Company, Summer (1913).

[35] A large number of small London manufacturers produced ranges which included very fashionable 'tailored' dresses and soft tailored suits. *The Draper's Trade and Fashion Guide*, 1912, London.

[36] *The New Dressmaker: With Complete and Fully Illustrated Instructions on Every Point Connected with Sewing, Dressmaking and Tailoring,* New York: The Butterick Publishing Company (1921).

[37] References to historical and social aspects of cutting can be found in the journals, *Textile History*, *Design History*, and *Costume*. For specific documentation of cutting history, see books by the following authors: Janet Arnold, Claudia Kidwell, Kevin Seligman and Norah Waugh.

### Chapter 2 Fabrics, Measurements and Tools

[1] Winifred Aldrich, *Fabric, Form and Flat Pattern Cutting,* Oxford: Blackwell Science (1997), p. 202.

[2] Peter Judd, 'Base Fabrics Used in Interlining Construction', *Textiles*, No. 4 (1992), p. 14.

[3] CEN, European Committee for Standardization documents on sizing and John Winks, *Clothing Sizes – International Standardisation*, Manchester: The Textile Institute, (1997).

### Chapter 3 The Bespoke Jacket

[1] Most of the books which describe tailoring techniques are American, but they can be obtained through the main clothing book suppliers R. D. Franks Ltd, London. A selection are listed below:
Claire B. Shaeffer, *Couture Sewing Techniques* (1994)
Cecilia Podolak, *Easy Guide to Sewing Jackets* (1995)
Connie Long, *Easy Guide to Sewing Linings* (1998)
Roberto Cabrera and Patricia F. Meyers, *Classic Tailoring Techniques – A Construction Guide for Womenswear* (1986)
Threads Magazine, *Jackets, Coats and Suits* (1992).

### Chapter 4 The Engineered Jacket

[1] Other books and videos describe the cutting and manufacturing process of tailored jackets, for example: Gerry Cooklin, *Pattern Cutting for Women's Outerwear,* Oxford: Blackwell Science (1994); Don Clark, *Pattern Cutting – Level 2* (video 1996); Martin Shoben, *The Art of Jacket Pattern Cutting,* London: (video 1999).

### Chapter 5 The Engineered Process of Manufacture

[1] Alison Beasley, 'Size and Fit: Procedures in Undertaking a Survey of Body Measurements', *Journal of Fashion Marketing and Management*, Vol. 2 No. 1 (1997).

Printed and bound by CPI Group (UK) Ltd, Croydon, CR0 4YY

16/04/2025

14658506-0005